OFF THE BEATEN PATH® SERIES

ELEVENTH EDITION

CONNECTICUT
OFF THE BEATEN PATH®

CINDI D. PIETRZYK
REVISED BY ERIC D. LEHMAN

Globe
Pequot
Essex, Connecticut

All the information in this guidebook is subject to change. We recommend you call ahead to obtain current information before traveling.

Globe Pequot

An imprint of The Globe Pequot Publishing Group, Inc.
64 South Main Street
Essex, CT 06426
www.globepequot.com

Copyright © 2026 by The Globe Pequot Publishing Group, Inc.

Off the Beaten Path is a registered trademark of The Globe Pequot Publishing Group, Inc.

All rights reserved. No part of this book may be reproduced in any form or by any electronic or mechanical means, including information storage and retrieval systems, without written permission from the publisher, except by a reviewer who may quote passages in a review.

British Library Cataloguing in Publication Information available

ISSN 1539-8641
ISBN 978-1-4930-9240-6 (paper)
ISBN 978-1-4930-9241-3 (electronic)

Contents

Acknowledgments v
Introduction 1
The Heartland **8**
The Litchfield Hills. **66**
Gateway to New England. **100**
Coast & Country **139**
The Quiet Corner. **194**
Index 217
About the Author 228

Acknowledgments

Authors often say a book can't be written without the help of many people, but I'm not sure readers always appreciate just how true that statement is. Trust me, it's true! When I agreed to write this edition, my first thought was, "How will I find places to include?" As I began my research, I thought, "How am I going to fit all of this into one book?!" Connecticut is one of those little spaces that packs a whole lot of punch. There are so many hidden gems that uncovering them all would be impossible for one person. In that vein, I'd like to thank all those people who gave me suggestions, sent me in the right direction, visited places for me, and answered my questions.

Specifically, I'd like to thank Stephen Wood of CTMuseumQuest.com for blazing a path through Connecticut. There weren't many places I discovered that Steve hadn't already visited. His write-ups were always helpful and entertaining. Check out Steve's blog and follow his ramblings around the state.

A huge thank you to all the grassroots community groups who have pulled together and saved so many historic sites. Without them, there might not be a Connecticut off the beaten path.

Thanks to everyone at GPP who do what they do so well!

And finally, I need to thank my husband, Steve, and my daughters for once again putting up with my hours away from them, the missed moments, and the frantic scramble to meet my deadline. Your love and support got me through the late nights and moments of thinking I'd never get it done. We got it done.

CONNECTICUT

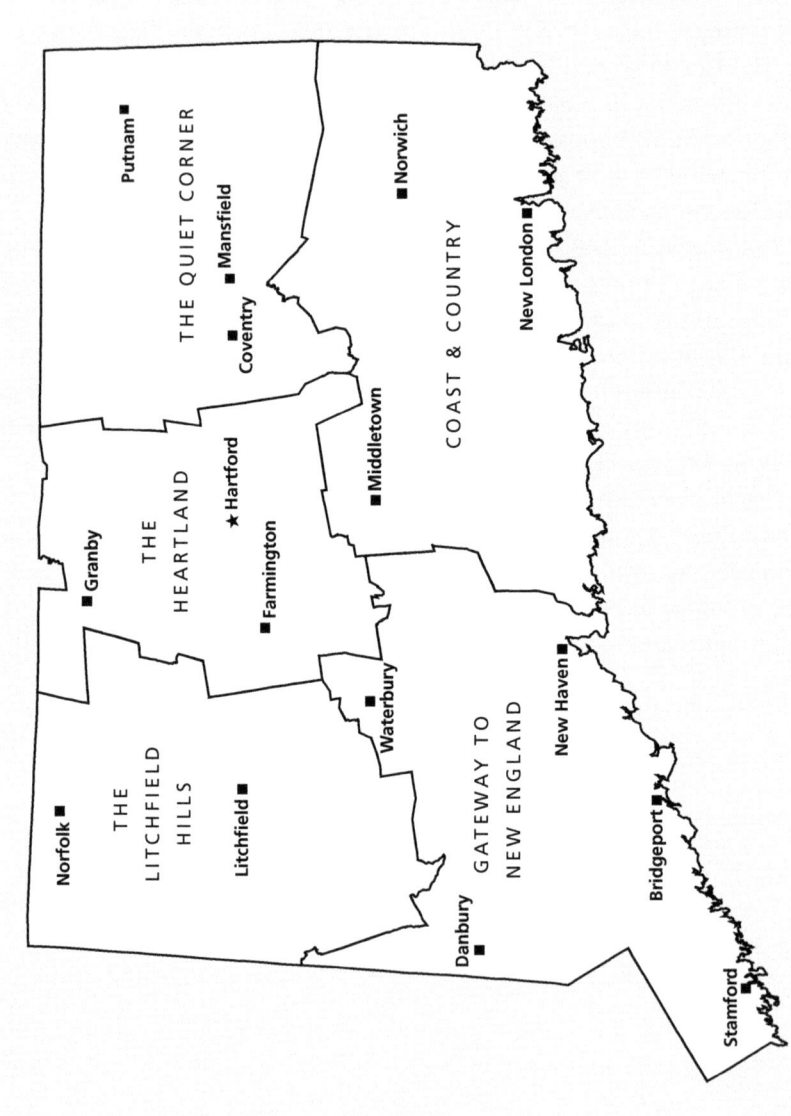

Introduction

Twenty years from now you will be more disappointed by the things you didn't do than by the ones you did do. So throw off the bowlines, sail away from the safe harbor. Catch the trade winds in your sails. Explore. Dream. Discover.

—Mark Twain

Nestled between the much larger states of New York and Massachusetts, Connecticut is certainly "off the beaten path." Our state occupies only a bit more than 5,000 square miles along the coast of Long Island Sound, making it the third-smallest state in the Union. But nowhere in America can the traveler find so representative a history, so rich a culture, and so great a physical diversity packed into so small an area.

Connecticut's history is rich and varied. The Native Americans who lived in the region for millennia before the arrival of the first Europeans called it Quinnehtukqut ("Beside the Long Tidal River" or "Long River"). About 20,000 Native Americans lived in the area when the Dutch discovered the Connecticut River in 1614. As settlers and natives clashed, many of the tribes were forced to work together, and tribal lines were blurred. Many Native peoples who live today have a mixed heritage from more than one of these tribes.

English Puritans from Massachusetts began to move into Connecticut in 1633, and in 1638–1639, the towns of Hartford, Windsor, and Wethersfield adopted the Fundamental Orders of Connecticut, setting up a government for the new Connecticut Colony. About the same time, the colony of New Haven was founded farther west along the coast of Long Island Sound. The two colonies were joined in 1662, and the state gained—roughly—its current outline.

Since then, the history of Connecticut has largely marched with that of America. The state has played a vital role in American experiences, such as the settlement of the frontier, the winning of the Revolutionary War, the adoption of the Constitution, the Union victory in the Civil War, and that vast technological upheaval known as the Industrial Revolution.

Connecticut's part in the American pageant has left a lasting mark on the state. Its towns have been ravaged by America's wars. Its language and culture have been molded by the nation's immigration patterns. Its

constitution state

Connecticut is called the "Constitution State" because the Fundamental Orders, a governing principle based on the will of the people, is considered one of the first written constitutions of a democratic government. You can see these orders at the Museum of Connecticut History in Hartford.

> ### Connecticut River
>
> The Connecticut River is one of 14 waterways designated American Heritage Rivers by former vice president Al Gore.
>
> The Connecticut River is 410 miles long—about 5,551 football fields.
>
> Today's Connecticut River came into being between 10,000 and 13,000 years ago, after the Wisconsin Glacier receded from the New England area.

geography has been altered by the spread of industrialization. Its economy has been shaped by the growth—and demise—of such industries as whaling, railroading, shipbuilding, and textile manufacturing. It has been, in many ways, a microcosm of America itself.

Sometimes known as the "Land of Steady Habits," Connecticut has taken as its official designation the title "Constitution State." George Washington called it the "Provision State" because it fed his army during the darkest days of the American Revolution. It is also called the "Nutmeg State," a sobriquet just as common as the official designation and perhaps more representative of Connecticut's history and culture; the name "Nutmegger" was often applied by the residents of neighboring states to Connecticut peddlers, who were famous for selling bogus nutmegs carved from local wood in place of the imported (and more expensive) real thing.

Whatever you call it, Connecticut is a land of odd contrasts and strange delights that have accumulated over centuries. Modern Connecticut has something to excite the whim and tickle the fancy of almost every traveler. Its diverse geography runs the gamut—from the sandy beaches and teeming marshlands of its coastal plains to the fertile meadows of its central lowlands to the forested hills of the eastern and western uplands, to the craggy granite cliffs that characterize its northwestern reaches. The many eras of its history are enshrined not only in countless museums, galleries, and restorations but also in numerous historical structures that are still part of the everyday lives of its people; this is, in fact, one of the few places in America where you can find real Cape Cod saltboxes, Victorian Gothic mansions, and Art Deco roadside palaces of the early automotive era all happily residing cheek by jowl.

Because of this, residents of Connecticut take their history seriously. Again and again strong Yankee ingenuity has been put into action, as dedicated Nutmeggers in hundreds of historical societies work to save historical property after historical property. This community action has resulted in the wonderful museums and galleries or historic neighborhoods you'll have the honor of exploring as you traverse our great state.

The densely populated cities along Connecticut's southwestern coast and the navigable portions of its major rivers are home to many of the state's inhabitants and give the state an urban flavor that stands in stark contrast to its rural uplands. This clustering of settlements along coasts and rivers explains why, even though Connecticut is the seventh-most densely populated state in the US (with an overall density of almost 740 persons per square mile), roughly 60 percent of the state is forest land. Most of the trees in these forests are northern hardwoods about 60–100 years old, and they are purely glorious in fall. In addition, approximately 12 percent of Connecticut is farmland.

In terms of amenities for the traveler, Connecticut has few equals. Though modern accommodations abound, this area, like most of New England, is famous for its quaint inns and bed-and-breakfasts (or B&Bs), many of which are housed in buildings that have been around longer than the state. The eclectic cuisine, both cosmopolitan and casual, reflects the cultural and gustatory gifts brought to the state by succeeding waves of immigrants. Its great wealth and emphasis on tourism make Connecticut a shopping paradise; establishments range from some of America's largest and most attractive malls, to mom-and-pop operations offering only-in-Connecticut crafts, to factory outlets that fairly shout "bargains."

For the traveler who likes to venture off the beaten path, Connecticut is an especially satisfying venue; you will constantly discover the odd, the interesting, and the truly unique tucked away in the most unexpected places. Whether it be a mere whimsy, such as a roadside rock painted to look like a startlingly realistic giant frog, a truly spine-chilling gothic mystery, such as Groton's Gungywamp, or something just plain honest and daring at East Haddam's Two Wrasslin' Cats Coffee House, you can never be entirely sure what you will find around the next bend.

We like to think of Connecticut as representing all the best of America in vest-pocket size: gilded beaches that would be the envy of California; rolling hills better than any in Virginia; pastoral farmland that makes you think you're in Indiana; downtown chic that rivals New York; and some of the friendliest people on Earth. A truly dedicated traveler could experience the full diversity of the state in one day. You could jump-start your day with an espresso in West Hartford, drive down to the shore for a few hours of sun and sand capped by a lunch of fried clams or lobster at the shore, and take an afternoon jaunt up into Litchfield County to browse the antiques shops before driving over to the Quiet Corner for a hayride through its fields and glens. You'd be tired, but you could do it.

Geography isn't the only source of variety in Connecticut. Its northerly location and long coastline conspire to produce a multiplicity of seasonal variations in the weather. Each season brings its own wonders and offers its own characteristic activities. Winter means New England main streets dressed for the holidays, pure white candles glowing in many-paned windows. Spring is the season for strolling along one of eastern Connecticut's back roads, watching farmers plow rolling farmlands, listening to the first few notes of birdsong, and sniffing the green tang of growing things in the air. Summer is a time for the shore; for golden beaches, the hiss of the waves, the crunch of fried seafood, and the sugary-sweet smell of cotton candy. Fall means amber and cinnabar hills, quintessentially New England white clapboard churches set against the fiery reds of nearby sugar maples, and the sweet taste of fresh-pressed cider and cider-glazed doughnuts.

Regardless of the season, traveling in Connecticut is easy. Interstate highways crisscross the state, with I-95 (the Connecticut Turnpike) running the length of its shore, I-91 bisecting the state from north to south, I-395 winding along its eastern border, and I-84 running from Danbury through Waterbury to Hartford and then through the northeastern counties to the Massachusetts Turnpike. The interstate highway system is complemented by an excellent system of state highways. However, traffic congestion has become an increasingly prevalent problem, especially during the summer, so you should build in extra time if you are planning to attend an event that has a specific starting time. More often than not, this book takes you off the interstates and puts you on the smaller roads that evolved with our state's history from Indian trails to two-lane paved roads. Some of these back roads may seem isolated. But never fear; no matter how far into the outback it feels, you're never more than half an hour from a major highway that will quickly return you to more populated areas.

Clearly, no one book can do justice to Connecticut's 350 years of history or to the diverse delights packed into this one small state. Thus, you won't find detailed descriptions of the well-known delights of Mystic or the popular casinos at Foxwoods or Mohegan Sun. Nor do we devote much space to the major attractions in the state's larger cities. These items are well documented online. Instead, we offer a directory of out-of-the-way places you might not know to look for if you're not native to the area. We've done the research for you and pulled it all together in this one convenient place. What is that historic building you're passing? Where does that trail lead? Where should I eat? Is that antiques store really worth the stop? If it's funky, funny, little known, or out of the way, you'll probably find it here.

For the purposes of this book, we've divided the state into five chapters, matching Connecticut's major geographic, historical, and cultural divisions. Within those chapters there are smaller sections to help keep things organized. We suggest that when planning a trip, you pull out a Connecticut state map and look at all the surrounding towns. Decide where you'd like to go, then use a nifty route planner, in which you plug in street addresses (all of which we have provided for you), and have the computer map your route for you. You can see at a glance the best way to see everything on your list and how much time it will take.

In today's world, social media sites are invaluable for up-to-the-minute news on all your favorite places. We strongly suggest you "like," "follow," and "subscribe" to places you plan to visit. This way you'll know about special events, pricing, and closings ahead of time.

Fall Foliage

In most of Connecticut, fall foliage hits its peak around Columbus Day, though areas across the north rim see peak color a little earlier. Starting in late September, you can get a daily fall foliage update by visiting ct.gov/deep/site/default.asp and clicking on the Fall Foliage link; you can even sign up for text and/or email updates. Some of the most popular spots to leaf peep include towers in parks like Sleeping Giant or Talcott Mountain, but we'll be sure to point you in the direction of the lesser traveled ones, like the top of the vineyard at Sharpe Hill or the stone labyrinth of Gay City State Park.

Food in Connecticut

Here in Connecticut, our cuisine is an amalgam of rugged colonial dishes leavened with ethnic foods, the heritage of the immigrants who helped transform our state. It all makes for a diverse and heady cuisine. Try to sample some of these emphatically Connecticut foods when you visit.

Chowder. The origins of its name, *chaudière* (large kettle), may be French, but this hearty soup is all New England. You won't find as many fish chowders in Connecticut as in other parts of New England, but we make stellar clam chowders.

New England clam chowder is a milk- or cream-based soup full of potatoes, onions, whole clams, and salt pork and seasoned with thyme. It's probably the version you think of when someone mentions clam chowder.

Rhode Island clam chowder is New England clam chowder lightened with just enough pureed tomatoes to turn the soup a rosy pink.

Connecticut clam chowder is a bracing, briny broth loaded with clams, potatoes, and onions—no milk or cream.

Manhattan clam chowder is a tomato-based veggie soup with a few clams.

Lobster roll. In some New England states, a lobster roll is lobster salad (cold lobster, mayonnaise, seasonings) served on a toasted hot dog bun. But in

Connecticut, a lobster roll is a spiritual experience: fresh, hot lobster meat, dripping with melted butter, served on a sesame-seed hamburger bun or toasted hot dog bun. Invented in Milford in the 1930s, the Connecticut Lobster Roll is one of the state's signature dishes. Be sure to try one, and don't forget the extra napkins for wiping butter-drenched chins and fingers.

Hamburgers. New Haven's Louis' Lunch is the oldest hamburger stand in America, and its vertical grill, toasted bread, and ban on ketchup have made it iconic. Steamed cheeseburgers were also invented in Middletown in the 1920s or even earlier, at a place called Jack's Lunch. In 1941, steamed burgers were served by John O'Rourke, owner of O'Rourke's Diner. In 1959, Ted's restaurant opened in Meriden as a family-operated business, pioneering the steam box and trays that are used at steamed cheeseburger joints throughout central Connecticut.

Indian pudding. A robust dessert dating back to colonial times, it's a mix of cornmeal, molasses, and warm spices cooked for hours at a low temperature until thick and amber-colored. Some heretics add raisins or apples, while most serve it with vanilla ice cream or a rivulet of heavy cream. The Griswold Inn in Essex usually has Indian pudding on its fall and winter dessert menu.

Pizza. New Haven is the pizza capital of Connecticut, maybe of the entire US. New Haven pizza, called "abeetz," was invented in 1936 by Frank Pepe, who built a tile-encased coal-burning oven that bakes at high heat. This gives the crust a scorched, caramelized umami that is matched by the chewy center. He used high-quality ingredients, including local clams, creating the "white clam pie" that is so famous today, complete with freshly shucked littleneck clams. The taste of clams is subtle and works well with olive oil, garlic, freshly grated cheese, and the hint of coal. If you don't like clams, don't worry: These days there are hundreds of New Haven apizza options, as its popularity spreads across the nation. Pepe's and Sally's (started by Frank's nephew Sal) are the traditional top choices among New Haven pizza palaces, with spots like Modern Apizza, Zuppardi's, and the Little Rendezvous close behind.

State Symbols

- **Official designation:** Constitution State
- **Indian name:** Quinnehtukqut—"Beside the Long Tidal River"
- **State motto:** He who is transplanted still sustains
- **State flower:** mountain laurel
- **State bird:** American robin
- **State tree:** white oak
- **State animal:** sperm whale
- **State insect:** praying mantis

- **State mineral:** garnet
- **State song:** "Yankee Doodle"
- **State ship:** USS *Nautilus*
- **State shellfish:** eastern oyster
- **State composer:** Charles Edward Ives
- **State fossil:** *Eubrontes giganteus,* an 18-foot-long carnivore
- **State hero:** Nathan Hale
- **State heroine:** Prudence Crandall

Places to Stay & Places to Eat Price Codes

At the end of each chapter are area accommodations and restaurants you'll want to check out.

The rating scale for accommodations is based on double occupancy and is as follows:

Inexpensive: Less than $100 per night
Moderate: $101 to $200 per night
Expensive: More than $200 per night

The rating scale for restaurants is based on the price of an entree without beverages, desserts, tax, or tip, and is as follows:

Inexpensive: Less than $10
Moderate: $11 to $20
Expensive: More than $20

Please remember, these are rough guidelines and should not be considered actual rates. Always call ahead to confirm. For museums and places that charge admission, we have indicated if an admission is charged but not how much, as those change often. We have also indicated if a museum is a member of the Blue Star Program, which gives active-duty military members and five members of their family free admission from Memorial Day through Labor Day.

The Heartland

The upper Connecticut River Valley is a broad, fertile meadowland ideal for farming and grazing, and the state's Puritan settlers were naturally drawn to it. It was the first part of Connecticut to be colonized, and those original settlements thrived and expanded until they finally merged to form what is today Greater Hartford, a vibrant metropolitan area of over a million people.

Bounding Hartford County's urban and suburban core on the north and west are the rural Tobacco and Farmington Valleys. To the east is pastoral Tolland County, and to the south are New Haven County and Connecticut's Coast & Country areas. Within these rural boundaries is Connecticut's heartland, the seat of its government and one of its most important commercial centers. As you might suspect, the majority of the attractions in this area are historical and cultural; in addition, you can find the commercial activities and entertainments of a large metropolitan area.

THE HEARTLAND

The Capital

Hartford

Officially settled in 1635, **Hartford** was important in the 19th century as a center of the abolitionist movement and the tobacco industry. A hub of activity, Hartford played an integral part in shaping our nation's history. Merchants traded molasses, spices, coffee, and rum along with the tobacco from warehouses throughout the city. The Colt Firearms Factory, maker of the Colt Revolver, "the gun that won the West," called Hartford home.

That history can be explored at the **Museum of Connecticut History** (231 Capitol Ave.; 860-757-6535; museumofcthistory.org), which has a great collection of items from our state's past, including an exhibit on the role Connecticut and its residents played in World War I; so many guns from so many years of Colt Manufacturing's history; Memorial Hall, where the portraits of the state's past and present governors hang; and the Mitchelson Coin Collection, reportedly one of the best in the world. Open Mon–Fri 10 a.m.–4 p.m., closed weekends and holidays. Call ahead to be sure. There are metal detectors as you enter the building, which you will have to pass through. When you do enter, the Connecticut Supreme Court is on your right, the Connecticut State Library is on your left. Straight ahead you will see a double staircase that leads off in both directions and will likely be roped off. The museum is located directly through the center of these staircases.

One of the most interesting exhibits here is the **Connecticut Freedom Trail Quilt Project**. Connecticut residents fought for freedom on more than one front throughout the state's history. While some went to battlegrounds throughout the region and fought on the front lines, many stayed home and fought for freedom on a different level—a secret, underground level. People from across the state created squares for the final product, each piece representing one of the sites along the trail. Quilting is a long-standing tradition, in fact, quilts were often hung outside safe houses to alert those in need that help was available within.

When you are done exploring the museum, head across the street to the State Capitol building. With its eight-sided gilded cupola gleaming in sunlight, **Connecticut's State Capitol** (210 Capitol Ave; 860-240-0222; cga.ct.gov) greets your eyes when you come into Hartford by way of I-84. Designed by Richard M. Upjohn, primarily a cathedral architect, this High Victorian Gothic–style colossus—completed on its hilltop site in 1878—is a marble-and-granite riot of pinnacles, turrets, columns, bas reliefs, statues, heraldic emblems, arches, and porticoes. In addition to state executive offices and legislative chambers, the capitol building offers a variety of historic exhibits, including the figurehead from the USS *Connecticut*, which sailed around the world on a goodwill mission ordered by President Theodore Roosevelt in 1907. The ship was destroyed in 1923, but the figurehead was spared and presented to Connecticut to be displayed. You'll also find a model of the *Hartford*, built by a US Navy veteran with one arm! It took him two and a half years of patience and determination to complete. History buffs may know it was from the *Hartford* that Admiral David Farragut commanded the famous words, "Damn the torpedoes, full speed ahead!" in 1864.

Tours are funded by the League of Women Voters of Connecticut Education Fund. Tour hours are Mon–Fri 9:15, 10:15, 11:15, 12:15, and 1:15; you can take a self-guided tour Mon through Fri, 8 a.m. to 5 p.m. Tour information can be found in the Capitol outside room 101 and also on the first floor of the Legislative Office Building, near the west entrance. The Capitol and Legislative Office Building are closed on weekends and major holidays.

If you haven't had your fill of history yet, stop by **Connecticut's Old State House** (800 Main St.; 860-240-5340; ctoldstatehouse.org), especially if you have little ones in your group who need to expend some energy. The hands-on children's exhibits in the Emily Seymour Goodwin Holcombe Center on the bottom level of this historic building will surely do the trick. Emily Holcombe was a dedicated activist and preservationist who organized many campaigns to save Connecticut landmarks and preserve our history, including working diligently to save the Old State House when it was marked for demolition. Here at this center, antsy little ones can build their own capitol on the Lego table; explore a farmyard with interactive, child-size farm animal statues, and more! They will also want to see the two-headed calf at the **Museum of Curiosities**, where you will also find sharks' jaws, a stuffed cobra, a crocodile's head, drawers full of birds' eggs, and wide-ranging diverse exhibits that were part of the former collection of local painter Joseph Seward. But first, take the time to explore the original state House of Representatives on one side of the upper level and the chamber of the state Senate on the other. There's an inspiring speech by P. T. Barnum that you can read aloud and feel as if you're speaking to a group of aspiring lawmakers and making a difference, but mostly it's just cool to stand where our forefathers stood hundreds of years ago as our state was taking shape. On the lower level you'll also find an informative exhibit on the *Amistad* and the trial that ensued.

The building itself has a long and interesting history. Construction began in 1792 but was not completed until 1796 due to various financial obstacles. It has faced the wrecking ball many times, but each time Nutmeggers rallied and saved this important part of their history. In 1961, the Old State House was named a National Historic Landmark. Closed Sun and Mon, open Tues–Sat

12 p.m.–5 p.m., with extended hours until 8 pm every Thurs, July–Nov. You can take a guided tour or opt for a tour on your own.

Hartford is often referred to as the "Insurance City," a reputation that dates back to the city's thriving merchant district, from which many ships set sail to England and other far-off ports. As business grew, so did the need for protection from pirates, storms, and accidents. In 1810, the Hartford Fire Insurance Group was created, and it still operates today. Other insurance entrepreneurs followed suit. In 1846, the Connecticut Mutual Life Insurance Co. of Hartford was formed even as local clergy declared the practice of insuring lives immoral. They came around, however, when in 1851 religious leaders joined business and civic leaders in founding the American Temperance Life Insurance Company. The Hartford Steam Boiler Inspection and Insurance Company came along in 1864, and by 1898, the first automobile insurance policy, at a staggering cost of two cents, had been issued by Travelers Insurance Company. Hartford's insurance companies continued to prosper and build their reputations by paying in full and on time when claims arose.

As you're driving through downtown Hartford, be sure to head down American Way where you can view **The Phoenix Mutual Life Insurance Building**. The "boat building," as it's popularly known, was designed and completed in 1963 by Harrison & Abramovitz, a New York architectural firm also credited with designing New York's Lincoln Center and United Nations headquarters. It is the world's first two-sided office building and is now on the National Register of Historic Places. Its graceful, green glass walls house a company with quite a history. Formed in 1851 as the American Temperance Life Insurance Company, the company originally offered insurance only to those who abstained from alcohol consumption. As the years went on and the temperance movement faded, the company changed its name to the Phoenix Mutual Life Insurance Company. Among their clients were Andrew Johnson, Hannibal Hamlin, Schuyler Colfax, and Abraham Lincoln.

From here you can take a stroll across the river and back on Hartford's **Riverwalk**. One of the highlights of this walk is the statue of Lincoln himself shaking hands with Harriet Beecher Stowe, the author of *Uncle Tom's Cabin*. This 2006 statue by Bruno Lucchesi commemorates the 1862 meeting between Lincoln and Stowe, when the president reportedly said, "So, you're the little woman who made this big war." That may have been a slight exaggeration, but the impact of *Uncle Tom's Cabin* on public opinion about slavery in the 1850s can hardly be overstated.

Back on the Hartford side of the river, you'll find what looks vaguely like a National Guard armory but is actually one of Hartford's most distinguished cultural institutions: the **Wadsworth Atheneum** (600 Main St.; 860-278-2670;

thewadsworth.org). Founded in 1842 by Daniel Wadsworth, the Atheneum is our nation's oldest continuously operating public art museum. The mock-Gothic "armory appearance" constitutes the central part of an architectural grouping of the museum's five connected buildings that includes Renaissance Revival and Tudor-style add-ons. The Wadsworth Atheneum's holdings near 50,000 works are thanks to donations from many prominent families as the museum grew and took shape. Wadsworth originally wanted to create a gallery of fine arts, but the vision turned into an atheneum, which includes scholarly works, books, artifacts, and more.

The museum features three levels of exhibits. The first level includes early to mid-20th century European and American art, Contemporary and post–World War II art, as well as some Chinese, Medieval, and Renaissance art. Level two brings you back to the 1600s through 1865 and includes the Samuel Colt collection, which was donated by his wife, Elizabeth Hart Jarvis Colt, in 1905. You will also find **The Amistad Center for Arts & Culture** on the second floor, which includes thousands of pieces of history that evidence the important role African Americans played in our history. You'll find posters, photos, books, and various changing exhibits throughout the year. Then head to the third floor to explore more than two centuries of American art, including an exhibit on Sol LeWitt, one of our many local-born artists that has achieved worldwide fame.

Current hours are Thurs–Sun 12–5 p.m. There is an admission fee, but the museum offers free admission on the second Sat of the month if you arrive between 10 a.m. and 1 p.m. Admission is also free from 4 to 5 p.m. Wed through Sun. Many local libraries also offer free passes. The Atheneum is a Blue Star participating museum, and veterans are admitted free year-round. The museum is always holding special events and special offers, so check the website.

Just outside the Atheneum is Connecticut's own sculptor Alexander Calder's **Stegosaurus**. You really can't miss this huge, red steel construction that towers over the Alfred E. Burr Memorial Mall, a pocket park between the

connecticut freedomtrail

Churches have regularly played an important part in our state's civil history. When people need a place to contemplate, grieve, come together as a community, or just question or affirm life in general, our churches offer sanctuary. Three such churches on Hartford's Main Street are listed on the National Register of Historic Places. If you'd like to stop, sit, and contemplate for a spell, they are the *Metropolitan A.M.E. Zion Church* (2051 Main St.), the *Union Baptist Church* (1921 Main St.), and the *Faith Congregational Church* (2030 Main St.).

> **AUTHOR'S FAVORITES**
>
> Trinity College Chapel
> Old New-Gate Prison & Copper Mine
> Taine Mountain Preserve
> Elizabeth Park Rose Garden

Wadsworth Atheneum and Hartford City Hall. This 50-foot-tall treasure was built in Waterbury and installed in Hartford in 1973 as a memorial to Alfred E. Burr, founder of the *Hartford Times*. In 2016, the structure received a facelift overseen by artist Abigail Mack in collaboration with the owners of the artwork, the Ella Burr McManus Trust (Alfred was Ella's father). Workers carefully removed decades of paint right down to the steel. A zinc-based primer was then applied and new coats of red paint, carefully matched to Calder's original color, were added. The pedestrian areas around the sculpture were cleaned and *Stegosaurus* once again stands proud.

Just 2 short miles from the Wadsworth Atheneum you'll find **The Austin House** (130 Scarborough St.; 860-838-4046; thewadsworth.org/collection/austin house), former home of A. Everett Austin Jr., Atheneum director from 1927 until 1944 and founder of Trinity College's fine arts department. This sprawling mansion sits among other grand residences and fancy pants buildings, but the joke is on them because this architectural oddity is a mere 18 feet in depth (although it is 86 feet long). Austin died in 1957 at the age of 56 from lung cancer. His wife, Helen Goodwin Austin, remained in the house. In 1985, she and her two children donated the house to the Atheneum. Tours take place on the third Thurs of the month at 11 a.m.; Reservations required. Admission fee is $35 and includes same day admission to the Wadsworth. Elevator service is not available.

As you continue north from the Atheneum, turn left onto Gold Street and watch for this unexpected and ingenious work of art. Carl Andre's **Stone Field** sculpture has always been a subject of conversation in Hartford. It consists of 36 large rocks arranged in rows on a slope of lawn. Some critics consider it a statement of minimalist art; some witty citizens call it Hartford's Meadow Muffins. When Andre conceptualized the sculpture, he claimed he wanted to offer city residents a refuge from the noises of the city, a place in which to contemplate and relax. George Athanso, the city's mayor at the time, didn't buy the idea and thought the sculpture would cause the city to be a laughingstock. Of course, it didn't help matters that after using a scant $13,000 to quarry and transport the boulders from a Bristol quarry, Andre pocketed the remaining $87,000 of the $100,000 commission he was paid to create the work of art. See, as we said, ingenious.

Freedom Fighters and Groundbreakers

Old North Cemetery (N. Main Street at Mather Street) contains the graves of numerous African American Civil War soldiers. Some served in the state's all-Black 29th Regiment, some were from the 31st Regiment US Colored Troops, and some came from other units. Many of the headstones have since gone missing, but at one time there were almost 30 military-issued headstones here. Take notice of headstones that are generally made of marble (or granite) and have a rounded top; these are usually military issue.

Also located in Old North Cemetery is the grave of *Mary Townsend Seymour*, a civil activist and leader in Hartford. She is credited with cofounding the city's chapter of the National Association for the Advancement of Colored People (NAACP), fighting for women's rights, and being active in local and state politics. In fact, she was the first Black woman to run for a state office. Seymour fought tirelessly throughout her life and in 2006 was inducted into the Connecticut Women's Hall of Fame. You'll find her family plot on the left side of the drive if you enter the cemetery from Main Street and walk toward the back gate.

Since you're in the area and cemeteries are your thing (as they are mine, welcome to the club), be sure to stop and explore *Spring Grove Cemetery* (2035 Main St.). Here you'll find the final resting place of *William Henry Jacklyn*, Hartford's first African American firefighter, along with that of *Laurent Clerc*, founder of the American School for the Deaf. Both cemeteries are open from dawn to dusk.

After you contemplate a while in *Stone Field*, walk over to the 4-acre **Ancient Burying Ground** (60 Gold St.; 860-337-1640; theancientburyingground.org). This cemetery was created in 1640 and holds the bones of some of Hartford's most prominent citizens, including Thomas Hooker. It's also the site of the **African-American Memorial** that honors the unmarked graves of more than 300 African Americans who are buried here. If you're a fan of early American art, the tombstones are a treasure trove of colonial death imagery and epitaphs. Hours are 8:30 a.m.–5 p.m. daily. May be closed on holidays and due to weather. Walking tour brochures can be found on the website.

Next to the State Capitol building on Jewell Street is **Bushnell Park** (166 Capitol Ave.; bushnellpark.org), the oldest publicly funded park in the country, and one of the first plots of land in America acquired through eminent domain for use as a park. The vision of **Rev. Horace Bushnell**, the park was first known as City Park and was designed not by Frederick Olmsted as many think, but by **Jacob Weidenmann**, a Swiss-born architect. Olmsted was busy on New York's Central Park when Reverend Bushnell asked him to work on the project, and he recommended Weidenmann instead. Now, more than a hundred years later, the renamed Bushnell Park continues to be "a place of life and motion," as its creators intended. Fun activities are always taking place somewhere in the park, but there are also plenty of places to sit quietly and enjoy the beauty. Whatever your plans, definitely take the time to explore this park's treasures, including the 1914 **Bushnell Carousel** (1 Jewell St.; 860-585-5411; thecarouselmuseum.org), whose 48 antique Stein and Goldstein horses revolve beneath 800 twinkling lights. The band organ is a refurbished 1925 Wurlitzer, and yes, you really can try to catch a brass ring. While the park is open year-round, the carousel closes from Jan through Mar. It is run by the **New England Carousel Museum**. The carousel is usually open 12–5 Sat and Sun, Apr–Dec., $2/ride.

In his original design for the park, Weidenmann included a whopping 157 varieties of trees and shrubs, spanning more than 1,000 specimens from across the world. Over the years, that number sadly shrunk to less than 340 due to disease, neglect, and damage. Thanks to the efforts of the **Bushnell Park**

The Historic *Hartford Courant*

Founded in 1764 by *Thomas Green*, the *Hartford Courant* (once the *Connecticut Courant*) is America's oldest continuously published newspaper. It is, in fact, older than our nation. It has been around long enough to report the Boston Tea Party as breaking news, and was a pro-patriot publication, a rarity, considering Boston newspapers were shut down by the Crown and much of what was coming out of New York was pro-British.

Green was a printer and worked diligently to keep the fledgling paper afloat. He owned a storefront out of which he sold dry goods and clothing and ran the newspaper out of an office in back. He had an assistant, Ebenezer Watson, who eventually purchased the business from Green. Watson ran the paper until 1777, when he died of smallpox. His wife, Hannah Bunce Watson, then stepped in to keep the paper going. This was no small feat considering Hannah had five young children to care for and the Loyalists were chomping at her heels; they burned down the paper mill she used and would not allow the *Courant* to be exported to the colonies. Hannah fought the good fight for two years before getting help from her new husband, Barzillai Hudson, in 1779.

The paper continued to play an important part in the country's news-making machine and the history recorded therein is priceless. In 1783, Connecticut resident Noah Webster published his Blue-Backed Speller in the *Courant*. In 1796, a Virginia farmer named George Washington advertised in its real estate section to lease part of his land at Mount Vernon. In the mid-19th century, the paper enthusiastically supported Abraham Lincoln and proclaimed his victory in 1860. At the turn of the 20th century, the paper presented its Sunday edition, something that would become a household tradition across the area and continues today with a circulation in excess of 180,000. In 1954, it ran a doomsday scenario that proclaimed "Hartford Destroyed," with smaller print explaining that it hadn't actually happened. In 2013, the *Courant* won a Pulitzer Prize for its coverage of the shootings at Newtown, Connecticut.

Foundation, the number of specimens has risen to 750 in recent years. So, as you're strolling through the park, see how many of the more unusual specimens you can find, like the largest turkey oak (*Quercus cerris*) in New England, a 500-year-old Chinese Toon (*Cedrela sinensis*), or the first-generation offspring of the state's original Charter Oak. Readers are welcome to attempt this search on their own by picking up a free tour brochure at the Capitol Building, but for those wanting a little help, check out the half-hour guided "Tree Tours of Bushnell Park," which run seasonally. For more information, visit bushnellpark.org. Various volunteer-led tours are available throughout the year, so check the website for the latest availability.

hartfordtrivia

In 1687, Governor Edmund Andros, appointed by the British Crown to oversee Connecticut, demanded colonists return the royal charter that made Connecticut a separate colony. Hartford colonists hid the charter in a towering oak tree, since called the Charter Oak. When the Charter Oak finally toppled in 1856, it was 1,000 years old.

From May until the end of Oct, you not only can walk beneath the 1886 **Soldiers & Sailors Memorial Arch**, but if you happen to be in the park between noon and 1:30 on a Thurs, you also can take a tour of the monument and learn little-known facts such as that the ashes of arch creator George Keller and his wife are buried in the east tower. Also be sure to check out the 8-foot-tall statues set into the arch, representing residents who walked away from their lives to fight in the Civil War. You'll find a student, a farmer, a freed slave, a stone mason, a carpenter, and a blacksmith.

In the eastern portion of the park, near the pond, is an 1874 statue of **Horace Wells**, a Connecticut dentist who is a hero for pioneering the use of nitrous oxide anesthesia in 1846. Wells went on to have a few difficulties, including experiencing a bad episode after overuse of chloroform. He unfortunately committed suicide in 1848 but was posthumously recognized for his achievements in 1870. He continues to be celebrated seasonally at the **Hartford Stage** in a play titled *Ether Dome*, all about his life and tragic death.

The 1899 **Corning Fountain** was a gift from John Corning (of Corning Glass Works of New York). He commissioned this beautiful 30-foot-tall fountain to honor his father who operated a gristmill in Hartford. Keep exploring to find the 1874 bronze monument to **Israel Putnam**, the Connecticut resident who is credited with the famous line, "Don't fire until you see the whites of their eyes," on Bunker Hill in 1775. When you come across a statue of a torch-holding angel, check out the size of her feet! This is the **Spirit of Victory**, a **Spanish-American War Memorial** that pays tribute to the soldiers who fought in the Spanish-American War from 1898 to 1899. The feet needed to be made so large to keep the statue standing upright.

If you're done exploring Bushnell Park and want to get out of the elements for a bit, head south to Summit Street and the campus of ***Trinity College***. When here, don't miss the ***Trinity College Chapel*** (300 Summit St.; 860-297-2126) built in 1932 and boasting stained-glass windows, a cloister, arches, and carved pews in keeping with the best medieval tradition. The chapel's most interesting elements are 78 ***hand-carved oak pews*** that face each other across the nave. It took more than 30 years to complete all the carvings, most of which were the work of ***J. Gregory Wiggins***, originally of Pomfret. Wiggins was a self-taught wood carver who began his trade as a young boy when he and his brother used to whittle wooden soldiers to play with. Wiggins was a friend of Trinity President Remsen Brinckerhoff Ogilby, who held the position from 1920 to 1943. He once told Ogilby that he wanted to create humorous pieces for the church since "the act of smiling in church should not be considered a crime." Take the time to appreciate his carvings even as you take in the beauty of the chapel. The Charter Oak Pew shows Captain Joseph Wadsworth hiding the Connecticut Colony's royal charter in an ancient oak tree to prevent its recall by Royal Governor Edmund Andros (not a beloved figure in Connecticut history). Hours are 9 a.m.–5 p.m., Sun–Sat.

Elizabeth Park (1561 Asylum Ave., West Hartford; 860-231-9443, ext. 104; elizabethparkct.org), which first opened in 1904, is home to the first municipally owned rose garden in America. The park itself, however, has been around since 1897 and was made possible when Charles Murray Pond donated his country estate to the city of Hartford. The park is named in honor of his wife, Elizabeth Aldrich Pond. Although Theodore Wirth designed the park, he consulted with the firm of Frederick Law Olmsted, and his influences can be seen throughout the property along with Wirth's. Today the property consists of 101 acres (90 of those were Pond's) and is lovingly cared for and maintained by the ***Elizabeth Park Conservancy***, which was formed in 1977 and brought the park back from serious disrepair. They continue to work as nonprofits and raise funds to keep the park not only beautiful but also thriving. Due to their efforts, the park is now listed on the National Register of Historic Places and is visited by thousands annually.

The approximately 15,000 rose bushes are at their peak between late June and early July. The many varieties of roses come in all sizes and hues, and the mingled scents, from the sweetly scented traditional American hybrids to the elegantly fragrant damask roses, are indescribable.

The park also features amazing gardens with flowers of all varieties, including a perennial garden, a tulip and annual garden, a shade garden, and a horticulture garden. Fans of history and architecture should make time to explore the ground's historical buildings, many original to the Pond farm. Even the restrooms are architecturally interesting, built and designed in 1935 by Hartford architects Smith & Bassett. There are also six tennis courts, lawn bowling, basketball courts, playgrounds, and ball fields.

Elizabeth Park is open daily, year-round, dawn to dusk. Admission is free, but the conservancy always appreciates donations. Check their website for more information on the myriad special events and fundraisers happening throughout the year.

Just to the southeast of the park, you'll find the **Connecticut Museum of History and Culture** (1 Elizabeth St.; 860-236-5621; chs.org). Founded in 1825 and designated a Blue Star Museum, it offers exhibits that help visitors learn about history and understand today through interpretation of the past. The museum has rotating exhibits, including one on how our state fared and changed through World War I, one on signs for inns and taverns of the state, and more. Hours Tues–Sat 10 a.m.–5 p.m., Thurs until 8 p.m.; Sun 12–5. Admission.

Continue a few blocks to the southeast and you'll find a little piece of paradise, where back in 1874, the great American humorist and novelist **Mark Twain** (aka Samuel Langhorne Clemens) began living in Hartford in a rambling, 3-story, 19-room Victorian mansion that he had built to his eccentric specifications. In 1881, he had the place redecorated in an even more eccentric style by Louis Comfort Tiffany. For the next quarter century, this was the Twain family summer home, which Twain himself often described as "part house, part steamboat." It was the place where the author wrote some of his best works, including *The Adventures of Tom Sawyer, The Adventures of Huckleberry Finn, The Prince and the Pauper,* and *A Connecticut Yankee in King Arthur's Court.*

The restored **Mark Twain House and Museum** (351 Farmington Ave.; 860-247-0998; marktwainhouse.org) is now a museum and storehouse of Twain memorabilia. The unmistakable redbrick building, with its startling three-color slate roof, many gables, monumental chimneys (it has 18 fireplaces), and flamboyant exterior walls painted in red and black Chinese stripes and trimmed in dark red, looms over the Farmington Avenue commuter traffic. Inside, the unique rooms have been restored as close to their 1881 condition as possible. About half of the original furnishings remain or have been acquired, including Twain's Venetian bed, whose ornate headboard so intrigued the author that he slept with his head at the foot of the bed so he could see the intricate carvings.

marktwaintrivia

Twain was fascinated by technology and incorporated many of the day's latest inventions in his home, including central heating and gas lighting fixtures. So it is fitting that the new museum center at the Mark Twain House was the first Leadership in Energy and Environmental Design (LEED)–certified museum in the country and the first LEED building in Connecticut. Among the many cutting-edge environmental features are the geothermal walls as the predominant cooling source.

Twain's ill-advised investment in a typesetting machine called the Paige Compositor resulted in such a devastating financial loss that he was forced to leave his Farmington Avenue home and move his family to Europe.

The Adventures of Tom Sawyer was the first novel in America to be written on a typewriter.

While the Twain family spent many happy years at this house in Hartford, Twain himself experienced a lot of heartache. He and his wife lost their first son, Langdon, to diphtheria at the tender age of 2 in 1871, the same year they moved to Hartford. They had a daughter that same year (Susy) and two more daughters (Clara in 1874 and Jean in 1880) and spent the next 17 years at this home. In 1891, the Twains moved their family to Europe while keeping ownership of the Hartford house. In 1896, on a trip back home to Farmington Avenue, Susy contracted meningitis and died at the age of 24. The family never returned to the house, unable to be where they had lost their beloved daughter and son. In 1904, Olivia passed away from an illness. In 1909, Jean died from complications due to epilepsy. Twain was left with only Clara until he died a year later in 1910 at the age of 74.

This Blue Star Museum features a welcome center, exhibition galleries, gift shop, a theater, and classrooms. While the welcome center and exhibits are self-guided, admission to the Twain family home is by guided tour only. There are a variety of tours to choose from, including holiday tours (highly recommended), Graveyard Shift Ghost Tours (learn what *Ghost Hunters* investigators discovered . . . if you dare), "Get a CLUE" tours, and the Living History House tours. Visit the website for more details. Open 7 days a week 9:30–4:30, last tour at 3:30 p.m. Closed on major holidays. Tickets should be purchased in advance.

Across the lawn from the Mark Twain House is the home where Twain's friend and famous author Harriet Beecher Stowe once lived. Today, the **Stowe Center for Literary Activism** (77 Forest St.; 860-522-9258; harrietbeecherstowe.org) has a visitor center in an 1873 carriage house, The Stowe House, a museum shop, beautiful historic gardens, a research library, and the Katherine Seymour Day House. Day was Stowe's grandniece, and she was responsible for the creation of the Harriet Beecher Stowe Center in 1941. Purchasing and moving into Stowe's house in 1927 (it had passed out of the family upon Stowe's death in 1896), Day lived there until her death in 1964, collecting all things related to her aunt and creating much of the collection you see today. This collection of artifacts and buildings offers a vivid glimpse into Stowe's life, the life of the woman who helped galvanize the abolitionist cause with her novel *Uncle Tom's Cabin*.

There are specialty tours and events throughout the year at the center, including Spirits at Stowe: An Otherworldly Tour (Oct) and The Preservation Tour, which focuses on the Victorian finishes in the house. The grounds of the Stowe Center are open year-round, dawn to dusk. The Stowe House is open year-round, Thurs 10 a.m.–3 p.m.; Fri and Sat 10 a.m.–4:30 p.m. Admission. Free for active military during the summer. Not every building on-site is handicapped accessible.

West Hartford

Granby has ponies, East Granby has turkeys, **West Hartford** has cows, which makes sense considering this is where CowParade Holdings Corporation is located. There were actually two cow parades in town, one in 2003 and one in 2007, and money raised benefited numerous charities. You can see some of the herd still in town.

But, of course, cows are not all that this swanky town has to offer. First settled in 1679, West Hartford stands in the shadow of Hartford but has a personality of its own: from the upscale Blue Back Square, where one can spend hours strolling the sidewalks and exploring the myriad shops and eateries, to the down-home **Westmoor Park**.

Proud of its history, town officials installed a sign on **Goodman Green** (Farmington Avenue and South Main Street) that lists 39 historic West Hartford sites with a short history and a map location for all. The green itself is a historic site, too. Donated to the West Hartford Parish of the Congregational Church by Timothy Goodman in 1747, this parcel of land has long been the center of activity for this community. Now maintained by the town (but still owned by the parish), Goodman Green is host to special town events and ceremonies. While traffic can be busy on both Farmington Avenue and South Main Street, the green is worth the visit. For a preview of the list, visit westhartfordct.gov.

Across Farmington Avenue from Goodman Green in Veterans Park, you will find **Connecticut Veterans Memorial**, a memorial to all members of the US armed forces from King Philip's War to the present. This circular memorial of black granite is titled "The Wall of Peace," and symbolizes the passage of time. Each conflict involving the US is reflected with a breaking of the wall. The names of West Hartford residents who were killed are etched in the stone. There is also a Walk of Remembrance that leads to an inner area of reflection.

A short trip up Farmington Avenue and down Trout Brook Drive brings you to **The Children's Museum** (180 Mohegan Dr.; 860-231-2824; thechildrensmuseumct.org), a great hands-on place to visit with the kids. They claim it's "where science and nature are fun," and they're right! Most kids we know like the giant walk-in kaleidoscope, but just as many love Conny the Whale, the giant, walk-in sperm whale (which is, of course, Connecticut's state animal). Voted *Hartford Magazine*'s "Best Kids' Attraction," the center offers the NASA-funded Blue Planet Red Planet exhibit, a planetarium (separate admission required), a wildlife sanctuary (very cool with lots of neat animals to see), an indoor forest that changes with the seasons, Turtle Town and Lizard Lair where critters can be seen and studied, and so much more. There are hands-on rooms, too, for those little ones with the wiggles. Open Wed–Fri 9:30 a.m.–3:30 p.m.; Sat 1 p.m.–5 p.m.; Sun 10 a.m.–4 p.m.; Closed Mon and Tues and major holidays. Admission for adults and children age 2 and older.

South of the museum is **New Park Brewing** (485 New Park Ave.; 860-232-2033; newparkbrewing.com), whose creations include Foliation, a pale ale brewed with flaked wheat and pilsner malt, and Expression Ten, with flavors of fresh pine needles, orange peel, and grapefruit. They have regular can releases, as well as food truck visits that are listed on their website. Monthly events include a Soul Brunch, which offers an array of soul, jazz, and R&B music, and includes a food truck and coffee roasters to complement the beer offerings. There's also a Funk Night that showcases special musical guests. The brewery is open Tues–Thurs 4 p.m.–9 p.m.; Fri 12 p.m.–10 p.m.; Sat 11 a.m.–10 p.m.; Sun 11 a.m.–6 p.m.

If you head north from the museum or Goodman Green, you can visit 162 acres of natural diversity at **Westmoor Park** (119 Flagg Rd.; 860-561-8260; westmoorpark.com). It's a great place to take the kids or the nature lover in your family. You will find a demonstration farm complete with farm animals; seasonal flower, herb, and vegetable gardens; a wildflower meadow; two ponds; an indoor discovery room with a parrot, geckos, turtles, and lizards; and 3 miles of nature trails all tended to by knowledgeable and talented staff. The park was made possible by the generous gift of Charles and Leila Hunter, who bequeathed the property to the town. The farm is open daily 9 a.m. to 4 p.m. year-round. The trails open at 7 a.m. and close at dusk. Fishing, picnicking, and dogs are not permitted in the park.

Newington

The town of **Newington** got its start as an industrial enclave of Wethersfield. The source of the town's first industry is portrayed on its town seal. Go ahead, go take a look. We'll wait.

Yep, you saw that right. It's a waterfall. A really, really small waterfall, about 15 feet actually. But **Mill Pond Falls** (123 Garfield St.) is where everything started for the fledgling settlement. In 1677, before Newington was Newington, four men secured the right to build a sawmill on Mill Pond so they could make barrel staves (the beveled sides of the barrel). They must have been onto something; the business lasted for a century before the wood supply dwindled and the business diminished. Today, the falls are surrounded by Mill Pond Park, a gathering place for many in town with a playground, sports fields, and walking trails.

newington trivia

Newington means "new town in the meadow," and residents adopted it as they made their departure from Wethersfield.

Wethersfield

East of Newington is **Wethersfield**, once known as "Oniontown" because the crop, especially the red onion, grew so well within its confines and its scent permeated everything. In fact, the red onion still has a strong presence here. And, while Wethersfield boasts the motto of "ye most auncient towne in Connecticut," it is actually one of three towns settled in 1635, the first year of our colony. Wethersfield shares the distinction with Windsor and Hartford, each represented by a grapevine displayed on Connecticut's flag.

There is a friendly rivalry between the residents of these towns as to who was first; but no matter if it was first or not, Wethersfield was an important port on the Connecticut River as the town grew. Then, in 1692, a flood changed the course of the river forever and destroyed all but one warehouse in the prosperous river town. Adjustments needed to be made; the former shipping port was now a cove and the river was deep enough to allow ships to bypass Wethersfield and sail right into Hartford. Industrious residents shifted their port from the newly formed cove out to the new river side (the area that is now Rocky Hill), allowing them to remain active in the shipping industry into the 19th century.

Today, Old Wethersfield, the remnants of the original town, has more than 300 historic homes, many bearing the names of early sea captains and some dating back to before the Revolution. With so much history in one place, it's difficult to decide where to begin. The **Wethersfield Historical Society** (150 Main St.; 860-529-7656; wethersfieldhistory.org) offers some good advice on interesting narrated tours and exhibits to whet your appetite.

You can also choose to explore the **Wethersfield Heritage Walk**, a 3-mile, self-guided tour of many of the historic sites. There are interpretive plaques along the walk that provide more information as well. To find an online map of the heritage trail, head to the town website (wethersfieldct.gov). You can park for free at the **Keeney Memorial Cultural Center** (200 Main St.; 860-529-7656; wethersfieldct.gov), where you will find more maps, public bathrooms, drinking fountains, historic exhibits, and a museum shop.

During the walk, stop in at the **Webb, Deane, and Stevens Museum** (211 Main St.; 860-529-0612; wds.org), including the 1752 Webb House where George Washington and Rochambeau met to formulate plans for the last campaign of the Revolutionary War. Next door was the house of Silas Deane, a member of the first Continental Congress and one of the most tragic figures of the Revolution. Originally one of the most ardent patriots, friends with George Washington and Benjamin Franklin, he helped negotiate the treaty with France. But he lost faith when Congress charged him with financial impropriety based on spurious evidence concocted by a jealous rival. His despairing private letters were intercepted, probably by his secretary (who was a British spy), published in the newspapers, and his reputation was destroyed.

The third house in this triple museum, built in 1788 by Isaac Stevens, is full of period antiques. Behind the museum lies a nice herb garden in a large open space. Open May to Oct, Wed to Sun, 10 a.m.–4 p.m. Guided tours available at 11 a.m., 1 p.m., and 3 p.m.

Also on Main Street you'll find the **Old Wethersfield Country Store** (221 Main St.; 860-815-4705; owcsct.com), named "Best General Store in New England" by *Yankee Magazine* in 2017, for good reason. Inside, you'll find a delightful menagerie of local food and products; 300 kinds of candies and chocolates (yep, 300); more than 70 different types of cheese; a nice selection of non-GMO, vegan, gluten-free, and organic foods; toys, gifts, and gift baskets for every occasion; and oh so much more, including ice cream. Owners Megan and John Jakubowski, who opened the store in 2014, are always looking for suggestions from their customers of what they'd like to see in the store. As the *New England Traveler* says, this store "takes the hit-and-miss out of finding locally made goodies and gifts." Open Tues–Sat 10 a.m.–6 p.m.; Sun 10 a.m.–5 p.m.

If you have a seafood lover among you, you need to stop at **City Fish Market** (884 Silas

wethersfield trivia

Wethersfield was the site of the first documented witch trials in America, featuring nine accusations and three executions between 1648 and 1668. The hysteria and neighbor-versus-neighbor drama of these accusations were fictionalized in Elizabeth George Speare's 1958 classic young adult novel, *The Witch of Blackbird Pond*, which won the Newbery Award Medal that year. The real victims were Mary Johnson, who confessed under pressure, and John and Joan Carrington, accused and executed for witchcraft.

Deane Hwy.; 860-522-3129; cfishct.com). Part fish market, part seafood restaurant, City Fish has been a fixture on the Silas Deane Highway since 1967. Fresh seafood is available daily in their market, having been trucked in from Massachusetts seaports. If you don't see what you're looking for in their vast freezer cases, just ask; chances are they might have it in the back. If you'd rather have the cooking done for you, have a seat in the restaurant and enjoy the huge portions and friendly service. The retail counter is open Mon–Tues 9 a.m.–5 p.m.; Wed–Fri 9 a.m.–6 p.m.; Sat 9 a.m.–5 p.m., and the kitchen is open Tues and Sat 10 a.m.–5 p.m.; Wed–Fri 10 a.m.–6 p.m. City Fish also supplies many area restaurants with fresh seafood, so don't be surprised when you see their orange/yellow trucks on the highway going to and fro.

Last but not least, you must pay tribute to the town's past as a "seed capital," at **Heirloom Market at Comstock Ferre** (263 Main St.; 860-257-2790; heirloommkt.com). Since 1811 seeds have been sold from this spot on Main Street, and from 1838 to 2016, the business operated under the name Comstock Ferre and Company, the longest continually operating company of its kind in the US. Today it is also a wonderful cafe where you can get a delicious breakfast and lunch, from scones to smoothies. In the attached grocery store you can still find (among other things) open-pollinated, pure, non-GMO seeds of the highest quality, heirlooms that you won't find anywhere else. Open Tues and Wed, 7 a.m.–5 p.m.; Thurs and Fri, 7 a.m.–8 p.m.; Sat 8 a.m.–8 p.m.; Sun 8 a.m.–4 p.m.

Rocky Hill

Leaving the 19th century behind, we travel to nearby **Rocky Hill,** and to another time in our history.

In 1966, while clearing ground for the construction of a new state building in Rocky Hill, bulldozer operator Ed McCarthy uncovered some unusual rocks. They had strange markings and scorings on them. It turned out that these were the tracks of dinosaurs that prowled the area 185 million years ago. In those days, this part of Connecticut was a mud flat on the shore of a huge lake, rich in fish and small crocodilians—good eating for a growing dinosaur.

After covering the initial excavation to preserve 1,500 tracks, the state excavated an additional 500 tracks, enclosed them in a geodesic dome, added an audiovisual facility that offers a neat presentation, and called the result **Dinosaur State Park** (400 West St.; 860-529-8423; dinosaurstatepark.org). Inside the dome, you'll be greeted by a full-size reconstruction of a carnivorous dinosaur called *Dilophosaurus*, but the big attraction is the amazing collection of tracks. Most of the impressions are three-toed, and they run up to 16 inches long. There's also a hands-on Discovery Room with many things to explore.

> ### connecticut trivia
>
> Purchase a Heritage Pass at Dinosaur State Park, Fort Trumbull (in New London), or Gillette Castle (in East Haddam) and receive unlimited admission into all three parks during the entire calendar year for two adults and four children.

The 80-acre park also has 2 miles of nature trails and picnic tables, and a place where you can make your own dinosaur casts out of plaster (check the website; you'll need to bring your own supplies). Open Mon to Sun, 9 a.m. to 4:30 p.m. Admission.

The **Rocky Hill Historical Society** (785 Old Main St.; 860-563-6704; rhhistory.org) is located in the 1803 *Academy Hall*, the former school designed and built by architect Abraham Jaggers to teach sailors the art of navigation. The society has a few interesting exhibits showcasing artifacts from Rocky Hill's history, including a Danforth Pewter collection. Open Sat, 12:30–3 p.m., or by appointment. There is no charge to visit.

The **Rocky Hill–Glastonbury Ferry** (293 Meadow Rd.; 860-625-8473), spanning the Connecticut River and linking one part of Route 160 (Ferry Lane) to the other, has been in operation since 1655. That makes it the oldest continuously operating ferry in America. It's also a good place to cross the river if you want to avoid the usually heavy traffic around Hartford's bridges. Service is provided by a tug called the *Cumberland*, which tows a barge called the *Hollister III*.

In 2011, this ferry, along with the Hadlyme–Chester Ferry, was almost shut down by the state in an effort to reduce the ever-present deficit. Nutmeggers again rallied—politicians were motivated, grassroots groups sprung up, voices were heard, and the decision was reversed. The Rocky Hill–Glastonbury ferry operates (weather permitting) Mon–Fri, 7 a.m. to 6:45 p.m., Apr 1 through Nov 30. Cost is $5 per vehicle on weekdays and $6 on weekends, and $2 for pedestrians and bikers; special commuter rates are available.

And, since you'll be taking the ferry, why not stop at **Still Hill Brewery and Tap Room** (1275 Cromwell Ave., Building C, Unit 9; 860-436-6368; stillhillbrewery.com) and taste the creations of Scott Barbanel before leaving town. While relatively new to the professional brewing scene, Barbanel is no stranger to making home brews. He began experimenting at his family home on Still Hill in Glastonbury, carrying on the tradition that gave the hill its name back in the day when one of Glastonbury's founding fathers operated a still there. Although Scott was not brewing moonshine, his beers consistently drew compliments from his family and friends, and they encouraged him to make the leap into professional brewing. He did. He opened the brewery and tap room early in 2016 and says it's his job to "craft high-quality kick-ass beers," and that it's our job to enjoy them. Well, okay, if we have to. Still Hill is open Thurs–Fri 4 p.m.– 9 p.m.; Sat 2 p.m.–8 p.m.; Sun 2 p.m.–6 p.m. Time to go to work.

The Collins family of **Fair Weather Acres** (1146 Cromwell Ave.; 860-529-6755; fairweathergrowers.com) has farmed the Connecticut River Valley for more than a century. The present generation, Chris and Mary Collins and their son Billy, started Fair Weather Acres in 1988 and went on to become the largest green bean grower in New England. In 1997, Fair Weather Acres relocated to the site of the original Collins Farm and business boomed until superstorm Irene hit the state in 2011. True to their roots, the Collinses recovered from the damage, diversified their business, and today they thrive once more. Their farm produces more than 200 varieties of fruit, vegetables, and herbs. They have a farm market, offer a CSA program, and host a large annual festival in the fall. The farm stand is open 8 months of the year Sun–Sat 8 a.m.–6 p.m.; Kitchen open daily 11 a.m.–2 p.m. Check website for kitchen menu.

East of the River

Glastonbury

Though in some ways a suburban town, **Glastonbury** is home to many farms and orchards. A complete list with addresses and crops they offer, as well as a crop calendar can be found on the Glastonbury town website (Glastonburyct.gov). Many of these farms have pick-your-own options or roadside stands. It's always a good idea to have cash with you in small bills, as sometimes the farm stands are on the honor system and no one is there to give you change. If you're lucky enough, you'll choose to visit one of the two farms whose crops also include grapes. For example, the **Joseph Preli Farm & Vineyard** (235 Hopewell Rd; josephprelifarm.com) has a farm stand *and* a winery. Head to the farm stand to pick up some fresh garlic, fresh-cut flowers, radishes, plums, or yellow squash. Or maybe you want to pick your own blueberries or blackberries. Then you can head to the vineyard and find the outdoor tasting area. Sounds good, right? The winery usually opens May–Nov (weather permitting), 12 p.m.–6 p.m. every day except Tues. Please check website for any change.

Crystal Ridge Winery (257 Belltown Rd.; 860-657-1004; crystalridgewinery.com) is another fine wine choice. This vineyard was established in 2004 on a 200-acre estate in South Glastonbury. In 2018, Crystal Ridge added a tasting room where you can do a tasting of five wines (Estate Tasting) or four (Reserve Tasting) of their red, white, and rosé wines, made right on the premises. The winery is truly a family venture with everyone lending a hand to make things run smoothly. Matriarch MaryAnn James passed away in 2016 after a battle with cancer, and the family continues in her honor.

Open year-round, but hours change seasonally. Usually open Thurs–Fri 3 p.m.–8 p.m.; Sat 12 p.m.–8 p.m.; Sun 12 p.m.–5 p.m. Check Instagram, Facebook, and Google for most up to date hours.

East Hartford

East Hartford is home to the ***Hockanum River Linear Park Trail*** (hockanumriverwa.org), a 4.5-mile trail that runs from Hillside Street to the Meadow Hill Station on Pitkin Street. Parking is available at designated spots along the trail and on the website the trail is mapped and broken into sections according to these parking places.

One of the parking places is a destination in itself. **Great River Park** (301 East River Dr.; riverfront.org/parks/great-river-park) is part of the movement to recapture the riverfront, and it's lovely. It features an amphitheater in which many special events and concerts take place, sculptures, nearly 2 miles of walking trails that are paved and lighted, a boat launch, and access to fishing in the river. And, if you choose, you can walk across the **Founders Bridge Promenade** into Hartford from the park. Parking is free and off street, but may be limited during special events. The park is open year-round.

Family is always welcome at the table, but food needs to earn its place. That's the motto at ***Granny's Pie Factory*** (103 School St.; 860-291-1164; grannyspiefactory.com), owned and operated by Joan and Anton Harovas along with their son, Niko. They make pie—and only pie—and they do it right. Believing that traditions are made around the family table, they want to make it a little easier for people by giving them a delicious reason to gather around that table. Any one of their pies will bring family members out of the woodwork and off their electronics. Give them a try and reconnect with your loved ones. Open Tues–Fri 10 a.m.–5 p.m.; Sat 9 a.m.–1 p.m.

Manchester

Manchester was originally home to the Podunk Indians and didn't see English settlers until 1673. The area then proceeded to go through an identity crisis as it grew into what is today one of the most densely populated towns in the state. It was part of Hartford for a while, known as the Five Mile Tract; then it became Orford Parish and was part of East Hartford. This was about a decade before the turn of the 18th century, and there were about 1,000 residents in the area, including ***Captain Richard Pitkin*** who, along with his sons, had supplied gunpowder to the Continental army. As a thank you to the Pitkin family for their service, the newly minted State of Connecticut awarded the family a 25-year monopoly on the manufacturing of glass. The ***Pitkin Glass Works***

was formed in 1783 and dominated the glass trade in the area until about 1830, mainly manufacturing bottles, flasks, and inkwells. The remains of the glass works building can still be seen on the corner of Putnam and Parker Streets.

While you're there at the corner of Putnam and Parker, turn west toward the traffic island. There, hidden within a stand of arborvitaes is a sign that designates this as the site of the 1775 **Pitkin Tavern**. It was here, the sign says, that Richard Pitkin and his wife Dorothy fed 26 Manchester volunteers who "answered the Lexington Alarm." Mrs. Pitkin is also credited with feeding General Rochambeau's army in 1761 as they headed to Yorktown. So not only did the Pitkins supply gunpowder to the troops, they kept them fueled with food as well!

The Pitkin family was joined by other families who made their living in the area. According to the **Manchester Historical Society**, the town had two churches (Congregational and Methodist), five schools, four taverns, five saw- and gristmills, one unsuccessful copper mine, three paper mills, and several woolen and cotton factories throughout the years. The town applied for incorporation in 1812 but was not successful until 1823, when Orford Parish officially became the town of Manchester.

One of the more successful manufacturing endeavors in Manchester belonged to a gentleman named **Richard N. Mather**, who owned and operated Mather Electric. Originally in Hartford, Mather moved his business to Manchester when he built an impressive new mill on Hilliard Street in the summer of 1887. At that time, generators and light bulbs were the backbone of Mather Electric. Mather was known in the industry as an "electrical genius," securing more than 20 patents in his life, including one in 1883 for the first generator. His light bulbs, known then as "lamps," graced the Chicago Opera House in 1885 when they made the switch from gaslights. Mather continued to enjoy success for the next 10 years before trouble struck. In 1893, a company called General Electric accused Mather of infringing on Thomas Edison's patent for the light bulb. Mather struck back, saying that GE wanted a monopoly on the industry and was trying to put him out of business.

The battle raged in the courts for close to a year before Mather had to stop making his light bulbs. At one point, even the streetlights in the north end of the city went dark. Mather Electric revamped and reorganized and continued making machinery for a time in its fancy building on Hilliard Street, but the company and the man were never the same.

As a way to make ends meet, the company leased some of its building space to other manufacturers, including the Norton Electrical Instrument Company, a company that built "horseless carriages," and a typesetting equipment manufacturer named Unitype. The Orford Soap Company rented space on

Hilliard Street after their Oakland Street building was destroyed by a fire in 1899. They liked it so much that they ultimately purchased the entire plant from Mather in 1903.

In 1980, the Train Exchange and Miniature Corner operated here, featuring a miniature railroad room on the second floor. Today, **Time Machine Hobby** (71 Hilliard St.; 860-646-0610; timemachinehobby.com) occupies the building and continues the tradition of the upstairs train room, with the **Silk City Model Railroad Club** coming in every first and third Sun of the month from 1 p.m. to 4 p.m. to build, add on to, and operate the huge layout, which is now the largest in New England.

Downstairs on the first floor you will find many toys and hobbies from today and yesteryear, from model cars to spud guns, from therapy putty to stuffed animals, from board games to card tricks. Stop in and enjoy the toys and trains, but also take a moment to appreciate the building and the history it has witnessed. They are open year-round Thurs–Mon 10 a.m.–6 p.m.

Manchester's **Fire Museum** (230 Pine St.; 860-649-9436; thefiremuseum.org) is home to the **Connecticut Firemen's Historical Society**. On March 20, 1970, a group of firemen met with the intent of collecting and preserving artifacts of firefighting history. Manchester's town manager, Bob Weiss, alerted the society members that the old fire station in his town was slated to be demolished unless a suitable use for it could be found. The members jumped at the chance and in the spring of 1979 the society signed a 100-year lease for the property, which was in desperate need of some love. It took four years, a state grant, hundreds of hours of work from volunteers, and a little help from the US Navy Sea Bees for the museum to finally open. The dedication took place on October 29, 1983, 13 years after the idea was first conceived.

Inside, you'll find old leather fire buckets, ornate marching hats, wooden water mains, and a rare 18th-century fire warden's staff among other artifacts on the museum's three floors. There's even a collection of old prints and lithographs of fires, from the pre-photographic era when the artist and lithographer were as important as the reporter to the process of communicating the news. The museum is open from the second Sat in Apr through the second Sat in Nov, noon to 4 p.m. Fri and Sat. Other dates and times may be available by appointment. Suggested donation of $5 for adults; children under 12 are admitted free.

If you have time to drive around Manchester, take note of these two houses should you pass by them (both are now private properties, so you must admire them from the street). The first is the **Walter Bunce House** (34 Bidwell St.), which was built by **Alpheus Quicy**, an African American stonemason, and is the only such building of his that still stands today. Quicy, his father, and his brother are credited with building important fieldstone homes and several dams in the Manchester area.

The second home of note is the **Hart Porter House and its outbuilding** (465 Porter St.), built sometime between 1840 and 1845 and believed to be a stop on the Underground Railroad due to a full basement in the outbuilding that is accessible only through a trapdoor. Porter worked as a farmer and married Martha Miner on January 12, 1837, in the same Manchester Methodist Church where Frederick Douglass spoke in 1843. The church's pastor, Reverend V. R. Osborn, often preached the importance of the abolitionist movement, and it appears that Hart Porter must have heard him, going to remarkable lengths, at great risk to himself, to help others find freedom.

If you are in the area and have the kids with you, why not let them burn off some energy with a visit to the **Lutz Children's Museum** (247 S. Main St.; 860-643-0949; lutzmuseum.org). Founded by a former art teacher and located in a former school building, this place is designed for children. The emphasis here is on "please touch" science and natural history exhibits including live animals rescued by the museum. If the animals can be rehabbed, they are cared for and released back to the wild, or if their injuries are such that they would not be able to care for themselves, they become residents of the museum. There is also an art exhibit with rotating collections, often in partnership with area teachers who show their students' artwork here. The museum also sponsors several excellent programs throughout the year including classes, trips, outreach programs, and summer camp. Open year-round, Tues–Fri 9 a.m.–4 p.m.; Sat and Sun noon to 4 p.m. Museum closed between 12 p.m. and 1 p.m. Tues–Fri. Admission except for those younger than 1.

After all this running around in Manchester, relax in **Wickham Park** (1329 Middle Turnpike West; 860-528-0856; wickhampark.org). This is a private, nonprofit organization, founded by Clarence and Edith Wickham. It will cost you to park your car, but you will also pay at many state parks on summer weekends. Wander through 250 acres of gardens, open fields, woodlands, ponds, an aviary, a nature center, and a sensory garden. Play disc golf, picnic, or take the fun hiking trail with your kids. Open Apr through Oct, daily 9:30 a.m.–sunset.

Bolton

Take a walk or cycle the **Hop River State Park Trail** (multiple entry points; 860-295-9523; ct.gov/dot), which begins on Colonial Drive in Manchester and extends through **Bolton** all the way to Windham County. Over 20 miles long, Hop River Trail runs along a former railroad line with a spur trail heading north into Vernon. The trail is mostly gravel and dirt, making for an exciting day out on your mountain bike (avoid trying a street bike on it) or for a very long walk (you can just take small sections at a time). In the winter, this is a prime spot for cross-country skiing. It's not all flat, though: Bolton Notch has over 300 feet of elevation gain each way.

Now that you've worked up an appetite, why not stop at **Munson's Chocolates** (174 Hop River Rd.; 860-649-4332; munsonschocolates.com)? Begun in 1946 in Manchester as the Dandy Candy Company, Munson's now boasts chocolates spinning around the earth on the international space station. The largest retail chocolate manufacturer in Connecticut, this is still a family business now into the third generation. They have 10 stores throughout the state, but the original is here in Bolton. Get your fill of chocolate truffles, nut bark, and cordial cherries, as well as more snackable candy bars, fudge, peanut brittle, chocolate-covered pretzels, and turtles. The store is open every day, and if you want great Connecticut-made chocolate, get it here. Retail hours are Mon–Fri 9 a.m.–7 p.m.; Sat: 10 a.m.–6 p.m.; Sun: 11 a.m.–5 p.m.

Down the road is the **Fish Family Farm** (20 Dimock Ln.; 860-646-9745; fishfamilyfarm.com), a 211-acre dairy farm that Munson's uses for its wonderful milk chocolate. However, you will probably be more interested in the ice cream, sold year-round by the quart in their freezer: vanilla, maple walnut, coffee, peanut butter, cherry vanilla, chocolate chip, and more. Open Mon–Sat, noon to 6 p.m.

The Tobacco Valley

East Windsor

The **Connecticut Trolley Museum**, **Connecticut Fire Museum**, and **Connecticut Motor Coach Museum** (58 North Rd.; 860-627-6540 for Trolley Museum or 860-649-9436 for the Fire Museum) in **East Windsor** offer you the opportunity to visit three great museums for one price in one location. How can you beat that?

The Trolley Museum is run by the nonprofit **Connecticut Electric Railway Association** and has a collection of more than 70 pieces of rail equipment, some dating back to 1869. The collection includes freight and passenger cars, interurban cars, elevated railway cars, locomotives, and more. While most of the trolleys are from New England and Canada, there are some from as far away as Illinois and Ohio and one from Rio de Janeiro. The museum offers a car-barn tour and a 3-mile trolley ride. Special events are held throughout the year including Storytime Mondays and Lego building contests. There are also special holiday rides, including Winterfest in December, which features leisurely rides along a 1.5-mile route decorated with twinkling colored lights. Santa has also been known to make an appearance.

The Connecticut Fire Museum is operated by the **Connecticut Antique Fire Apparatus Association** and has a collection of about 20 fire trucks built between the early and late 20th century. The adjacent Motor Coach Museum, also run by the Connecticut Antique Fire Apparatus Association, has a variety of transit buses on display.

The museums are open sporadically depending on the season, but weekends are your best bet. Check their website thefiremuseum.org for the latest. Admission.

Windsor

Once upon a time, every town had a place like **Bart's Drive-In** (55 Palisado Ave.; 860-847-4053; Beergardenatbarts.com). Today they are scarce, but you'll find one in **Windsor**. Bart's started as a hot dog stand, eventually expanded to include an indoor dining area, and has now expanded even further to include the Beanery Bistro right next door. Whether you're craving a chili dog, fresh fish, an ice cream cone, or maybe a gourmet coffee and a muffin, you'll find it here. Watch for Seafood Sunday, when all seafood is delivered and prepared fresh daily. There are picnic tables that overlook the river, and you can usually spot anglers fishing from the shore or in boats, so after a meal it's fun to sit awhile and watch or stroll down the sidewalk that runs along the river. Open Mon–Sun 7 a.m.–6 p.m., carryout hours 7:30 a.m.–5:30 p.m.

The **Windsor Historical Society** (96 Palisado Ave.; 860-688-3813; windsorhistoricalsociety.org) was founded in 1921 and continues to preserve the town's history and share it with all those who visit. The society operates a museum and library where you can explore and discover myriad permanent and changing exhibits, including old journals and maps, an 1800 highway survey, and an original payroll list of the Windsor residents who answered the rebel alarm in Boston in spring 1775. The museum also contains a variety of Native American relics and a display of Americana. Open Wed through Sat, 11 a.m. to 4 p.m. Admission.

The society cares for two historic houses in Windsor. The first, the **Dr. Hezekiah Chaffee House** (108

windsor trivia

Settled on October 4, 1633, Windsor claims to be the "oldest English settlement in Connecticut," though Wethersfield disputes this claim.

In 1647 Alse Young of Windsor was the first person to be hanged for witchcraft in New England.

Windsor resident Amy Archer-Gilligan was the inspiration for the elderly poisoners in the play and movie *Arsenic and Old Lace*. She ran a boarding house on Prospect Street and poisoned some of her pensioner tenants with homemade wine.

Palisado Ave.), was built around 1767 and was home to the doctor and his family. It is said that John Adams had dinner here in 1774. The house now belongs to the town of Windsor, and the society began leasing it in 1992. They opened the first floor to the public in 1993 as a museum with period furnishings and household items. Visitors can also learn about the lives of slaves owned by Chaffee, including Elizabeth Stevenson, who was emancipated, and Nancy Toney, who was the last surviving slave in the state when she passed away in 1857.

Dr. Chaffee's offices were attached to the family's home and are available for viewing today. Visitors can view medical instruments and learn about medicinal practices during that time. Chaffee's daughter, Abigail, was married to Colonel James Loomis. Their son, James Chaffee Loomis, went on to become a senator and founded the **Loomis Institute** along with his siblings. Back then the institute separated boys and girls, and The Chaffee House housed the girls' division, which went on to become the Chaffee School. The two branches reunited in 1970 to form the **Loomis-Chaffee School**.

The historical society also manages **The Strong-Howard House** (96 Palisado Ave.). This historic home (formerly the Fyler House) experienced a bit of an identity crisis when it was renamed in 1999. The house was scheduled to be demolished in 1925 but was saved thanks to the efforts of the historical society, which raised $750,000 for restorations. In their research to do just that, the society discovered that while the home sat on land belonging to Lieutenant Walter Fyler, the current structure was actually built by the Strong family 118 years after the Fylers were in residence and later substantially updated by Captain Nathanial Howard. Hence, the new name.

The house now reflects the way of life at the beginning of the 19th century, but you don't have to be careful of fragile artifacts in this museum. In fact, touching and exploring is encouraged! That's because the furniture and household objects are actually accurate reproductions, carefully researched and created to reflect the time period. So go ahead and sit on that bed! Both houses can be toured Wed through Sat 11 a.m.–4 p.m. when the Historical Society is open.

Run not by the town's historical society but by the DAR is the magnificent **Oliver Ellsworth House** (778 Palisado Ave.; 860-688-8717; ellsworthhomesteaddar.org), named for one of the most important residents of Windsor, of Connecticut, and maybe of America. He helped author the Constitution, served as one of Connecticut's first senators, wrote the Judiciary Act, and was appointed by George Washington as third Chief Justice of the Supreme Court. In short, he was one of the founders of this country, and the fact that his homestead still exists here just above his beloved Connecticut River is a gift to us in this present day. In the words of Ellsworth himself, "I have visited several countries, and I like my own the best. I have been in all the States of the Union, and Connecticut is the best State; Windsor is the pleasantest town in the State of Connecticut and I have the pleasantest place in Windsor. I am content, perfectly content, to die on the banks of the Connecticut." Open on the third Sat from May to Sept, 11 a.m.–2 p.m.

Ellsworth has been unfortunately forgotten, even in his home state. But for him, the work was its own reward, and the fact that the system of law he helped create has lasted so long would be reward enough.

Windsor Locks

For anyone interested in the history of aviation, the **New England Air Museum** (36 Perimeter Rd.; 860-623-3305; neam.org) in nearby **Windsor Locks** is a must. The museum features an extensive collection of aircraft, memorabilia, and exhibits housed in three large heated or cooled (depending on the need) hangars. Some of the larger aircraft are kept outdoors. One of the oldest aircrafts is a beautiful wood-and-canvas Bleriot XI monoplane, dating from 1911. There is also an extensive collection of World War II fighters and bombers, and even supersonic jets. The museum also features smaller items of interest, including a variety of engines, cockpit simulators, and a collection of flight memorabilia. Many of these items, acquired from area aerospace companies, can't be seen anywhere else. Don't miss their Open Cockpit and Veterans Day programs; they are a family favorite. Open Tues–Sun 9 a.m.–4 p.m.; last admission at 3:30. Closed on holidays. Gift shop. Admission. Museum passes cannot be used on special event days.

Going back in history to a slower time and place, the **Windsor Locks Canal** (Canal Road; 860-242-1158; www.ct.gov/dep) is a great little walk along the riverside. Built in the 1800s, this short canal alongside the Connecticut River is really a workaround for boats traveling the Enfield Rapids. The walking trail is along the old towpath that hovers between the canal and the river. Walk, or skate, or bike as long as you like on the easy 5-mile length and dream about the old canal days of Connecticut.

Suffield

One of the most famous residents of **Suffield** was dietary reformer Reverend Sylvester Graham. Born in 1794, he invented the Graham diet in 1829, including fresh vegetables, fruit, high fiber breads, and small portions of eggs and dairy. For him, meat, alcohol, and spices were avatars of "sin," and his diet was a way to fend off "impure thoughts." He lectured around America, gathering

west suffield trivia

West Suffield is the site of the first cigar factory in the country, which was built in 1810. The factory site is now marked by a mere gravestone-like monument on the front lawn of a residence on Ratley Road, just south of Spruce Street in West Suffield.

many followers, who liked this strange combination of Puritanism and vegetarianism. Because he banned spices, the recommended diet was quite bland, but his "Graham flour" recipe for hard, pure, dark bread, caught on anyway. This bread was later reworked and sweetened into that essential ingredient for s'mores, Graham Crackers.

At our next cookout we'll ignore the fact that marshmallows and chocolate would have been banned under Sylvester's program.

One of the places Graham might have visited is the restored 1764 home on Suffield's beautiful Main Street (Route 75), now the **King House Museum** (232 S. Main St.; 860-668-5256). The building features six original fireplaces and is filled with period furnishings, including a four-poster bed that formerly graced the Jonathan Trumbull house in Lebanon. Displays include an assortment of Bennington pottery, a tinware collection, and, appropriately enough for the Tobacco Valley, a collection of cigar and tobacco memorabilia. The King House Museum is open Wed and Sat, May through Sept, from 1 to 4 p.m. Admission is free, but donations are welcome.

Enfield

About 20 minutes east of Suffield is the town of **Enfield** and the site of Connecticut's only community of Shakers. This community thrived in Enfield from 1792 to 1917. Based on the premise of direct communication between man and God, Shakers did not believe in praying through a church, priests, or other men of the cloth, but members would sit and meditate until they received a sign from God personally. At this point, they would begin to tremble or shake, hence the name "Shaking Quakers," which was eventually shortened to Shakers and adopted by the group. While it may have started off as a derogatory term, it came to symbolize quality and integrity.

Facing serious opposition in England, in 1774 Shaker leader Ann Lee set sail for America with some of her supporters and began spreading word of their religion on the shores of America. First visiting Enfield in 1781, Mother Ann, as she was known, was met with opposition and barely escaped being tarred and feathered. She risked a second visit the following year and again met with opposition that broke out in serious riots. Not to be deterred, however, Ann returned to Enfield in 1783. While this visit was much more peaceful than the previous two, Mother Ann would not live long enough to enjoy it. She died the following September at the age of 48. She had planted the seeds in this community, however, and in 1792, the first Shaker community was established in Enfield.

Throughout the years, the Enfield community grew to include five families who lived on nearly 3,000 acres in town. The group held true to its beliefs in feminism, pacifism, and freedom. It became an important stop for fugitive slaves in their quest for justice, as evidenced by a diary of a member that chronicles the visit of Sojourner Truth. The community thrived through the first half of the 1800s, but then the stringent demands of the religion (including celibacy) began to take their toll, and one by one the families disbanded, merged, or moved to other established Shaker communities.

Today, only a few buildings built and owned by this Shaker community remain. Some are privately owned, and the rest, unfortunately, are on the prohibited grounds of the state Department of Corrections facilities on Shaker Road. Visitors can, however, learn more at Enfield Historical Society's **Old Town Hall Museum** (1294 Enfield St.; 860-745-1729), open Sun 1 p.m.–5 p.m., May–Oct, and the **Martha A. Parsons House Museum** (1387 Enfield St.; 860-745-6064), open by appointment, or by visiting enfieldhistoricalsociety.org. Admission is free.

Like every other successful business, Powder Hill Farm in Enfield was feeling the need to diversify to survive. For this working dairy farm, the 1990s brought falling milk prices and struggling times. Owners Jack and Mavis Collins decided to open **The Collins Creamery** (9 Powder Hill Rd.; 860-749-8663; thecollinscreamery.com) in 1997. The business took off and today is managed by Jack and Mavis's daughter and son-in-law, Tony and Michele Bellafronte, which is funny because Tony doesn't eat ice cream. They do just fine, however, by offering more than 20 flavors of the richest, creamiest ice cream we have ever tasted. For those of you who can't handle the high-test stuff, there is also frozen yogurt, fat- and sugar-free, and soft serve. While there is no indoor seating, you are welcome to stay and enjoy your frozen treat at the picnic tables among the beautiful farmland. Open daily in season, noon to 8 p.m. Remember to bring cash; they don't do plastic here.

East Granby

When **East Granby** was first settled in 1664 it was known as the Turkey Hills Ecclesiastical Society, and the town really embraces this history. The turkey is on the town seal, there's a Turkey Hills Road that runs through town, and in 2008 when the town was celebrating its 150th birthday, they took a page from Granby's campaign of the painted ponies called "Giddy Up to Granby," but they put their own spin on it and trotted out the turkeys. Fiberglass turkeys, that is. Sponsors were able to decorate their turkeys to their liking, and these Toms started popping up all over town. There are about 40 total, each standing about 5 feet tall; you will see them outside of businesses and on private lawns. See how many you can find!

One place you won't find a turkey is the **Old New-Gate Prison & Copper Mine** (115 Newgate Rd.; 860-653-3563). "Copper mine" and "prison" are not usually two things linked together, but such is the case here. Originally chartered as the first copper mine in America in the early 1700s, the town's mine didn't produce the results necessary to make it profitable, although not for lack of trying—50 years of trying! Work was finally abandoned in 1750 and the mine, with all its holes and tunnels, sat empty for over 20 years until 1773, when it was decided by the General Assembly that the dark, dank environment might be just the place to deposit criminals. On December 22, 1773, New-Gate Prison (its notorious namesake being in London) welcomed its first prisoner—John Hinson. (He escaped 18 days later, but he was still the first!) The prison operated as our nation's first state prison until 1827 and during that time gained a reputation as "the worst hell-hole in North America." The site is now a National Historic Landmark and a State Archaeological Preserve. It was reopened to the public in July 2018 after an 8-year restoration. Inside the 12-foot-tall stone wall, a small prison yard includes a guardhouse, the ruins of a chapel, two workshops, a cell block, and an entrance to the dank passageways of the underground copper mine, where the prisoners were confined, often claimed by disease, suicide, or insanity. Some people say that spirits of the men and women who met their demises here still haunt the tunnels to this day. Visit if you dare! Open May to Oct; Fri–Mon 10 a.m.–4:30 p.m.; closed Tues and Wed; Thurs reserved for group tours. Admission for those older than 12; Blue Star Museum.

Across the street from the prison stands the **Viets' Tavern**, an 18th-century house that was home to Captain John Viets, first warden of the prison, and his wife, Louis Phelps, who prepared food for the prisoners at one time. Captain Viets died in 1777 of smallpox at the age of 65. He and his wife are both buried near the tavern; their tombstones can be seen there. Tours of the unrestored tavern will be offered after restoration is completed, anticipated in 2026.

You'll spot the "Viets" name elsewhere in town. Take a ride to **East Granby Farms Recreation Area** (79 North Main St. [Route 187]) and head to the entrance where you can't miss the bright blue silo with the words "L. H. Viets & Sons Cattle & Horses" painted on it. The L. H. is Leon Hastings, the son of Anna and Charles Viets, who owned the 500-acre farm that is now the recreation area. When the farm ceased operating, the town acquired the land and turned it into a recreation center and park. As a nod to its former use and owners, they decided to leave the silo and adorn it with a mural of the farm.

The bungalow style house located at the park entrance once belonged to Leon's parents. It was a **Gordon Van Tine mail-order house** that the Viets ordered late in 1920. Gordon Van Tine houses, manufactured home kits that needed to be assembled (like IKEA furniture), rivaled Sears in the mail-order home business. Charles presented Anna with the deed on Christmas morning as a gift to her. They lived in the smaller house on the farm while one of their sons and his family lived in the main farmhouse.

If you need a glass of spirits to calm your nerves after visiting with spirits at the prison (see what we did there?), then **Brignole Vineyards** (103 Hartford Ave.; 860-653-9463; brignolevineyards.com) can help you out. This 15-acre, family-owned vineyard boasts a beautiful new winery. They offer different events throughout the year, so be sure to check their Facebook page and website for the latest. Even if you choose to simply enjoy your wine on their beautiful deck, you really can't go wrong! Open Mon–Fri 1 p.m.–7 p.m.; Sat 12 p.m.–7 p.m.; Sun 12 p.m.–6 p.m.

Granby

You will see many places in **Granby** that reference Salmon Brook, the earlier village named for the eponymous brook that runs to the east and south of the village. Whether the stream was named for the settlement or vice versa, we're not sure. Maybe you can find out with a stop at the multi-house **Salmon Brook Historical Society** (208 Salmon Brook St.; 860-653-9713; salmon brookhistoricalsociety.com). You can start at the 1732 **Abijah Rowe House**, donated to the historical society in 1966 by Colton sisters Mildred and Carolyn, whose father had purchased the house in 1903. The house has been restored to what it would have looked like in the early 19th century. Period furniture from the area was donated and added to original features of the house, including a corner cupboard in the parlor and the front door. Upstairs there is a collection of Victorian artifacts, such as antique dolls. The Rowe House is believed to be the oldest structure left from the original British settlement. Also on-site is the 1790 **Weed-Enders House**, home to the society's office and museum store. This primitive saltbox house was moved from its original location in Enders State Forest to the society's property in 1974. Once there, it was restored to its original condition as a farmhouse with a Victorian parlor containing a stereopticon and an Edison Phonograph.

Your next stop at the museum can be the 1870 **Cooley School House**, the only remaining one-room schoolhouse in town (at least the last one that hasn't been renovated into a private residence or store). This building was moved to its current location in 1980 after being donated to the society by Merrill Clark, whose mother was a teacher at the school. It now gives visitors a good idea of what a 19th-century schoolroom would have looked like.

The last building on our tour is the newest, the 1914 **Colten-Hayes Barn**. Built by tobacco farmer Fred M. Colten, the barn holds a lot of history, including antique tools, Native American artifacts, a replicated village store, exhibits on the history of voting in town and the town churches, and so much more. Like we said, you can literally walk through history. Public tours are Sun 2 p.m.–4 p.m.

A trip to Granby is not complete without a visit to the 300-year-old **Dewey-Granby Oak** on Day Street, off Route 20. This tree, while not the biggest or even the oldest tree in the state, is probably the coolest. It's prominently displayed on Granby's town seal, which appears on everything from official stationery to town vehicles. It even has its own website (salmonbrookhistorical.org/granby.htm), which tells you all about this beautiful tree that has seen so much. In fall, the oak is especially attractive and worthy of a photograph or three.

Once you've had your fill of history, perhaps a stop at **Grassroots Ice Cream** (4 Park Pl.; 860-653-6303; grassrootsicecream.com) is in order. This artisan ice cream shop, as they like to call themselves, is located in the old Avery's General Store and is family-owned and -operated by Lee and Eliza Florian and their children.

The business name has special meaning for the Florians. They tragically lost their 2-year-old son to a disease called adrenoleukodystrophy, a disease that could have been treated had their newborn been screened. Determined to spare other families the pain they were going through, the Florians formed a grassroots campaign to have a bill passed in Connecticut requiring the screening. Due largely to their efforts, the bill requiring newborn screening for adrenoleukodystrophy passed in the Connecticut Legislature on July 3, 2013. Grassroots Ice Cream opened the next day.

By experimenting and coming up with unique flavors, from Pear Lavender sorbet to Banana Caramel Cup to Boysenberry Jasmine, the Florian family has amassed an almost cult-like following. When one flavor runs out, they just replace it with a different one. Open through the summer, every day 11 a.m.– 9 p.m. Winter hours depend on the weather, so be sure to check their Facebook pages before traveling. They have four other locations in Connecticut; check website for more info.

As you drive around town, watch for the smattering of life-size painted ponies. These were part of the 2006 fundraiser called "Giddy Up Granby" hosted by the **Granby Artists Association** (granbyartists.org). Each horse (and there are more than 40) has a name and a theme. A drive along Salmon Brook Street will bring you past "State Line Colt" by Sally Melrose at State Line Propane (500 Salmon Brook St.), "Stargazer," by David Guarco and Julie Wilson Foster at State Line Oil (514 Salmon Brook St.), and "Meadow Mare" by Diane Bannon, which stands not in a meadow at all but under the porch for the residents at MeadowBrook of Granby (350 Salmon Brook St.). "Sparky & Friends," painted by Rosemarie Mendes, can be found outside the Salmon Brook Veterinary Hospital (136 Salmon Brook St.) if you are heading back that way. Some folks make a day of finding as many horses as they can. We've given you a start. Good luck!

When you've just about had your fill of painted ponies, find your last one of the day outside **Cambridge House Brew Pub** (357 Salmon Brook St.; 860-653-2739; cbh.beer). This horse, aptly named "IPA," was purchased through the donations of Cambridge's patrons, and he stands guard at this pretty laid-back brew pub that has been creating delicious concoctions since 2005. As an example of just how laid back they are, they have a job opportunity on their website called "I'll do anything" for those who know they want to work in a brew pub but aren't exactly sure what they want to do. Hours are Sun 11:30 a.m.–8 p.m.; Closed Mon and Tues; Wed and Thurs 11:30 a.m.–9 p.m. and Fri and Sat 11:30 a.m.–10 p.m. They offer takeout and you can listen to live music most weekends.

If you're in a shopping frame of mind, you'll find your fill at **Old Mill Pond Village** (383 Salmon Brook St.; 860-653-3433; oldmillpondvillage.com). This cool conglomeration of shops includes the **Big Red Gift Barn** that is jam packed with everything you'd expect to find in a New England gift shop—clothes, jewelry, home decor, jams, jellies, and kitchen items. Then there's **The Christmas Shop**, which will transport you to December the minute you walk in the door, even if it's a 100°F August day outside. This shop also carries enough Halloween decorations to satisfy any fan, a selection of outdoor decorations from garden flags to porch benches, and a nice assortment of indoor furniture, too! Even if you don't purchase anything, you can walk off some of that Cambridge Brew. Open Tues through Sat, 9:30 a.m.–5:30 p.m.; Sun, noon to 5 p.m. Closed Mon. Check the website for vacation closings before traveling.

If you like to stroll through rooms full of items from years gone by, don't drive by **Salmon Brook Shops** (563 Salmon Brook St.; 860-653-6587) without stopping. While it admittedly doesn't look like much from the outside, the inside is packed with stuff. You can browse through old records, estate jewelry, furniture, postcards, books, linens, dishes, movie posters, advertising art, and more. Former First Lady Laura Bush stopped by here a few years back on her way to a speaking engagement. The staff said she was polite and personable as she perused the store with her security detail in tow. So, if Mrs. Bush deemed this store worthy of a stop, then we concur! Open 11 a.m.–5 p.m. every day except Wed.

Another great place to stop at in the area is **Sweet Pea Cheese** (151 East St.; 860-653-4157) in North Granby. Located on the Hayes family farm known as the **House of Hayes**, this operation churns out cheese and other products made from their own goats and cows. They regularly supply local restaurants and their products can be found at many farmers' markets throughout the state. After eight generations of family farming, we're pretty sure they know what they're doing! Open daily, 10 a.m. to 7 p.m.

If you're ready for an amazing farm-to-table experience, visit **Lost Acres Orchards** (130 Lost Acres Rd.; 860-653-6600; Lostacresorchardcom.wordpress.com). Purchased in 1975 by Ginny and Tom Wutka, these lands have been producing fruit since 1812! The Wutkas have expanded the orchards and found new ways to share them with visitors. The family operates a Farm Kitchen, which offers fresh soups, hot and cold sandwiches, salads, and even pizza, all made with the freshest ingredients. If you love what you had for lunch, there are plenty of pastries in their bakery for you to take home and enjoy later.

Don't be fooled by the relaxed atmosphere, though. Running an orchard is a busy, year-round endeavor. Rhubarb is harvested in May; June brings the berries (strawberries, blueberries, and raspberries); in July there's basil, parsley, and early vegetables; August is peach season; and September through October brings apples, pumpkins, squash, and mums! September also brings the beginning of cider time and the pressing continues until the apples run out, which is typically right around the holidays. Then it's time for baking pies and cookies. The winter months find the Wutkas making apple butter and other jams and jellies, as well as hot soup for the restaurant. When it begins to warm enough, they start the vegetable seedlings in the greenhouse, and the cycle starts all over again. Phew.

The bakery is open year-round, Wed through Sun, 9 a.m. to 5 p.m.; the deck is open, weather permitting, May through Oct. Please note that while the Wutkas grow many crops, the apples are the only ones that are pick-your-own.

If you're in the area on a weekend evening, continue down the road to **Lost Acres Vineyard** (80 Lost Acres Rd.; 860-324-9481; lostacresvineyard.com), a completely separate business with no relation to the orchards and completely worth a stop. Husband and wife team Kevin and Michelle Riggott purchased the land in 2008 and two years later opened the tasting room. Tastings of the white, red, rosé, and apple wines are available and include five choices and a complimentary glass to take home. Once you choose your favorite, you can move to the deck overlooking the vineyards to enjoy it al fresco or sit fireside and listen to the live music that's offered some nights. Guests can bring in their own food or purchase a cheese plate or antipasto right there at the vineyard.

The Riggotts are big supporters of the arts, and they choose artists each year and feature their art in the vineyard's tasting room as well as hosting the Granby Land Trust's annual Juried Art Show. They also hold special events throughout the year, so be sure to check the website often to see what's coming up next! Open Apr through Dec, Sat, noon to 6 p.m., and Sun, noon to 5 p.m. Also Fri 12 p.m.–6 p.m. beginning May 10.

If you opted to head west from the Salmon Brook Historical Society on Route 20 (Simsbury Road) instead of north, you have other options. If the kids are with you and they need to burn off some energy, head to **Holcombe Farm** (111 and 113 Simsbury Rd.; 860-844-8616; holcombfarm.org) where you will find 312 acres that are home to a working (and historic) farm, recreation areas, and miles of trails on which to explore and enjoy nature. According to the website, you should head east for easier walks through fields and forest and head west for more challenging hikes up ridges and along the brook. Whichever you choose, birdwatchers in your group will be thrilled with the more than 60 species of birds that live at the farm, and if you're lucky, you'll see other wildlife too, including deer, turtles, and more. If **geocaching** is your thing, you'll find several caches at the farm as well. You can download a map from the website to take with you. The trails are open year-round from dawn until dusk.

To the west along Route 219 (Barkhamsted Road) you will find **Enders State Forest** (Route 219; 860-379-2469; ct.gov/deep), Connecticut's 29th state forest and home to the beautiful, tumbling **Enders Falls**. The original 1,500-acre property was a gift from the Enders family in memory of their parents, John and Harriet Enders. Today the park contains more than 2,000 acres (thanks to land acquisitions by the state) and is enjoyed by thousands of visitors.

While the forest neighbors **McLean Game Refuge** (109 Salmon Brook St.), hunting is allowed only in certain areas of the park per the original deed from the Enders family. It is important, though, for you to be aware of hunting season and who else might be out there with you. The Connecticut DEEP's website (ct.gov/deep) provides information on when and where hunting is allowed. There are other cautions, as well. The purple-blazed trail takes hikers to the waterfalls, and we urge those headed that way to enjoy the waterfalls from a distance. The rocks above and around the falls are wet and slippery and can be dangerous. Stay on the trail and keep an eye on all those in your party, especially the young ones who may scamper off for a closer look at the beautiful falls that cascade over jumbles of rocks and form pools upon pools. It's not unusual in the warm weather to see adventure seekers sliding down the rocks and plunging into the refreshing pools below, but this is something that really shouldn't be attempted without proper equipment and training. The nearby Lost Acres Fire Department even does special training exercises in the area so they can be prepared for the numerous rescue operations they are called out to annually. Nature deserves to be respected for all its beauty and danger.

The park is open from 8 a.m. to sunset year-round. There is no fee and there are no facilities at this state park.

The Farmington Valley

Simsbury

Simsbury was settled in 1648 by a group of Windsor families who acquired the land from the Massacoe Indians. They called their new settlement Massacoh Plantation, a name that was eventually changed to Simsbury when the town was incorporated by the Connecticut General Court in 1670. In March 1676, when King Philip's War began to heat up, the entire village of about 40 dwellings was destroyed by Wampanoag Indians. The Wampanoag uprising was over by August, but it took two years for reconstruction to begin. Once it did, Simsbury quickly became an important factor in Connecticut's economy and politics. The first copper coins in America were struck here in 1737, and the first steel mill in America was built here in 1744. Hundreds of residents fought in the American Revolution, including Major General Noah Phelps, who, as America's first spy (he was just a captain then), entered Fort Ticonderoga in disguise to gather information for Ethan Allen; Allen then proceeded to capture the fort. By the 1820s, the town was a major stop on the Farmington Canal, which ran along the route of today's Hopmeadow Street (Route 10).

Pettibone's Tavern has been a fixture in Simsbury since 1780, when it was built for Captain Jonathon Pettibone Jr. Situated conveniently along the major travel path from Boston to New York, the tavern saw its fair share of travelers, including George Washington, John Adams, Harriet Beecher Stowe, and Ethan Allen.

The house, however, was not a happy family home. Captain Pettibone

simsbury trivia

Simsbury's main avenue, Hopmeadow Street, gets its name from the fields of hops that once grew where the street runs today.

In 1737, Simsbury's Samuel Higley developed the first copper coinage in America. The Higley copper was worth two and sixpence (42 cents) in paper currency. The coin's motto was "I am good copper."

The first safety fuse, used for mining and exploration, in America was made in Simsbury in 1836 by Richard Bacon. Bacon ran the mine at New Gate and entered into a partnership with the English firm of Bickford, Smith & Davey.

was a whaling captain who sailed far out to sea for long stretches of time. His wife, Abigail, stayed home alone in the big house. As the story goes, Abigail took up with another man, and one evening the captain returned home early and found his wife with her lover. He allegedly killed them on the spot with an axe. Historical records don't really bear the whole story out, but it is interesting to speculate.

Throughout its long history, the building was alternately tavern and private residence. A tunnel from its basement to the basement of an old red colonial home across the street suggests it may have been a stop on the Underground Railroad at one time. Today, the tavern has been transformed into **Abigail's Grille & Wine Bar** (4 Hartford Rd.; 860-264-1580; abigailsgrill.com), an upscale gathering place for good food and good wine. The restaurant's resident ghost has been known to give diners a friendly pat or poke now and again. Is the ghost Abigail Pettibone? Or perhaps someone who lost his life in pursuit of freedom in that bricked-over tunnel? Whoever this friendly ghost is, it has become a Farmington Valley tradition, with radio disk jockeys often spending All Hallows' Eve at the restaurant reporting on ghostly doings.

Open for lunch Mon–Thurs, 11:30 a.m. to 3 p.m.; for dinner Mon–Thurs, 3 p.m. to 9 p.m.; Fri and Sat, 3 p.m. to 10 p.m.; Sun brunch 11 a.m.–2:30 p.m., dinner 2:30 p.m.–8 p.m.

The **Simsbury Historical Society** (800 Hopmeadow St.; 860-658-2500; simsburyhistory.org) owns nine buildings on a 2-acre complex in historic Simsbury, including **Phelps Tavern, Phelps Barn, Hendrick Cottage**, and a one-room schoolhouse. Explore these period buildings and enjoy interactive exhibition galleries that show visitors what it was like to be guests at the Captain Elisha Phelps House between 1786 and 1849, when it was an inn. Three successive generations of Phelps tavernkeepers are chronicled, along with the social history of New England taverns. Back then, Connecticut towns were required by law to have at least one tavern to accommodate travelers, who arrived by horse, stagecoach, and canal boat. Museum hours are limited and tours are offered only on Sat or by appointment. The grounds and gardens are open year-round during daylight hours. Admission. Blue Star Museum.

For much of Simsbury's early history, **Talcott Mountain** cut the region off from the meadowlands of the Connecticut River Valley to the east. This isolation ended when the Albany Turnpike was hacked across the mountain, but that knife-edge of rock looming dramatically over the landscape remains a state of mind. Though separated by only a mile, Simsbury, Avon, and even Farmington to the south have far more in common with the small towns to their west than with the suburbs east of the mountain.

There has been a tower atop Talcott Mountain for most of the past 200 years. The first was built in 1810 and was the inspiration for John Greenleaf Whittier's poem "Monte Video." It was destroyed in a windstorm in 1840, but other structures followed until finally, in 1914, businessman Gilbert Heublein built a fourth tower atop the mountain, a grand white 165-foot-high edifice of steel and concrete anchored in the rock. For 20 years **Heublein Tower** was a summer home for the Heublein family. Today, the mountain and its tower are all part of **Talcott Mountain State Park** (Route 185; 860-242-1158). Four states are visible from the top of the turret on a clear day, but first you have to climb. The main public access route is off Route 185. A road leads partway up the mountain to a parking area, from which you can hike the 1.25-mile trail to the top. The early part of the climb is fairly steep, though there are benches for resting. Once you reach the tower, you'll have to make another climb up the stairs to the top; there are no elevators.

The park is open year-round from 8 a.m. to sunset. Heublein Tower is open 10 a.m. to 5 p.m., Thurs through Mon, Nov through Sept. For the month of Oct, they extend their hours from Wed through Mon, 10 a.m. to 5 p.m.

When leaving Talcott Mountain, turn left on Route 185 and drive west toward Route 10. A mile or so west of the access road, you'll come to an old iron bridge. On your right is a huge, witchy-looking tree whose branches loom over the road like some spectral presence. This is the **Pinchot Sycamore**, reputedly the oldest tree in Connecticut, and certainly the largest. Right before the bridge is the entrance to a small park where the tree resides. Take the turn slowly, as it's a bit steep as you enter the park. The tree is named for conservationist Gifford Pinchot and was dedicated to him in 1965. You'll be in awe as you stand under the tree that sports a 23-foot-diameter trunk. You have to stop and wonder about all this beautiful sycamore has seen in its history.

On your way to Canton from Simsbury, in West Simsbury, you'll find two farms worth a stop. The first is **Tulmeadow Farm Store and Ice Cream** (255 Farms Village Rd.; 860-658-1430; tulmeadowfarmstore.com), owned by the Tuller family since 1768. They sell a delightful selection of produce, like lettuce, arugula, chard, tatsoi, basil, tomatoes, cucumbers, peppers, scallions, broccoli, bok choy, sweet corn, squashes, zucchini, cucumbers, green beans, and eggplant, as well as their grass-fed beef. However, you are probably here for their ice cream store, which they opened in 1994, to try one of the 50 flavors of award-winning, 16 percent butterfat ice cream. Open mid-Apr through Oct, 9 a.m.–9 p.m., but note that the ice cream window opens at noon.

Down the road is **Flamig Farm** (7 Shingle Mill Rd.; 860-658-5070; flamigfarm.com), home of the famous backwards "EGGS" t-shirts, which are ubiquitous in this part of Connecticut. This small 10-acre farm was founded in

1907, going through eras of dairy and egg retail. Today, though, this is a great place to bring your children for the legendary petting zoo. Open Apr through Nov, daily, 9 a.m.–5 p.m.

Canton

Canton, like so many Connecticut towns, has a ghost. This one is supposedly in the shape of a Revolutionary War messenger who disappeared in the vicinity while conveying a payroll from Hartford patriots to French officers aiding the Americans. After a bleached skeleton was found under the Canton Tavern, where the man was last seen alive, stories began circulating that the innkeeper had murdered the hapless messenger and stolen the money. Shortly thereafter, people started seeing a headless horseman, presumed to be the ghost of the paymaster, riding west along the Albany Turnpike (US 44) toward Saratoga. They still do. So if you're down by the Canton Golf Course some dark and foggy night, and you notice that your headlights are shining through a ghostly horseman and his steed to illuminate the road beyond, don't pay it any mind. It's just the **Headless Horseman of Canton** on his perpetual journey.

In the southern part of Canton on Route 179 is the village of **Collinsville**, which received its name from the Collins Company, an 18th- and 19th-century manufacturer of axes and machetes that were sold around the world. The story of the Collins Company is recounted in a series of exhibits in the **Canton Historical Museum** (11 Front St.; 860-693-2793; cantonmuseum.org). This small museum houses a re-created 19th-century general store, post office, barber, and blacksmith shop. There are collections of period clothing, furniture, household items, even a Civil War casket. There is also a striking 2,000-square-foot railway diorama accurately showing Collinsville and Canton as they appeared circa 1900. It is managed by the **Farmington Valley Railroad Society**. Open June through Nov, Fri, Sat, and Sun, 1 p.m. to 4 p.m.; Dec through May, Sat and Sun, 1 p.m. to 4 p.m. Admission.

Nearby in one of the old factory buildings is **Antiques on the Farmington** (10 Depot St.; 860-693-0615; antiquesonfarmington.com), a multi-dealer shop with furniture and accessories displayed in room settings so you really feel as if you've walked back in time. Browse slowly and you may just find a bargain. Open daily, 10 a.m. to 5 p.m.

Roaring Brook Nature Center (70 Gracey Rd.; 860-693-0263; roaringbrook.org) is affiliated with the Children's Museum in West Hartford and aims to foster the relationship between humans and nature. They offer guided nature walks, hikes on snowshoes, maple-sugaring demonstrations, bird walks, and summer nocturnal walks on 5 miles of trails. If you want to go it alone, you can, as there are trail maps available in the Nature Center Store and on their website. They hold special events, too, throughout the year, including concerts and a Halloween children's fair. Open year-round; hours vary due to school schedules (check their website).

And since you are so committed to going off the beaten path, why not try travel by canoe or kayak on the Farmington River? **Collinsville Canoe and Kayak** (41 Bridge St.; 860-693-6977; collinsvillecanoe.com) is a family-owned business that occupies the old Miner Lumber Company building in historic Collinsville. Starting small, they have expanded to 10,000 square feet, with numerous classes and rentals for all experience levels. If you want to buy a canoe or kayak, this is also the place to come. You can try out the equipment in the river right behind the store. How's that for customer service? Open Wed to Fri, 10 a.m.–6 p.m.; Sat and Sun, 10 a.m.–5 p.m.

Avon

Crossing into **Avon**, follow Town Farm Road to its end. If you turn right, you will quickly happen upon **Fisher Meadows** (800 Old Farms Rd.), a 205-acre natural area for hiking and walking, biking, fishing, canoeing, and picnicking. There are also recreational ball fields here. You have your choice of trails and you can download a map at Avon's town website (avonct.gov). The trail around Spring Lake is a good, flat walk. For a more strenuous hike, take the trail along the Farmington River, which offers lots of up-and-down walking, so it's not a good walk for small kids or tots in strollers. In the spring and summer, both trails offer great opportunities to spot wildflowers, such as the Virginia waterleaf, a declining species that is protected in Connecticut. Feel free to bring Fido, but please be sure he stays on his leash; it's the rule.

If you turn left onto Town Farm Road, you travel the narrow, winding roads past **Avon Old Farms School**. This private school for boys was designed by Theodate Pope Riddle of Hill-Stead Museum fame. The buildings are modeled after cottages in Great Britain's Cotswolds. There are no tours of the campus for the public, but you can drive through the campus to look at the buildings.

Heading north past Avon Old Farms along Nod Road, you'll eventually come to the **Pickin' Patch** (276 Nod Rd.; 860-677-9552; thepickinpatch.com). The land here has been farmed since 1666 and operates as a family-friendly farm stand and pick-your-own place. In 2012, when the Avon Cider Mill went out of business, the Pickin' Patch acquired their name, equipment, and product lines, adding cider doughnuts, jams, jellies, and more to their repertoire of items available. The farm stand opens when the pansies start to bloom and stays open until Christmas Eve; open 9 a.m. to 6 p.m. daily. There is a crop calendar on their website, so you can check and see what's in season when. On Oct weekends, you can take a free hayride to the pumpkin patch or book a group hayride during the week for a small price and receive a sugar pumpkin, cider and doughnut holes, and a souvenir cider sipper. Perfect for those gorgeous New England fall days.

If you continue west on US 44, you'll pass **Old Avon Village** (1–45 E. Main Street; 860-680-5298; avonvillagemarketplace.com), where you'll see a huge Hitchcock-style rocking chair that is something of a local landmark. People give directions based on proximity to the rocker, and rival high school students often "chair-nap" it to celebrate a football victory.

This area of our state saw its first Congregational church organized in 1652. The **West Avon Congregational Church** (280 Country Club Rd.; 860-673-3996; westavonchurch.org), built in 1751, is the descendant of this congregation. But as more settlers arrived and the population grew, the community began to spread out. Residents found the trip along the Farmington River from their homes to the village of Farmington too arduous and dangerous in the winter months. They requested and were allowed to build their own church, known as the "Lord's Barn." Unfortunately, the structure burned down in 1817, and today, only a marker remains to show the location on a knoll near the end of Reverknolls Road, about 1 mile north of the Cider Brook Cemetery.

By that time, however, plans for a new meetinghouse to serve the growing community were already under way—if only residents could agree on a location. Unable to come to a decision, the two groups began to diverge. Changes occurred within the General Assembly that allowed additional congregations to form. The society on the east side of the river assumed the title of Third Church in Farmington and their church was built, with the help of none other than David Hoadley, the future builder of many New England churches at the intersection of what are now Routes 44 and 10.

Just west of the junction of Routes 44 and 10 North is Avon Park North, where you'll find the **Farmington Valley Arts Center** (25 Arts Center Ln.; 860-678-1867; artsfvac.org). Home to the **Fisher Gallery and Shop** and about 20 artists' studios, this arts center showcases pottery, basket weaving, printing, painting, leatherworking, and silversmithing. The center believes in promoting the arts and giving visitors the chance to experience the creative process from start to finish. What a wonderful way to inspire your inner artist! Studios are open the first Sat of every month from noon to 4 p.m., and at the discretion of the individual artists. The shop and gallery are open Mon, 10 a.m. to 2 p.m.; Tues through Fri, 10 a.m. to 4 p.m.; Sat, noon to 4 p.m.; they are closed for major holidays.

The **First Company of the Governor's Horse Guards** (280 Arch Rd.; 860-673-3525; ctfirsthorseguard.org) is the oldest cavalry unit in continuous service in the US, tracing its lineage back to 1658, when the Connecticut Colony founded a troop of mounted guards. In 1788, the Horse Guards were reformed as a company of Light Dragoons, modeled on the Royal Regiment of Horse Guards in England. When Connecticut joined the Revolution against the British Crown, the new state took over the Horse Guards. In those days, the unit's main function was to escort and protect visiting dignitaries, and it acted as an honor guard to President George Washington when he visited Wethersfield in 1789.

The unit saw somewhat more dangerous service as a mounted unit in the War of 1812 and the Spanish-American War. In 1916, it patrolled the Mexican border during operations against Pancho Villa. Dismounted and reorganized as a machine-gun battalion, it served in seven major engagements in France during World War I. At the end of the war, the Horse Guards were remounted as the 122nd Cavalry Squadron of the Connecticut National Guard; four days after Pearl Harbor, they became the 208th Coast Artillery and served as an antiaircraft unit in the South Pacific.

Today, the Horse Guards' duties are once again mainly ceremonial, making appearances at presidential and gubernatorial inaugurations. All horses are donated, and they include just about every breed except Clydesdales. On Thurs from 7:30 to 10 p.m., the public is invited to watch the unit practice its drills. These consist of intricate, beautifully choreographed precision maneuvers, often accompanied by music. The Horse Guards hosts an annual Open Horse Show in June as well as various community programs. The Second Company of the Governor's Horse Guards holds its summer practices in Newtown; see the Danbury entry in "Gateway to New England" for details.

Around the corner on Route 167, you can see the **Old Horse Guard Barn**, which dates back to 1880 and is currently being leased from the state by the Avon Historical Society. The society recently put a new roof on the building, which was used to house the Guards' horses from 1954 to 2002. They hope to use the barn to house exhibits in the future.

Miller Farms (308 Arch Rd.; 860-673-3258; millerfarms.us), next to the Horse Guards headquarters, is a fourth-generation operation that produces some of the best turkeys in the region, but fresh birds are available only during the fall and winter holidays. At Thanksgiving, Miller's pitches its "turkey tent," an outdoor bazaar full of special goodies for your holiday table, including their "Turkease," a semi-boneless turkey that cooks three times faster than a whole turkey and "slices like a dream," according to Miller's. The turkeys sell like hotcakes, so call ahead to order. Outside the holiday season, Miller Foods sells other meats such as hams and smoked turkeys plus natural pet food in their market. Open Mon through Fri, 9 a.m. to 5 p.m.; Sat, 9 a.m. to 3 p.m.; Sun, 9 a.m. to 1 p.m.

Once a large dairy farm, **Riverdale Farms Shopping** (124 Simsbury Rd.; 860-677-6437; riverdalefarmsshopping.com) in Avon is now the site of one of the more interesting shopping centers in the area. This complex occupies several low hills under the eye of the Heublein Tower, atop Talcott Mountain to the north and east. Nineteen barn-like buildings, some original and renovated, some new, now house offices, stores, restaurants, and boutiques—and new ones are opening all the time. Most of the stores are crafts, gift, or fashion stores, but you'll also find a yoga studio, pet groomers and pet supply stores, dance studios, and so much more.

Burlington

Burlington is home to the beautiful 1,148-acre **Nassahegon State Forest**, established in 1926 as watershed protection for the **Burlington Fish Hatchery** (34 Belden Rd.; 860-673-2340), which is still in operation today as the oldest fish hatchery in the state. They stock our waterways with brook, brown, and rainbow trout, as well as being the only producer of kokanee salmon fry.

Kokanee are a breed of the larger, Pacific Ocean sockeye salmon. Every fall, adult kokanee are transported from East Twin Lake and Lake Wononskopomuc in Salisbury to the hatchery for spawning. The eggs are incubated and the fry are cared for until late May when they are brought back to East Twin Lake, Lake Wononskopomuc, and added to West Hill Pond. It takes 3 years for the fish to mature into adults, which can be between 12 and 16 inches long. The hatchery estimates that their kokanee salmon program results in 20,000 to 30,000 hours of recreational fishing annually. The hatchery is open year-round, 8 a.m. to 3 p.m. daily. Tours can be arranged by appointment or you can simply stop in and check it out for yourself.

Known simply as the Burlington Block of the Nepaug Forest until 1942 when it was officially renamed the Nassahegon State Forest, this area offers great hiking, including a portion of the Connecticut Forest and Park Association's **Tunxis Trail**, which travels a total length of 79 miles from Southington to the Massachusetts border, but you can do a small portion of it through the forest. Make it a 2-mile out-and-back, or, if you have the option, leave a car at each end and cut the hike in half.

Before you head to your parked car (or get ready to retrace your steps to Punch Brook Road), turn right on Stone Road and walk about 140 feet. On your right, you will come to an **old stone jailhouse**. This is a remnant of a camp built in these woods in 1934 for men who traveled from town to town looking for work during that difficult economic time. This camp could accommodate up to 250 men, who were required to put in at least 24 hours of work a week in exchange for board and a weekly paycheck of 90 cents.

burlington trivia

To the south of Nassahegon State Forest is the Whigville section of Burlington, so named for a group of citizens who belonged to the Whig Party, the predecessor of the modern-day Republican Party. They attended a Whig Party Convention in the state capital and carried a sign proclaiming themselves residents of Whigville and it stuck.

Residents of Burlington who are old enough to remember say that sometimes these men came into town and caused quite a ruckus. Most likely this "jail" was a holding cell for those who might have had too much to drink or were not following the rules. They hung out here until they were under control again. In 1936, the Works Progress Administration (WPA) took over the camp, and men lived and worked there until about 1938 when the National Youth Administration took over. Other agencies used the camp from time to time until 1944, when it was put to use as a forest headquarters until 1971, when DEEP was formed. Today, nothing more than foundations and a chimney exist along with the jail, oddly still intact, right off of Stone Road.

The **Taine Mountain Preserve** (burlingtonlandtrust.org) is another great hike and further proof of how instrumental land trusts are in saving the open spaces in our state. In 2015, the **Burlington Land Trust** collaborated with the town and **Trust for Public Land** to purchase 150 acres that were adjacent to the 150 acres already in the preserve. Today, the 300 acres are managed by the land trust and are open for us to enjoy and appreciate. Two hikes are available: the almost-2-mile Perry's Lookout Loop and the almost-3-mile Taine Mountain Double Loop. The terrain can be rocky (and wet during a thaw or rain) and some parts are steep, but it's generally not too bad if you take your time and wear the right shoes. There are some incredible views to be had at the summit as well. Parking is available along Venture's Way and Ryan's Way; directions are available on the website.

Please be bear-aware when you take these hikes. There have been an increasing number of bear sightings in Connecticut as of late. The DEEP recommends, if you see a bear, to keep your distance, make your presence known by shouting and waving your arms and/or walk slowly away. Never feed the bears or any wildlife for that matter.

If ghost hunting is more your thing, then Burlington is your place. The first stop on our Burlington ghost tour is the **Seventh Day Baptist Cemetery** (Upson Road), but if you want to do more than drive by, you'll need to gain approval from the Burlington Police Department. A ghostly tale of a female apparition appearing and disappearing with a green mist at this cemetery has been told for years. There is speculation that the "Green Lady," as she is called, was Elizabeth Palmiter, who walked this green earth in the 19th century. One stormy night, when Mr. Palmiter didn't arrive home in a timely manner from a trip into town, Elizabeth supposedly went out to look for him. She didn't get far before drowning in a swamp. It is said that now Elizabeth roams the cemetery presenting herself to unsuspecting (or suspecting) visitors. There have also been stories of Mr. Palmiter roaming the graveyard with a lantern looking for his beloved. Alas, these are just stories. The reality of the situation is that the story of the Green Lady originated with a local camp leader who made up and told his campers the story all in good fun. But that doesn't mean there aren't other lonely spirits roaming the Seventh Day Baptist Cemetery.

The second stop on our ghost tour is the **Lamson Corner Cemetery** (Milford Street [Route 69]), where, the story goes, a hiker in the area noticed a young man standing at the top the hill of the cemetery and, thinking he was visiting a grave, called out to him to ask what time it was. He received no answer, and, in fact, the man turned and walked away. When the hiker, a bit perturbed, followed the man to get his answer, the man simply disappeared and where he stood was the grave of a World War II soldier. Numerous paranormal groups have visited the cemetery, getting a variety of results, all up to interpretation. So, if you're driving by and want to get out and take a stroll through the cemetery to pay your respects, just keep an open mind. Many of the gravestones are those of young children, possibly due to a smallpox epidemic. Perhaps this explains the sadness that seems to thicken the air.

On a brighter note, let's make our way to **LaMothe's Sugar House** (89 Stone Rd.; 860-675-5043; lamothesugarhouse.com), one of just a handful of real old-fashioned sugar houses left in Connecticut. Here, during February and March, visitors can tour a working house and see the whole process of "sugaring off." There's a big old sap boiler that cooks maple sap into syrup, which you can then see blended with cream and butter and poured into molds to make creamy shaped candies (like Santas or maple leaves), or mixed with other ingredients to make maple taffy. The sugar house sells syrup, maple candy, and maple fudge. Visitors always get a sample of some type of maple sweet. In Connecticut, the peak season for sugaring off is late Feb or early Mar, but LaMothe's is open year-round, Tues through Sat; 10 a.m.–5 p.m., Sun 12 p.m.– 5 p.m.

Farmington

We've found some unusual places in Connecticut, and we've even encountered some spooky places, but **Shade Swamp Sanctuary** (Scott Swamp Rd.) in **Farmington** takes the cake as unusual and spooky. Located right off busy Route 6 in Farmington, this abandoned zoo seems overhung with a prevailing sadness. The 800-acre preserve surrounding the old cages is owned by the state but maintained by the Farmington Garden Club. You can park next to the Shade Swamp Shelter that is visible from Route 6, and you'll see a sign for the Blue Trail and then blazes on the trail. All this is pretty normal until you enter the woods and start to see the cages. Some are simply metal that is now bent with age, and others are sort of dens that nature has begun to reclaim.

The state of Connecticut acquired 140 acres in 1926 as a donation from Walter W. Holmes. In 1934, the Connecticut Department of Fish and Game opened the Shade Swamp Sanctuary as a place for endangered or injured native birds and animals. Structures, cages, and dens for the sanctuary were built by the Civilian Conservation Corps (CCC) as was the Shade Swamp Shelter, which is now listed on the National Register of Historic Places. As word got out about what the state was doing, people started bringing non-native species to the sanctuary in hopes of finding them a home. Alligators, monkeys, parrots, bears, and more were brought here, but, of course, it was impossible to house them in this environment. The facility was shut down in the early 1960s because of suspected "illicit activity."

If you'd like to explore the rest of the area, you have two choices of trails. One is the blue trail, which begins at the shelter off Route 6 and brings you through the abandoned zoo and over a footbridge. You'll pass by a kame terrace, a geological formation that resembles a hill with a flat top. It's made of sand and/or gravel left by a glacier, and if you had stood there thousands of years ago, you'd be looking at a large lake instead of the deposits it left there. The blue blazes then take you back to the start of the trail—just under a mile and a half in all.

The longer white trail is located on the west side of New Britain Avenue, with parking near the gated entrance to the former DEEP site on the north side of Route 6 just west of New Britain Avenue. For your GPS, the address is approximately 198 Scott Swamp Rd. This DEEP headquarters is now decommissioned, and you'll see the buildings as you hike by. For maps and more information on these trails, visit Farmington's website (farmington-ct.org).

Nearby, in the midst of 278-acre **Farmington Memorial Town Forest** there is a **memorial to US Army pilot 2nd Lt. Vincent H. Core**. In the spring of 1945, Lt. Core was on a training mission when he began to have trouble with his P47 Thunderbolt. Knowing he would have to make an emergency landing, the level-headed airman directed his plane toward the town forest to avoid the more populated areas below. Unfortunately, Core was unable to regain control over his aircraft and he hurtled through the trees, perishing in the crash. A Boy Scout troop from Bristol erected the memorial in the 1970s as thanks to Airman Core and his level-headed decision that saved countless lives on the ground. In 2014, Boy Scout William S. Sanford chose to blaze a trail with orange markers to the memorial so people could find it easily and pay homage to Core. The main access to the memorial is from Red Oak Hill Road (107 Red Oak Hill Rd., opposite 120 Red Oak Hill Rd.). If you are not able to secure parking on Red Oak Hill Road, your other option is to park on the cul-de-sac of Reservation Road.

Hill-Stead Museum (35 Mountain Rd.; 860-677-4787; hillstead.org) is so Farmington that it is almost impossible to imagine it existing anywhere else. Housed in a white clapboard 1901 replica of a neocolonial house built in an 18th-century English farm style is an amazing collection of French impressionist paintings, prints, antique furniture, porcelain, textiles, and clocks.

Hill-Stead was originally home to Cleveland iron mogul Alfred Atmore Pope. In keeping with his wealth and pretensions, Pope made sure that when it was time for daughter Theodate to go away to school, his child was entrusted to a proper eastern institution: **Miss Porter's School** in Farmington. Upon graduation, Theodate persuaded her father to forsake the Buckeye State and move east to the Nutmeg State. She also talked him into springing for a new house designed by the then-trendy architect **Stanford White**, with a sunken garden designed by landscape architect **Beatrix Farrand**. And since Theodate had an abiding interest in architecture, she assisted White in designing the new family manse. White was either a good businessman or he was truly impressed with Theodate's work, because he cut his fee by $25,000 in appreciation of her help. Miss Pope went on to become the first woman licensed to practice architecture in the US.

Like so many American captains of industry, Alfred Pope was a collector. This was an age in which America's newly rich raided the homes and galleries of Europe for furnishings, often buying art and antiques in wholesale lots. The Popes were typical in this regard, and their tastes were certainly eclectic. Chippendale furniture, fine porcelain, contemporary bronzes, and pre-Columbian statuary all jostled for space in the Pope home. On the walls hung a Degas, a Manet, a Cassatt, and no fewer than three Monets. The piano was a custom-designed Steinway.

It was all gloriously excessive. And it is all still there, just as it was when Theodate died, leaving behind 50 pages of instructions for the house to be turned into a museum and maintained just as she left it. Hill-Stead Museum is open Tues through Sun, 10 a.m. to 4 p.m., with the last tour leaving at 3 p.m. each day. The grounds are open 7:30 a.m. to 5:30 p.m. Hill-Stead

farmington trivia

Farmington is home to Miss Porter's School, known for graduate Jacqueline Bouvier Kennedy Onassis.

has a wonderful gift shop with prints of works exclusive to it, such as Monet's *Haystacks* and Degas's *Dancers in Pink*. Admission. Blue Star Museum.

Just around the corner from the Hill-Stead Museum is the **Stanley-Whitman House** (37 High St.; 860-677-9222; stanleywhitman.org), a beautifully restored 1720 colonial homestead. The original house, built to a typical early 18th-century standard, has a central chimney flanked by two chambers on each floor; it was later expanded by the addition of a lean-to that gives it a saltbox shape. The wood-sided exterior was originally painted with a mixture of ox blood and buttermilk; the restoration has not gone to quite that extreme, but it otherwise seems authentic. Hinged access panels inside the house let you see details of the original construction and restoration. The house is filled with period furnishings and is surrounded by herb and flower gardens. Tours are offered Wed through Sun, noon to 4 p.m., with the last one leaving at 3:15 p.m. If there are five or more in your party, the museum asks you to call ahead to book a tour. The museum is open Wed through Fri, 9 a.m. to 4 p.m.; Sat and Sun, noon to 4 p.m. Admission. Blue Star Museum.

Farmington played an important role in the antislavery movement. Many abolitionists called the area home and offered their houses as stops on the Underground Railroad. In fact, Farmington gained the moniker "Grand Central Station" of the railroad. In 1841, the town hosted the slaves who fought for their freedom aboard *The Amistad* when they gained their freedom thanks to John Quincy Adams. Farmington abolitionists provided housing and education as well as raising money to get them back home. The **Farmington Historical Society** (138 Main St.; 860-678-1645; fhs-ct.org) offers monthly tours from May through Sept of places that played a part in helping the African Mendis and other slaves find freedom. There is a charge; details are on the website.

If you're in the Farmington area on a Wednesday, Saturday, or Sunday afternoon, don't miss a visit to the **Unionville Museum** (15 School St.; 860-673-2231; unionvillemuseum.org). The **Unionville** section of Farmington, located about 5 miles east of the center of town along Route 4, was an industrial center during the late 18th and early 19th centuries. Flints for Washington's army and guns for the War of 1812 were made here, as well as the pikes that Torrington native John Brown took with him to Harpers Ferry (he intended to use them to arm the Southern slaves he convinced to revolt). **The Luxor** was located on Water Street and was quite the treat for residents, although not as flashy as theaters in larger cities. This movie schedule alerts patrons that *High Sierra* (with Humphrey Bogart and Ida Lupino), *Victor* (with Fredric March and Bettie Field), and *Andy Hardy's Private Secretary* (with Mickey Rooney, Lewis Stone, and Ian Hunter), among others would be playing. It also shows the movie house's phone number as 288-3. Ahh, such was the life in 1941. The museum displays chairs from the former theater. Open 2 p.m. to 4 p.m. Wed, Sat, and Sun.

Central Connecticut

New Britain

New Britain got its manufacturing start making sleigh bells. From these modest beginnings the city gradually branched out in the early 1800s and into the manufacture of other hardware products, until it eventually came to be known as the "Hardware City." With the industrial age came waves of new immigrants seeking jobs in the tool works. The Irish came first, then the Germans and Swedes, then the Italians. The biggest waves, though, consisted of Eastern Europeans, including Lithuanians, Ukrainians, Armenians, and especially the Poles. Even after the hardware industry moved abroad, Polish immigrants continued to arrive in New Britain. Today, the city's population of first- and second-generation Poles is greater than that of many cities in Poland. They have contributed their music, their language, and their food to the city.

newbritaintrivia

The Copernican Observatory and Planetarium at Central Connecticut State University in New Britain houses one of the largest publicly available telescopes in the US.

In some places in New Britain, Polish is spoken almost as freely as English. And if you love authentic Polish food, the perfect place to go is **Podlasie** (188 High St.; 860-357-3051). It's like visiting a marketplace in Eastern Europe. You'll find Polish mineral water; dark, dense bread; newspapers; ingredients for Polish cooking; and some intriguing Polish chocolates on the shelves. The back of the store is given over to a dairy case (great country butter), a pastry case full of elegant-looking tortes and cakes, and a case for cheeses, herring, fresh meats, and cold cuts, many made in the store. Most of the shoppers are Polish, so you'll hear mostly Polish being spoken. There's usually at least one English speaker in the store who is happy to help you translate. Open daily 8 a.m. to 6 p.m. (There is another Podlasie in Bridgeport at 2286 E. Main St.; 203-335-0321.)

The Hardware City is not all about industry. There is also a true appreciation of the arts, evidenced by the *New Britain Museum of American Art* (56 Lexington St.; 860-229-0257; nbmaa.org). Established in 1903, this museum is the oldest in the US devoted solely to American art. Its more than 8,000 holdings include portraits by Cassatt, Stuart, Copley, and Sargent and the western bronzes of Solon Borglum, as well as works by the likes of O'Keeffe, Noguchi,

ANNUAL EVENTS IN THE HEARTLAND

FEBRUARY

Connecticut Flower & Garden Show
Connecticut Convention Center, Hartford
(860) 844-8461
ctflowershow.com

MARCH

Connecticut Spring Antiques Show
Hartford State Armory
360 Broad St., Hartford
(860) 345-2400
ctspringantiquesshow.com

APRIL

The River Run 5k & 10k Races
Iron Horse Boulevard, Simsbury
simsburyriverrun.com

MAY

Shad Derby Festival
Various places
windsorshadderby.org

JUNE

Travelers Championship
TPC River Highlands, Cromwell
travelerschampionship.com

JULY

Greater Hartford Festival of Jazz
Bushnell Park, Hartford
hartfordjazz.org

AUGUST

Plainville Hot Air Balloon Festival
Norton Park
197 South Washington St., Plainville
plainvillefireco.com/Balloon_Festival.html

SEPTEMBER

Berlin Fair
430 Beckley Rd., East Berlin
(860) 828-0063
ctberlinfair.com

Farm Fest
Hilltop Farm
1616 Mapleton Ave., Suffield
hilltopfarmsuffield.org/farmfest

Mum Festival
70 Memorial Blvd., Bristol
(860) 584-4718
bristolmumfestival.com

Old Wethersfield Arts and Crafts Fair
Cove Park, State Street, Wethersfield
(860) 529-7656
wethersfieldhistory.org/visit/wethersfield
-arts-and-crafts-fair

Southington Apple Harvest Festival
75 Main St., Southington Town Green
(860) 276-8461
southingtonahf.com

Suffield on the Green
Suffield Town Green
friendsofsuffield.org/suffieldonthegreen
.html

Wapping Fair
South Windsor Fairgrounds
75 Brookfield St., South Windsor
wappingfair.org

Wethersfield Cornfest
Broad Street Green, Wethersfield
(860) 721-6200
wethersfieldchamber.com/event/the
-cornfest

OCTOBER

Glastonbury Apple Harvest Festival
Riverfront Park
300 Welles St., Glastonbury
(860) 659-3587

Hartford Marathon
Begins at Bushnell Park
(860) 652-8866
hartfordmarathon.com

Max's 5th Annual HOPtoberfest
Rosedale Farms & Vineyards
25 East Weatogue St., Simsbury
rosedale1920.com/events/

Plainville PumpkinFest
1 Central Sq., Plainville
(860) 747-1965
plainvillepumpkinfest.com

NOVEMBER

Holiday Light Fantasia
Goodwin Park, Hartford
holidaylightfantasia.org
Runs Nov through Jan, proceeds to charity

Manchester Road Race
Main Street, Manchester
manchesterroadrace.com

DECEMBER

First Night Hartford
Bushnell Park, Hartford
firstnighthartford.org

Benton, and Wyeth. Its collection of American impressionists is second to none. Don't forget to take a walk in the park behind the museum, designed by Central Park landscape architect and Hartford native Frederick Law Olmsted.

The museum is open Mon, Tues (closed Wed), Fri, and Sat 10 a.m.–5 p.m., and Thurs 10 a.m.–8 p.m. Admission is charged except Sat from 10 a.m. to noon. This free window is a great time to introduce the kids to the art of this wonderful place without breaking the bank. Blue Star Museum.

New Britain's **Central Connecticut State University** is home to the small **Copernican Observatory and Planetarium** (1615 Stanley St.; 860-832-3399; ccsu.edu/astronomy), which offers free programs on a first-come-first-serve basis, on the first and third Sat of each month at 8 p.m. There is an obvious love of the subject matter by the presenters. It's a great way to gain an intro into all things astronomical. Did we mention it's free?

New Britain's moniker as the Hardware City is commemorated in the **New Britain Industrial Museum** (30 High St.; 860-832-8654; nbindustrial.org). It's a small but choice museum, put together by people who genuinely love New Britain and its industrial past. You can trace New Britain's past and see its future as you view the history of the companies that put New Britain on the map: Stanley Works, Fafnir Bearing, Landers, North & Judd, and American Hardware. Open Wed and Sat 1 to 5 p.m.

Taking the family to see a major-league baseball game is expensive. But here in Connecticut, you can get all the authentic appeal of America's pastime without having to sell your Mickey Mantle rookie card. You can sit close to the action, and chances are good you'll be able to snag a foul ball or a player's autograph. Best of all, you might discover the next Barry Bonds or Derek Jeter before the rest of the world catches on. Check out the **New Britain Bees** (New Britain Stadium, Willow Brook Park, 230 John Karbonic Way; 860-826-BEES; nbbees.com). The Bees are members of the Futures Collegiate Baseball League and are not affiliated with any major-league team. They play Apr through Sept and offer many kid-friendly activities, all at a fraction of the cost of a trip to New York or Boston.

Avery's Beverages (520 Corbin Ave.; 860-224-0830; averysoda.com) is another New Britain jewel. In fact, it's a wonderful Aladdin's cave of jewel-colored soda and mysterious Rube Goldberg machinery some readers might remember from their childhoods. At Avery's they bottle soda the way it used to be done back in the day, wooden carrying cases and all. The family has been bottling soda in the same red barn since 1904. Sherman F. Avery used to deliver his soda all over New Britain and beyond in a horse-drawn wagon before he went modern in 1914 and purchased a delivery truck. Today, they still make deliveries to restaurants and stores in nearby towns. You can also visit their own store to sample that high-quality soda pop made from only the finest quality ingredients, including real cane sugar (no sugar substitutes here!), and naturally pure well water. You can even try your hand at making your own, but beware—some results from that endeavor include bottles of Dog Drool Soda, Toxic Slime, and Monster Mucus. Um, yuck? Perhaps it's safer to stick to some of Avery's original recipes of cola, lemon-lime, ginger ale, and root and birch beer. Whatever your taste, you'll find it bottled in glass to preserve that old-fashioned flavor. You can even have personalized labels printed on your soda, a great idea for weddings or other special occasions. Avery's has such a fascinating history, and if you have the time, call ahead to arrange a tour of the bottling works. You won't be disappointed.

As you drive down Route 9 between New Britain and Farmington, you'll pass a hauntingly familiar sculpture of American Marines raising a flag. This is the **Iwo Jima Survivors' Memorial Park and Monument**. It is dedicated to 6,821 Americans who, during World War II, gave their lives in the desperate fight for the Pacific island of Iwo Jima, the place where it was said that "uncommon valor" was a "common virtue." The monument's sculpture re-creates the famous flag-raising by American troops atop Mount Suribachi. On special days, such as Veterans Day, the monument is decorated with an avenue of American flags. Open 24 hours daily.

Southington

If you have little ones with you, be sure to visit **Karabin Farms** (894 Andrews St.; 860-620-0194; karabinfarms.com). They've been in *Southington* since 1972, and what started out as a hobby for owners Michael and Diane Karabin has turned into a family-run, family fun place. Their children grew and went off to college but came back, one by one, to be involved in the business in some way. Together they have planted over 2,000 fruit trees and 10,000 Christmas trees. They offer pick-your-own apples, peaches, pumpkins, and Christmas trees (they also offer pre-cut ones). There are hayrides to the fields, live animals to visit (including funky-looking Highland cattle), snacks to be had at the snack barn, as well as an entire treasure chest of things to be discovered in the store. Throughout the year, along with the fresh fruit and vegetables, you can also find homemade pies, local honey, maple syrup, jams, pickles, and soup mixes. They also offer humanely raised (right on the farm) meat, seasonal flowers, including a huge variety of poinsettias at Christmas, as well as specialty soaps and candles. The farm is open daily Apr through Dec 23, 9 a.m. to 5 p.m.; Jan through Mar, Sat and Sun, 9 a.m. to 5 p.m.

Board & Brush (61 Center St.; 203-343-6445; boardandbrush.com/south ington) is a do-it-yourself workshop where you can go by yourself or with a group of friends and create home decor projects from scratch. No experience, supplies, or tools are needed; they are all provided for you. You choose the design and an instructor walks you through the process. It's sort of a like a Paint Night, but with wood. Owners Scott and Lisa Selby decided to start their own Board & Brush (they are a franchise) when Scott was looking for a change from his HR career and Lisa was looking to go back to work after raising their two sons. The timing was perfect, and they opened their doors on Center Street. While the bulk of their projects use wood, they also offer classes in glass, chalkboard, pillows, slate, and terra cotta. It's also BYOB, so make it a night. Visit the website to see upcoming classes!

The third farm in Southington is a crowd-pleaser. **Bradley Mountain Farm** (537 Shuttle Meadow Rd.; 860-385-GOAT; bradleymountainfarm.com) is a 200-year-old dairy farm built by Ichabod Bradley in 1813 and is on the registry of National Historical Places. They offer a premier goat-milk soap, courtesy of the herd of LaMancha, Mini-LaMancha, and Nigerian Dwarf goats. You can also enjoy a tour of the historic Bradley Home, with its 9 fireplaces and 7 authentic colonial murals. But the reason this farm is beloved by all is its offerings of goat-related fun. Kids of all ages (including adults who wish they were still kids) can schedule play dates to groom, cuddle, and walk your goat on a lead on the property. Goat strolls and hikes in the pastures are a popular form of relaxation, along with the popular "goat yoga." If you want to actually learn how to take care of goats rather than just cuddle with them, they have more hands-on instruction. Check their calendar for events on weekdays and evenings, with pick-up for soap you ordered, Sun 11 a.m –2 p.m.

Plainville

Back in the 18th century, Route 10 was the major thoroughfare passing through **Plainville**. It was down this road that Rochambeau's French army marched on its way to join Washington and travel to Yorktown and win the decisive battle of the American Revolution and head back to Boston. The location of one of the French campgrounds is marked by a small plaque on Main Street (Route 10) after the intersection of Hatters Lane (on the right) and before Winchell Smith Dr. (on the left, if you're going north). The plaque reads: "In 1781 and 1782 Jean Baptiste Count de Rochambeau and his French troops marched by here enroute to and from Yorktown, Va."

No matter the century, traveling creates an appetite, and there's no better place to stop than ***J. Timothy's Taverne*** (143 New Britain Ave.; 860-747-6813; jtimothys.com), just as travelers have been doing for centuries. The restaurant is housed in a building built in 1789, President George Washington's first year in office. Back then, the tavern was owned and operated by John Cooke. Cooke's Tavern became a well-known stagecoach stop for travelers of the day. When the time came, John passed the business and building down to his son, George, who lived there for almost a century, still operating the tavern. Upon George's death in 1923, his niece, Nancy Kirkham, inherited the tavern. In 1934, the tavern was transformed into a full-service restaurant, which it has been ever since. The Cooke family sold the business to current owners Tim Adams and Jim Welch in 1979, who are proud to carry on the tradition.

Today, under the name J. Timothy's, the tavern offers six public dining rooms and their infamous Dirt wings. Their wing sauce has been voted best in the country, with their buffalo wings taking second place, and they are proud of it! They even have directions on the website clarifying the correct method for ordering. They take their wings seriously. You've been warned. Open Tues–Thurs 11:30 a.m.–10 p.m.; Fri and Sat 11:30 a.m.–10:30 p.m.; Sun 11:30 a.m.–9:30 p.m.

Bristol

If you're looking for some great family fun, head east from Plainville to **Lake Compounce** (186 Enterprise Dr.; 860-583-3300; lakecompounce.com) in **Bristol**. Now the country's oldest amusement park, Lake Compounce has been serving up family fun and thrills since 1846 with its 427 acres, 20-acre lake, and myriad rides and attractions. There really is something for everyone, including a great portion of the park for the smaller children, with age-appropriate rides and shows. The more daring can choose from three coasters: the Zoomerang; Boulder Dash, voted number one wooden coaster in the world; and Phobia Phear Coaster, New England's first triple-launch coaster. If you're willing to

Going Up?

On your way to Lake Compounce, you may notice a tall, interesting-looking building jutting out of the trees. It looks a little like a transplanted skyscraper from the city. It is actually an elevator test tower. Located on the grounds of the Bristol Research Center, the tower is used by the Otis Quality Assurance Center. Topping out at 383 feet, the test tower is the tallest in North America.

get wet, there's Riptide Racer, Clipper Cove, Mammoth Falls, and much, much more, including Lights Out, which is a high-speed water slide in, you guessed it, the dark. For those of you who are looking for tamer options, check out the beautiful 1898 carousel. You'll find horses carved by Looff, Carmel, and Stein & Goldstein. There are 49 horses (27 jumpers and 22 standers), a goat, and two chariots. The original Wurlitzer organ still grinds out tunes for riders. Like we said, something for everyone. Open daily 11 a.m. to 8 p.m. Memorial Day through Labor Day and then sporadically from Labor Day until the end of Dec, during which the park offers some way-cool Halloween and holiday lights events. Be sure to check their website for admission costs and hours, since they may vary for different areas of the park.

Around the middle of the 19th century, Bristol was the center of clock- and watchmaking in the Northeast. At one time, the town supported 280 clockmakers, and in 1860, they turned out a total of 200,000 clocks. Today, the great clockworks are only a memory preserved in the town's ***American Clock & Watch Museum*** (100 Maple St.; 860-583-6070; clockandwatchmuseum.org). Within the walls of the 1801 Miles Lewis House and two modern additions, the museum manages to display a collection of more than 5,500 clocks and watches, including many made locally. This vast assemblage is organized by type and eras, so that as you take the self-guided tour from room to room, you can observe how the styles of clock cases changed to match furniture styles. Among the more interesting items are some oak clock cases from the 1920s and 1930s, which are exhibited together with the metal rollers that pressed the intricate designs into the wood. There are also lovely "tall" clocks, including some made by Eli Terry. There's even one clock whose workings are carved entirely from wood. The American Clock & Watch Museum is open Wed–Sun 10 a.m.–5 p.m.; Mon and Tues hours may be available by appointment. Admission. Blue Star Museum.

Clocks and watches aren't the only items collected in Bristol. Housed in a restored turn-of-the-20th-century factory building, the ***New England Carousel Museum*** (95 Riverside Ave.; 860-585-5411; thecarouselmuseum.org) contains some of the best examples of antique carousel art in existence, hundreds of pieces in all. Featured items include a collection of band organs, the entire carousel from Santa's Land in Putnam, Vermont, and a gorgeous pair of 1915 carved chariots, each encrusted with 1,500 glass jewels. The museum also has two art galleries and a fine history exhibit. This was the first museum of its kind on the East Coast, and many preservationists still consider it the best.

The main museum occupies the building's ground floor. Wood carvers and painters perform restorations on the second floor, and if you happen to be there while they are working, you can go upstairs and watch. The second floor also contains the **Museum of Fire History**, which is worth a visit and is included in the admission price. Open year-round, Wed, Fri, Sat, 10 a.m.–5 p.m.; Thurs 10 a.m.–8 p.m.; Sun noon–5 p.m. Closed major holidays but usually open for local school holidays. You can also reserve the museum for special events year-round, including themed birthday parties and weddings. Admission. Blue Star Museum.

One of the best attractions in Bristol is one you are unlikely to stumble across unless you're a native Nutmegger and you happen to be around at Halloween time (and happen to also read this book!). **Witch's Dungeon Classic Movie Museum** (103 E. Main St; 860-817-6095; preservehollywood.org) has been in operation for more than 50 years, and it all started with young Cortlandt Hull, who, as an ill child, spent time building model monster kits. As he grew up, he became fascinated with the theatrical transformations from human to monster. Soon Cortlandt grew bored with his models and hungered for more. He was disappointed with visits to different wax museums that just didn't do it for him, so he started creating his own full-size versions of his favorite monsters, and they seemed to take on a life of their own. It was a real family affair—Cortlandt's dad helped him with a building to house them in and built the backgrounds; his mom re-created many of the famous costumes for his creatures; his uncle acted as engineer—and the rest is history.

By the 1970s and 1980s, Cortlandt's skills had improved, and his "little" museum started to gain national attention from the likes of the *New York Times*, *National Geographic*, and *Ripley's Believe It or Not!* Members of the acting community took notice, too, and lent their support. Vincent Price, John Agar, and Mark Hamill all did special recordings for the museum. People from all over the country have come to visit this Connecticut treasure. Cortlandt's beloved creatures are now sought after and travel the country to star in their own special displays. Who knew all this would come from his interest in monster models?!

The museum is wheelchair accessible. Open Fri–Sun, 6 p.m.–9 p.m., bookings available through their website.

Places to Stay in The Heartland

AVON
Avon Old Farms Hotel
1 Nod Rd.
(860) 677-2818
Avonoldfarmshotel.com
Moderate to expensive

GLASTONBURY
Connecticut River Valley Inn
2195 Main St.
(860) 633-7374
crvinn.com
Moderate to expensive
Beautiful any time of the year in the Connecticut River Valley

SIMSBURY
Simsbury 1820 House
731 Hopmeadow St.
(860) 658-7658
simsbury1820house.com
Moderate to expensive
Rambling 1820 house with comfortable accommodations

Simsbury Inn
397 Hopmeadow St.
(860) 651-5700
simsburyinn.com
Moderate to expensive

Places to Eat in The Heartland

COLLINSVILLE
Crown and Hammer Pub
3 Depot St.
(860) 693-9199
crownandhammer.com
Moderate to expensive
Great pub-style food, live entertainment, and beautiful views of the Farmington River and dam

LaSalle Market & Deli
104 Main St.
(860) 693-8010
lasallemarket.com
Inexpensive
Great location with live music

HARTFORD
Trumbull Kitchen
150 Trumbull St.
(860) 493-7412
trumbullkitchen.com
Moderate to expensive
Contemporary restaurant for fusion cuisine; reservations are a must

PLAINVILLE
J. Timothy's Taverne
143 New Britain Ave.
(860) 747-6813
jtimothys.com
Moderate
Known for the best hot wings in America

SIMSBURY
Brookside Bagels
563 Hopmeadow St.
(860) 651-1492
Inexpensive, Open Tues–Sun, 6 a.m.–2 p.m.
Incredibly fresh bagels in interesting flavors, awesome selection of cream cheese and lox, creative sandwich combinations

SOUTH WINDSOR
Mill on the River
989 Ellington Rd.
(860) 289-7929
Millontheriver.net
Expensive
One of the most romantic restaurants in the state

The Litchfield Hills

Traveling west of Hartford, you'll soon find yourself in the uplands of **Litchfield County**, and as you drive north and west, you get deeper into the **Litchfield Hills**, a forested spur of the Berkshires. This area bordering New York on the west and Massachusetts on the north is typical New England: steepled white churches, romantic old inns, quaint antiques shops, and small establishments run by Yankee craftspeople. In recent years, this idyllic area has become home to many of the rich and famous, bringing with them upscale shops and nouvelle restaurants that give the farms and forests a cosmopolitan flavor.

The southern hills include the region's "Alpine Lake" country, an area reminiscent of Switzerland, with cool, forest-shrouded lakes and tranquil meadows. This region is home to some of the state's (and America's) best inns. On the western edge of the Litchfield Hills, separating them from the Taconic Mountains, is the Housatonic River. As it flows from the extreme northwestern corner of Connecticut to the populous areas of Fairfield and New Haven Counties, it transforms from a wild freshet that is surely one of the prettiest in New England to Connecticut's second-largest river. This land of woods and water is one of the most idyllic spots in the entire country, and many have spent a happy day—or lifetime—exploring its rills and dells.

THE LITCHFIELD HILLS

The Albany Turnpike

In the days before railroads and superhighways, Hartford and Albany, New York, were linked by a rutted roadway called the **Albany Turnpike**. This highway of sorts was the main route through the rugged northwestern uplands, and its location determined the patterns of settlement in this part of the state. Today, the successor to the old turnpike is Route 44, and anyone traveling through this part of Connecticut must pass over it.

New Hartford

One of the easternmost townships along the Litchfield portion of Route 44 is **New Hartford**, home to **Satan's Kingdom State Recreation Area**. The name's origin has been the subject of debate for years, but it likely was named for the bandits who used to hide out in the rugged, wooded countryside that flanked the turnpike and offered a perfect hiding place from which to ambush and rob the Hartford–Albany stagecoaches. Across the street from the recreation area is Satan's Kingdom Road, marked by a street sign . . . most of the time. As you can imagine, this sign is a temptation for modern-day thieves, and it routinely gets stolen. At one point, a new sign was put up, though it didn't read "Satan's Kingdom Rd." but rather "Statan's Kingdom Rd." Was this a typo or a deliberate attempt to dissuade would-be hooligans? Either way, that sign was stolen, too. Maybe they should just rename the road.

Within Satan's Kingdom you will find the popular **Farmington River Tubing** (92 Main St.; 860-693-6465; farmingtonrivertubing.com), which operates from Memorial Day through mid-Sept, outfitting people with life jackets and inflated inner tubes and sending them on down the river. Once you receive your equipment, you are literally on your own until you reach the outtake point 2.5 miles downriver. The company will not help you if you fall out of your tube, and they advise you not to stand up while navigating any of the three Class 1, 2, and 3 rapids you will encounter on your trip. They also recommend you do not leave the river until you finish the route. Tubing is not for everyone: Minimum recommended age is 10, minimum height and weight is 4 feet and 50 pounds, though the company leaves it up to your discretion. They suggest you wear shoes, and we suggest you pick a pair that will stay on your feet. Local fishermen have complained about the number of shoes they have "fished" out of the river, and the pollution just isn't good for anyone. Operation is weather permitting, so it's always best to call ahead before making the trip. Cash only.

Also located in New Hartford is the **Collinsville Antiques Co. of New Hartford** (283 Main St.; 860-379-2290; collinsvilleantiques.com). If you're wondering about the name (we were confused, too), it's because the company was formerly located in Collinsville, where it had operated since 1989. When new owners Doug and Cindy Szydlo purchased the business in 1995, they expanded it into the wonder it is today. Often voted Best Antiques Shop by the *Hartford Advocate* and *Hartford Magazine*, the shop outgrew its space in the old Collins Company. The town didn't want to lose the business, and it caused quite a stir, but it was time. In 2005, the company found its new home in New Hartford's Waring manufacturing building but kept the name as a nod to its beginnings. Open daily, 10 a.m. to 5 p.m.

Barkhamsted

North of New Hartford, Route 44 loops through **Barkhamsted**. If you're here during the cooler months, say, February or March, a visit to the **Kasulaitis Farm and Sugarhouse** (69 Goose Green Rd.; 860-379-8787) to watch the process and buy some tasty maple products is a must. If you miss sugaring off, stop by anyway and watch the lambs frisk and frolic in the spring pasture. Such sights are good for the soul. Open Mon–Fri, 5 p.m. to 8 p.m.; Sat and Sun 11 a.m.–4 p.m. See syrup being made in mid-Feb to the end of Mar. Phone ahead. Maple syrup sold year-round.

Something else that's good for the soul is watching New England's color change as she greets autumn in all her splendor. Barkhamsted's combination of sparse population, winding roads, heavy forest, and large lakes makes it one of the most dramatic parts of Connecticut for leaf peeping.

One of the best **fall foliage** jaunts through Barkhamsted starts north of the town at the junction of Routes 20 and 181 in Hartland. If you approach this intersection from the east on Route 20, you'll pass through West Hartland on the way. Don't let this confuse you; with typical Yankee contrariness, West Hartland is actually east of Hartland, so keep driving for another mile. At the intersection in Hartland, take Route 181 south. This road runs between the Barkhamsted Reservoir and the Farmington River, for much of the way under the limbs of the lovely **People's State Forest**.

At the tip of the reservoir, Route 181 meets Route 318. Take 318 east to **Saville Dam**, which separates Barkhamsted and Compensating Reservoirs, which are the chief suppliers of water for Hartford. The dam, named for Caleb Mills Saville, chief engineer, was built in 1940 and is 135 feet tall and 1,950 feet long. The dam really is beautiful at any time of the year with its castle-like structure and stonework. You can read more about the dam's history on the Connecticut history website (connecticuthistory.org). There's parking nearby and even on the dam itself; this is a popular spot to stop for pictures or a picnic.

AUTHOR'S FAVORITES	
Litchfield Distillery	The Daffodils at Laurel Ridge
White Flower Farm	Saville Dam

From the dam, continue east to Route 219. From there you can drive south to pick up Route 44, return west for more leaf peeping, or loop up to Route 20 in Granby.

If after reaching Saville Dam you're still in the mood for more fall color, head back west on Route 318 for a half mile beyond the intersection of Route 181. Turn right on East River Road. This will take you directly through **People's State Forest** along the banks of the West Branch of the Farmington, where even on the hottest day the tall trees and pines keep the forest shady and glade cool. This forest has a network of trails to explore, including the yellow-blazed **Jessie Gerard Trail**, on which you will find the site of a village that existed more than 270 years ago. Established in 1740 by Mary Barber and her husband, James Chaugham, this village was known as the Barkhamsted Lighthouse and became a regular stop for stagecoaches traveling through the area. Barber and her husband decided to move to this area of wilderness to escape her father, who was not happy that she, a white woman, married Chaugham, a Narragansett Indian. They, their children, and their children's children lived quite happily there for the next 120 years. Now a State Archaeological Preserve known as the **Lighthouse Archaeological Site**, the former village is not much more than a few cellar holes, but it is a stop on the **Connecticut Freedom Trail** and a continuing reminder of the ongoing fight for freedom from discrimination. The forest recreation area is open from 8 a.m. to sunset.

The nearby village of **Riverton** abounds with enticing stores and snack shops. You might, for example, wrap up your visit with a deli sandwich and Moxie from the **Riverton General Store** (2 Main St.; 860-379-0811; rivertonct .com). The store is open daily from 6 a.m. to 4 p.m., and you can eat at their outdoor seating area or have a picnic along the river.

Or perhaps you'll stop at **Greenwood Glass** (3 Robertsville Rd.; 860-738-9469; petergreenwood.com) to see what Peter Greenwood is up to at his studio, where he teaches and practices the art of glass blowing. Located in an 1829 church, the studio is open Tues through Sat., 9 a.m. to 5 pm.; it's always good to call ahead and make sure he's going to be there, though.

If you or someone in your group likes fishing, then don't miss **Uncle Aaron's Tackle Shack** (4 Robertsville Rd.; 860-307-7156), where you can pick up crawlers, worms, flies, or any other creepy crawly thing you'd need to land a prize fish. Uncle Aaron also has a collection of antique reels for you to check out. And any questions you have about fishing, Uncle Aaron is your guy. He'll make sure you have what you need. Open 6 a.m.–7 p.m. most days during fishing season.

Behind the General Store at the north end of School Street is the **David K. Leff "Hidden in Plain Sight Trail"** (ctmq.org/david-k-leff-hidden-in-plain-sight-trail). These sorts of local trails abound in Connecticut, off the beaten path, but this one really gives you a lot for little effort. Leff was an author, a legal advisor for the Connecticut General Assembly's Environmental Committee, and deputy commissioner for the Connecticut Department of Environmental Protection. He was the primary writer of the state's first green space plan and negotiated Connecticut's largest land acquisition, more than 15,000 acres, known as the Centennial Watershed Forest. He served on just about every board and was known throughout the state as a champion for the environment. You can tell how beloved he was by the community because the trail in his honor was cleared, blazed, and signed by several organizations working together: the Hartland and Barkhamsted Historical Societies, CT DEEP, Friends of People's State Forest, Friends of American Legion State Forest, and Farmington River Committees.

The short loop trail begins at the ruins of an old sawmill, which harnessed the Farmington River's power in the late 1700s before chairmaker Lambert Hitchcock built his factory (across from the General Store) and began producing furniture in 1818. A fabric printing mill took over the spot in 1837, and the Ward Family Mill was the largest employer to ever exist in Hartland. It burned in 1941, flooded in the 1950s, and was eventually deeded to the state. Today, you can walk this easy loop through the cellar holes of mill worker housing, along the raceway, and to the gate of the spillway. You can enjoy the ducks on the river and the maple trees. Leff's philosophy of "terranexus" is perfectly embodied in this mix of the human and natural worlds, of the past and the present.

Winsted

West of Riverton is the larger town of **Winsted**, with a long Main Street full of shops and restaurants. It is home to what is surely one of the most interesting hidden gems, the **American Mural Project** (90 Whiting St.; 860-379-3006; americanmuralproject.org). Inside this old factory building is the largest indoor collaborative artwork in the world, 120 feet long and 5 stories high with numerous levels to view it from. Its sprawling panels depict a history of American industry and the workers who have built the country over the past centuries. The Mural Project sponsors many educational programs, including an apprentice-style internship program. But for the casual tourist, this is simply a place to come and wonder. Open Fri and Sat, 10 a.m.–5 p.m.; Sun, noon–5 p.m., year-round.

Next door to the mural project is **Whiting Mills** (100 Whiting Street; 860-738-2240; whitingmills.com), once the largest hosiery manufacturer in the state, now transformed into something a little more familiar than a giant mural; it is a home for numerous craftspeople, specialty shops, and small businesses. Walk the beautiful old wood floors and browse the shops and artist storefronts to find woodworkers and woven arts, painters and photographers. Check out the sublime bookcraft creations at the Lil' Reading Room or make an appointment to learn Hollywood special effects at Tyler Green FX Studio. Open Mon to Sat, 10 a.m.–7 p.m.; Sun 11 a.m.–5 p.m. Hours of individual stores and artists may differ, so call ahead if you want to see something in particular.

Norfolk

Located at the junction of Route 44 and Routes 272 and 182, *Norfolk* was historically called the "icebox of Connecticut." With an elevation of 1,375 feet and an average mean temperature quite a bit cooler than the rest of the state, it's no surprise the town got this reputation, especially before central heating. The coldest temperature in state records was posted here on February 13, 1943: -37 degrees.

It's the music, though, for which this town is known today. Norfolk's love affair with music dates back to the 1890s when the **Litchfield County Choral Union** was founded by Ellen Battell and her husband Carl Stoeckel, whose father was the first professor at the Yale School of Music. The couple would hold concerts at their Litchfield Road mansion. In 1906, as the concerts (and the audiences) grew, the couple built a **Music Shed** in which to hold them. When Ellen died in 1939, her will stipulated that her estate and its facilities be used for Yale University's summer music school. Thus began an enduring tradition. For the last century, musicians from around the world have played at this amazing venue.

The first-rate acoustics of this Music Shed can still be enjoyed today at the annual **Norfolk Chamber Music Festival** (20 Litchfield Rd.; 860-542-3000; music.yale.edu/Norfolk), an event that is sort of like the more famous event at Tanglewood without the crowds. The concert schedule and participants vary from year to year, but they never disappoint, with Fri and Sat evening performances throughout July and Aug.

A musical legacy is not all this affluent but generous family left to the town of Norfolk. The shingle-sided, barrel-vaulted 1889 **Norfolk Library** was donated by Isabella Eldridge in honor of her parents, Reverend Joseph and Sarah Battell Eldridge. Isabella's sister, Urania Battell Humphrey, donated the 1888 **Battell Memorial Chapel** in the Church of Christ Congregational on Litchfield Road. It features priceless Tiffany stained-glass windows depicting the four seasons that were later donated by Ellen Battell Stoeckel in 1929. Mary Eldridge commissioned the 1889 *Joseph Battell Fountain* on the green, designed by high-society architect Stanford White, in honor of Mary's uncle Joseph. Mary Alice Bradford Eldridge also paid for the 1892 **Norfolk Town Hall**.

Norfolk was also home to many less fortunate people, including *James Mars*, who was born into slavery in Canaan, Connecticut, in 1790. Mars and his family escaped captivity and hid for many months at the homes of abolitionists in Norfolk, Connecticut. At the age of 21, he gained his freedom thanks to new state laws. He became a deacon of Talcott Street Congregational Church in Hartford and worked to improve civil liberties. He wrote his autobiography, *The Life of James Mars*, in 1864 to educate people about the existence of slavery in the North.

Mars died in 1880 at the age of 90. He is buried in the **Norfolk Center Cemetery** (15 Old Colony Rd.; 860-542-1775; norfolkcentercemetery.org) alongside his father, Jupiter Mars, who served in the American Revolution. Their stones are located to the rear and left of the first entrance into the cemetery. To the right of this entrance, near the wall next to Old Colony Road, is the grave of **Alanson Freeman**, who served in the all-Black Connecticut 29th Regiment of the Civil War.

Heading north on Route 272, you'll come to **Campbell Falls State Park** (Old Spaulding Road.; 860-482-1817), where you can see the Whiting River boil over rocks in a narrow gorge. You'll need to take a short hike to reach the falls; just follow the sounds of rushing water. The water drops in two levels, with a small pool in between and one at the bottom. The first level is a good place for a picnic among the weathered rocks. Campbell Falls is off Norfolk Road, just south of Southfield, Massachusetts, just before Spaulding Road. If you are traveling from the other direction, it's about 5 miles north of Haystack Mountain, on Route 272 in Norfolk.

Canaan

Although the festival in nearby Norfolk tends to be better known, the **Music Mountain Chamber Music Festival** (225 Music Mountain Rd.; 860-824-7126; musicmountain.org) is the oldest continuous chamber music festival in the US. Held in the tiny village of **Falls Village** in **Canaan** from mid-June to mid-Sept, this music festival offers 16 concerts each year. They are mainly held on Sun afternoons, but Sat evenings often bring jazz concerts and other

northcanaan trivia

Milo Freeland is credited with being the first African American to volunteer for the Union army during the Civil War. Freeland died in 1883, while living in East Canaan. A stone was placed in Hillside Cemetery on Route 44 in North Canaan in 1996 during a ceremony in his honor.

special events. Music Mountain was founded in 1930 as the permanent home for the Gordon String Quartet, and they have been offering chamber music ever since.

Canaan is also home to the most inaccessible part of the state, up on the plateau of **Great Mountain Forest** (200 Canaan Mountain Rd.; 860-824-8188; greatmountainforest.org). Great Mountain Forest (GMF) is one of America's oldest conservation legacy organizations and one of the largest conservation easements in New England. It encompasses 6,300 acres of working but protected conservation land in northwest Connecticut. The swamps and rough terrain of this high plateau kept loggers out, and so some areas contain remnant trees over 350 years old. Despite its reputation for being wild and remote, though, Great Mountain Forest has 13 miles of trails and adjoins pieces of the Housatonic State Forest and Centennial Watershed Forest, so the adventures here can seem endless. The administrative offices are open Mon to Thurs, 8 a.m.–1 p.m., but the forest is open sunrise to sunset every day. Get on your boots or snowshoes and take a true off-the-beaten-path adventure.

Salisbury

Beyond the Canaans in the town of **Salisbury** you can find **Mount Riga**, part of a system of peaks that marches north and west from Salisbury to the New York and Massachusetts borders. For many years, the iron-rich depths of these mountains were mined and supplied our nation with much-needed tools and weapons. The local community of mineworkers became known as the "Raggies," perhaps because they lived on Mount Riga. Many of these workers were immigrants, possibly from Latvia. They didn't know the culture, didn't speak the language, and kept mainly to themselves. Not feeling particularly welcomed by the Yankee locals, the Raggies lived quietly on the mountain well into the 20th century, even after the iron forges cooled. Today, there are myriad sources of information on this group of people, as descendants have begun to speak out and preserve their rich history and heritage.

If you'd like to hike to the summit of Mount Riga for the amazing views, there are many well-marked hiking trails to choose from. Near the summit is **Crying Child Rock**, which people say makes a soft crying sound just like an infant whenever the wind is right. Sit for a spell and listen.

If you turn north instead of south to Mount Riga on the Appalachian Trail here, you reach **Bear Mountain**, the highest peak in Connecticut (though the highest point is nearby on the shoulder of Mount Frissell, which peaks in Massachusetts). The views from the giant, 20-foot-high cairn of stones on top (built in 1885) are incredible. In the spring, look out for lady slippers lining the trail. If you continue north of Bear Mountain's peak, just steps across the border on the white-blazed Appalachian Trail in Massachusetts lies Sage's Ravine, one of the rare remaining sections of old-growth trees in New England.

salisbury trivia

The Appalachian Trail crosses the region, running over *Bear Mountain*, which at 2,316 feet is the highest peak in the state.

The highest point in the state is actually on the shoulder of *Mount Frissell*, at 2,380 feet in the northwestern-most corner of Connecticut. On the trail a half mile west of that spot is the tristate border, where you can stand on that mountain and (assuming that you are reasonably limber) place one foot in Connecticut and one foot in Massachusetts and bend over and put both hands in New York.

The Lakeville section of Salisbury is where you'll find **Lime Rock Park** (60 White Hollow Rd. [main entrance]; 860-435-5000; limerock.com), probably Connecticut's most famous racetrack for NASCAR speedsters. From time to time, you can see celebrities like Tom Cruise behind the wheel. For us regular people, it's a fun place to spend the day. Home to the **Grand-Am Championship Weekend** and the traditional Memorial Day weekend season opener, Lime Rock goes out of its way to please the fans. Always wanted to drive a race car? There are multiple ways you can get on the track. From individual options to group experiences, check out their website to see what might work best for you. They also hold special events, such as the Farm to Track Picnic & Pig Roast, Car Shows, Scout Days, and Fourth of July fireworks.

In 1924 and 1925 John, Olaf, and Magnus Satre immigrated to Salisbury from their native Norway where they were well-known Nordic ski jumpers and alpine and cross-country skiers. The brothers, probably missing their sport or wanting to share their skills, established the **Salisbury Outing Club**, teaching the art of skiing. They held their first competition in the winter of 1927. It drew more than 200 attendees and cemented their place in Salisbury. After a few successful years, the club had a rough time during the war years, but rose once again in 1945, this time named the **Salisbury Winter Sports Association** (SWSA) (80 Indian Cave Rd.; 860-850-0080; jumpfest.org). Today, the SWSA continues what the Satre brothers started on the hill that bears their name. They "teach the skills necessary for the enjoyment and lifelong pursuit" of Nordic ski jumping and alpine and cross-country skiing. They first hosted the **Eastern**

National Ski Jumping Championships in 1952 and continue to do so today. The association is an all-volunteer, nonprofit effort that works to foster a love of skiing and jumping, especially in the young (although you have to be at least 6 years old to start). They sponsor events throughout the year, including Friday Night Lights, a Target Ski Jumping competition that is followed by a Human Dog Sled Race, ski invitational, a Snowball Dance in February, a Junior Ski Jump Camp, a ski swap and sale, and more. Check out their website for dates and information.

Ethan Allen Way

Cornwall

Cornwall is one of those ubiquitous Connecticut towns with multiple villages with similar names. I swear, sometimes they do it just to confuse us. The town of Cornwall was incorporated in 1740, named after Cornwall, England. Located on the east bank of the Housatonic River, the town's population is less than 1,500 people, divided among five village communities: Cornwall Bridge, Cornwall Village, Cornwall Hollow, East Cornwall, and West Cornwall. They don't even have enough students to have their own school system (they are part of Regional District 1 and share schools with Canaan, Kent, North Canaan, Salisbury, and Sharon), yet they have three post offices. It truly is a beautiful town, if a little confusing to outsiders. The town's most famous attraction is the West Cornwall Covered Bridge, the largest and handsomest such bridge in Connecticut.

To find the **West Cornwall Covered Bridge** (not to be confused with the Cornwall Bridge, also in Cornwall), you'll need to find Routes 7 and 128, which intersect right at the bridge. Route 128 then takes you over the bridge and turns into Main Street in West Cornwall. There are lots of opportunities for picture taking around the bridge; just be careful of the traffic and be sure to park out of the way.

Originally designed by Ithiel Town, the bridge has been in continuous service over the Housatonic River since 1864. This is an impressive feat, especially considering the dangers it has faced. For example, it survived the flooding from the Hurricane of 1938, and Hurricanes Connie and Diane in 1955. In 1961, it stayed intact despite the severe ice jam that needed to be dynamited. In 1945, a 20-ton oil truck fell through the bridge floor, yet it held fast. The bridge is 172 feet long and

cornwalltrivia

The West Cornwall Covered Bridge is featured in the opening scenes of the 1967 film *Valley of the Dolls* as a symbol of New England.

15 feet wide and is one of only three remaining covered bridges in the state. Perhaps you'll cross it on your way to one of the post offices.

On the west side of US 7, a couple hundred yards south of the bridge, is something right out of an H. P. Lovecraft horror novel. There, jutting out from under a canopy of overhanging trees along the side of the road is a big rock painted to resemble a most lifelike giant frog whose leering mouth seems to be reaching for the occupants of the passenger side of the car. But don't worry, the story behind the painting of this rock is not menacing. It all started more than 60 years ago when Margaret (Marge) Grusauski Wilson was on her way home from high school and noticed that a Route 7 highway worker had painted two white eyes on the rock as an apparent joke. Marge went home and told her brother, John, about the rock, and the two of them decided to "do it up good." They went back later and added long rows of white teeth, ears, eyes, and a nose, adding black details. They chose a small black rock for the "monster's" hat. They were almost happy with their work, but something wasn't quite right. The next evening, Marge had a new partner in "crime" when she and her best friend, Marietta Baird, found a flat rock, painted it red, and gave the monster his tongue. **Monster Rock** was complete. They never spoke about it and no one knew who the culprits were. Marge eventually moved to Florida and held her silence for a very long time, while a few other people took credit for painting the rock. Finally, Marge told the whole story, so today, when you stop to take a picture, be sure to think well of Marge, her family, her friends, and her Monster Rock.

About a mile south of the covered bridge also on Route 7 is **Clarke Outdoors** (163 US 7; 860-672-6365; clarkeoutdoors.com), which offers kayaks, canoes, and rafts for those who want to try the river's whitewater. The knowledgeable staff give a safety talk before each trip and are happy to answer any questions you have. They offer guided and unguided tours on the Housatonic River, including a lovely trip under the covered bridge. Reservations for the guided rafting trips are a must. *Tip:* Prices are lower during the week. Shuttle service available. Be sure to check out the expressive anthropomorphic critters adorning Clarke's signs and vans. These are original **Sandra Boynton** paintings! They also have a retail store with a large selection of equipment, clothing, and books. Open Mar through Nov, Wed through Mon, 10 a.m.–4 p.m.; closed Tues and Wed.

cornwalltrivia

Famous *Law and Order* prosecutor Sam Waterston and *Chicago Med* doctor Oliver Platt both live in West Cornwall. If you see them, though, act cool! Don't blow it for us.

Five miles south of the Cornwall Bridge (the bridge, not the village) in Cornwall Bridge (the village, not the bridge) is the **Cornwall Bridge Pottery Store** (69 Kent Rd. South; 860-946-9679; cbpots.com), where you can see beautiful pottery at its source. Artist and owner Todd Piker invites visitors to wander through the kiln yard, watch potters at their wheels, and ask questions. Piker is a fount of knowledge, as he's been making and selling world-class stoneware since 1972. Much of Piker's pottery features a celadon glaze made from slag recovered from a local riverbed, where it was deposited by the ironworks that used to dominate the area's economy. None of the glazes, however, contain lead. Most items are decorated with simple blue or brown brushwork designs with an Asian flavor. The firing is done in a 35-foot wood-fired kiln and the flames give the finished pieces distinctive two-tone markings. The workshop is open for visits, but it's always best to call ahead for the best hours. If you're lucky, you'll find some seconds available for sale here.

If you happen to travel north along Route 7 and the Housatonic, be sure to stop at **Gold's Pines** (Route 128), a 56-acre plot of white pine and hemlock trees that contains the **tallest tree in the state** (at least it was as of the end of March 2016, when it was officially measured). The little forest was started by **Theodore S. Gold** in 1870. It was acquired by the state in 1941 and became part of the **Housatonic State Forest**. Gold's original stand of trees is believed to be almost 200 years old. The tallest tree is a white pine that was 158 feet tall when last measured. Access to the stand is off Route 128; the tree can be found on the west side of the trail before the trail curves to the right and passes a group of trees with species signs.

Nearby, you'll find **The Wish House** (413 Sharon Goshen Tpke [Rte. 128]; 860-672-2969; wishhouse.com), a whimsical store with the patchwork bear out front. The items in this store are eclectic and artfully arranged. You'll find gifts, clothing, books, soaps, linens, and a little bit of everything here, including Josh Bach ties, Anokhi bathrobes, Cornwall-made syrup, and more. Open Tues through Sun, 11 a.m. to 5 p.m. This is also where the **Cornwall Farm Market** (860-672-2969) is held every Sat, mid-May through early Oct, 10 a.m. to 1 p.m., on the lawn.

If you're a fan of things that go bump in the night, here's a ghost story from the area for you. In the early 1740s, a man named Thomas Griffis settled a few miles south of today's Cornwall Bridge village, in a place called Dark Entry Forest. The forest was located in the shadows of the mountains that surround the town. He was joined over the next few years by members of the Dudley family as well as other settlers and together they tried to subsist on the rocky land not particularly suitable for farming or livestock. Why they chose the spot they did is a mystery, but it seems an unfortunate choice. The settlement became known as ***Dudleytown*** and its citizens faced years of bad luck, illness, crop failures, and more. Whatever happened here centuries ago will likely never be known with any degree of certainty, but the village was abandoned and became one of New England's most famous ghost towns.

Today, the forest where Dudleytown is located is privately owned and trespassers will be ticketed by police for even stepping on the land. To learn more about the Dudleytown curse, we recommend picking up a copy of *Cursed in New England* by Joseph A. Citro (Globe Pequot).

Just east of Dudleytown is ***Mohawk Mountain***. The big draw here is skiing at ***Mohawk Mountain Ski Area*** (46 Great Hollow Rd.; 860-672-6100; mohawkmtn.com), but if that's not your thing, avoid the crowds and take a scenic warm-weather 2.5-mile stroll to the top of the 1,683-foot-high mountain in ***Mohawk State Forest*** (Rt. 4; 860-927-3238; portal.ct.gov). The view from the top is absolutely breathtaking.

The Mohawk Trail runs through these woods and can actually be accessed on Dark Entry Road and can be hiked through to Cornwall Village (or vice versa). While the Connecticut Forest and Parks Association closes this part of the trail around Halloween (for obvious reasons), it is open the rest of the year. Perhaps this is the perfect hike on which to ponder the fate of Dudleytown.

If you like walking, why not try it with a llama in tow? That's exactly the experience you can have with Cornwall's ***Country Quilt Llama Farm*** (860-248-0355; countryquiltllamafarm.com). Owner Debbie Labbe has proven that llamas can be perfect animal ambassadors, well suited to interact with people. Debbie started this llama farm in West Cornwall in 1988, taking two llamas on the road to meet preschoolers and seniors. Now, her experiences have become legendary. She offers llama walks with Snoopy, Harley, Rio, Robert, Bentley, Cooper, Jack, and Theo in partnership with White Memorial Conservation Center in Litchfield. You can stroll the trails and get to know these animals better. And maybe you'll learn something about yourself, too.

cornwalltrivia

In 1948, Mohawk Ski Area in Cornwall became the first ski resort in the country to make artificial snow. The first (unsuccessful) attempt involved trucking in 700 tons of ice from Torrington.

Kent

Main Street (US 7) in the town of ***Kent*** is known as ***Ethan Allen Way***, after the Connecticut hero who was born in the area. This street is lined for several blocks with restaurants, art galleries, antiques stores, craft shops, and more. You'll also find interesting establishments on Maple and Railroad Streets, but on Main Street try the new **Morrison Gallery** (60 N. Main St; 860-927-4501; morrisongallery.com), which is big enough to be a museum on the Connecticut Art Trail. For the literarily inclined, the **House of Books** (10 N. Main St.; 860-927-4104; hobooks.com) is a great place to nose around, with a perfectly curated selection of art, literature, history, and biographies. You should also check out the famous Kent Library book sale, which spills onto the sidewalks near the town center every sunny weekend of the summer.

A mile and a half north of Kent on US 7 is **Kent Falls State Park** (462 Kent Cornwall Rd. [Rte. 7]; 860-927-3238). The broad meadow and shaded picnic areas visible from the road are inviting enough, but you might be inclined to pass it by if you weren't specifically looking for a place to spread a picnic lunch. Don't. The best part of the park is a 250-foot tumbling waterfall that is easy to miss despite being one of the state's largest, especially when the foliage of high summer obscures it from view. If you like tramping through the woods, you can hike to the top of the falls, or if you prefer less demanding pleasures, you can simply sit out on the rocks in the lower pools and dangle your toes in the torrent. Even though the water may be a tad cool for toe-dangling come autumn, we highly recommend visiting the park after the leaves have turned and the summer crowds have thinned. The park is open daily in the summer, 8 a.m. to 7 p.m. The rest of the year it closes at sunset.

Tall Tales of Ethan Allen

Ethan Allen was a big guy (six feet, six inches tall) with a big thirst. According to one "tall" tale, on a hot August afternoon, Allen and his cousin Remember Baker, having overindulged, repaired to nearby shady woods to sleep it off. Baker was awakened by a strange noise, and he watched in horror as a rattlesnake bit his drink-befuddled cousin over and over. Before Baker could find a weapon to subdue the serpent, it moved away from Allen, gazed at Baker with a certain drunken stare, then wobbled its way into the bushes, where it collapsed in a stupor. Allen awoke refreshed from his nap, except for complaints about "these eternal, damnable, bloodsucking mosquitoes," which had disturbed his rest.

Ethan Allen's wife, Fanny, was, by all accounts, his equal in temper and independence. A story is told that Allen's friends became concerned about his drinking and decided to frighten him into leading a more temperate life. They wrapped themselves in sheets and hid beneath the bridge that Allen passed on his way home from his favorite tavern. Making the requisite booing, moaning, and keening sounds, they jumped out at their friend, only to scare his horse into rearing. Despite his snozzled state, Allen managed to control his mount and greeted the "apparitions" by proclaiming, "If you are angels of light, I'm glad to meet you. And if you are devils, then come along home with me. I married your sister."

About a mile north of Kent, you'll find a big maroon L-shaped barn set back a short distance from the west side of US 7. The ground on which it sits used to be the Kent town dump, but all that changed back in the 1970s. At that time, New Britain's Stanley Tool Company was looking for a site for a museum to house a collection of American tools and implements collected by noted artist and author **Eric Sloane**. Stanley wanted the state of Connecticut to run the place, but the state would accept ownership only if the museum's site was somehow historically significant. As it turned out, down at the foot of the hill behind the town dump in Kent were the ruins of an old blast furnace that produced pig iron during most of the 19th century. The presence of this jumble of stone made the dump suitably historical, so Stanley acquired the property and had Sloane design a building for his collection. Thus was born the Sloane-Stanley Museum, now known as the **Eric Sloane Museum & Kent Iron Furnace** (31 Kent-Cornwall Rd. [Rte. 7]; 860-927-3849; portal.ct.gov/ECD-EricSloaneMuseum). Open May to Oct, Fri to Sun, 10 a.m.–4 p.m.

The tools collected here, some of which date from the 17th century, have some historical interest as a link with everyday life in America's past, but Sloane vehemently rejected the image of himself as what he called "a nurturer of nostalgia." The contents of this museum should instead be viewed as oddly beautiful art. Sloane personally arranged and lighted the displays, and the resulting jumble of wooden bowls and woven baskets, yokes and mallets and pitchforks, axes and scythes, and weathered sawhorses has an internal order that is both pleasing and restful. It's as if each arrangement were a small work of art.

In addition to the fine tool collection, the museum also contains a recreation of Sloane's art studio with some of his works on display. And don't forget that historic blast furnace; it's the tumbled pile of rocks surrounded by the split-rail fence at the bottom of the hill behind the barn. Open May to June, Fri through Sun, 10 a.m. to 4 p.m.; June through Oct, Thurs through Sun, 10 a.m. to 4 p.m. Admission. Blue Star Museum.

Literally next door (they share a driveway), is the **Connecticut Antique Machinery Association** (31B Kent Cornwall Road; 860-927-0050; ctamachinery.com). This is really a collection of several history museums in one, spread out across a large campus and containing not only antique machinery like steam tractors and train cars but also the Cream Hill Agricultural School, with its original desks and library, and the Connecticut Museum of Mining and Mineral Science, full of native rocks and mining equipment. They also sponsor an annual festival at the museum, when they actually start up many of these machines, and the noise is incredible. The festival also features wood splitting, blacksmithing, broom making, and cider making. Antique cars and trucks fill the fields, and food is available from a variety of vendors. On normal days, the museum is open from May 1 to Nov 1, Wed to Sun, 10 a.m.–4 p.m.

Located just off US 7 about 4 miles south of Kent, **Bull's Bridge** is one of only a few remaining covered bridges in Connecticut and one of two that are still open to traffic (the other is in West Cornwall, also off US 7 a few miles north).

Bull's Bridge was built in 1842 and spans the Housatonic River between New York state and Connecticut on the river's eastern bank. George Washington didn't sleep here, but he did pass over the bridge, and he (or a member of his party) did manage to lose a horse in the Housatonic while doing so. If looking at the bridge gives you a sense of déjà vu, that's because it's probably been the source of more New England covered-bridge photographs on postcards and calendar covers than any other bridge in this part of the world.

After you cross the bridge, about 3 miles up the road on the **Schaghticoke Indian Reservation**, you'll find an old cemetery with many timeworn headstones, including one commemorating the last resting place of a "Christian Indian Princess." This tombstone belongs to **Eunice Mauwee**, born in 1756, the granddaughter of Chief Gideon Mauwee, the first recorded Sachem of the present-day Schaghticokes. She died in 1860 at the age of 104. As you explore other tombstones here, remember to show proper respect and not take rubbings without permission.

New Milford

South of Kent is the charming town of **New Milford**, with its iconic town green (complete with World War I tank) and numerous cafes and shops. But Sunday is the great day in this town, at least from May to October, because the **Elephant's Trunk Flea Market** (490 Danbury Rd.; 508-265-9911; etflea.com) brings thousands of people from New York and beyond to shop for bargains. Since 1976 this has been one of the largest outdoor markets in the state, with parking spaces for over 1,000 vehicles. The ever-changing set of dealers from all over the East Coast will bargain with you for glassware, vintage and new tools, vintage clothing, coins, decoys, antique toys, collectibles, furniture, Depression glass, jewelry, pewter, baseball cards, and more. They actually ban vendors who deal in counterfeits or knockoffs. Open end of May to Oct every Sun 7 a.m.–3:30 p.m. However, be aware that the doors close at 2 p.m. and there are no pets allowed. Admission.

The Hills

Goshen

They say that at one time, travelers passing through the Bridgeport area during the spring were shocked to see elephants plowing nearby fields; they were rented to local farmers by circus impresario **P. T. Barnum**. These days if you see an elephant strolling through a field along Route 4 in **Goshen**, it won't be plowing—the various circus animals on the property belong to **Commerford Zoo** (48 Torrington Rd.; 860-491-3421; commerfordzoo.com), which operates kids' fun fairs and petting zoos throughout New England. Commerford's animals have also been known to make an appearance at birthday parties and weddings, and have even been in a movie or commercial or two. You can't tour Commerford's, but at any given time, a fair number of the residents will be exercising and visible from the road.

Nodine's Smokehouse (39 North St.; 860-491-4009; nodinesmokehouse.com) is one of the best smokehouses in New England. It's also something of a Connecticut institution. Nodine's (it's pronounced no-DINES) carries many specialty items, ranging from smoked hams, turkeys, and chickens to the more exotic smoked pheasants, shrimp, and venison sausage. Nodine's more common meats can be enjoyed in made-to-order sandwiches. Open Mon through Sat, 9 a.m. to 5 p.m.; Sun, 10 a.m. to 4 p.m. If you see something you like but don't want to drag it along for the rest of your trip, never fear; they have a mail-order operation.

You'll need some dessert with that smoked meat, so why not stop at **Thorncrest Farm and Milk House Chocolates** (280 Town Hill Rd., Goshen; 860-491-4261; milkhousechocolates.net). At Thorncrest, they believe that "Chocolate should be just as fresh as tomatoes." The farm ensures the cows are fed the finest, sweetest hay and natural feeds. And then, wonderfully, almost magically, single-cow-origin chocolates are crafted from their milk. The farm's shop is open Mon to Sat, 10 a.m.–5 p.m.; Sun 10 a.m.–4 p.m. You can also visit the cows that produce this remarkable milk on Thurs through Sun, 10 a.m.–3 p.m.

And to wash down all that deliciousness? Goshen features one of the best wineries in the state, **Sunset Meadow Vineyards** (599 Old Middle St. [Route 63]; 860-201-4654; sunsetmeadowvineyards.com), with a perfect location for growing grapes, over 1,000 feet above sea level and a western-facing slope to catch the afternoon rays. Their estate and appellation bottles are worth the full tasting, and there's nothing better than sitting in their converted barn at the long tasting bar and nursing a bottle of smoky St. Croix or lemony Riesling. Open year-round, Mon, Thurs, and Fri 12 p.m.–5 p.m.; Sat 11 a.m.–6 p.m.; Sun 11 a.m.–5 p.m.

Torrington

No one driving past 192 Main St. in **Torrington** can possibly ignore the awe-inspiring symphony in Roman brick and rosy-red slate that occupies the property. At first, all you see is the big, round, 3-story corner tower. Then the eye begins to jump from dormer to porch to porte cochère, taking in the Victorian carvings, the intricate sashes, the many small details that speak of another age, when decoration for its own sake was a common element of American home-building.

The magnificent, 16-room **Hotchkiss-Fyler House** is now the headquarters of the **Torrington Historical Society** (860-482-8260; torringtonhistoricalsociety.org). It still displays the original mahogany paneling, hand stenciling, and parquet floors that made it such an opulent example of Victorian excess when it was built by **Orsamus Roman Fyler** back in 1900. The original furnishings, on display here, are almost as extravagant as the house itself. Several of the rooms feature wonderful little collections of art objects, including gold Fabergé spoons, Sèvres porcelain, Victorian art glass, and Meissen porcelain figurines. The Hotchkiss-Fyler House is open mid-Apr through the end of Oct, Wed through Sat from noon to 4 p.m. An adjacent museum devoted to local history is open mid-Apr through Oct, Thurs through Sat, 1 p.m. to 4 p.m. with guided tours on the hour. Admission. The Torrington Historical Society is open Wed–Sat, noon–4 p.m.

One of the nicest places to take a leisurely fall hike is located in **Burr Pond State Park** (385 Burr Mountain Rd.; 860-482-1817). The circuit around the 88-acre pond in the park is a pleasant walk. There's history in the park, too: It was the site of Gail Borden's first American condensed-milk factory. In 1856, Borden, who was from Torrington, created a way to preserve milk by condensing it; his creation was called the "milk that won the Civil War." A bronze tablet marks the place where the factory once stood before being destroyed by fire. Some of the trails are perfect for little ones or those not up to a strenuous hike. The 438-acre park also offers swimming, fishing, boating, and picnicking.

Torrington is also the birthplace of notorious abolitionist **John Brown**. While he wasn't successful in his attempt to free the slaves at Harpers Ferry, and paid for his efforts with his life, Brown certainly left his mark on our state's and nation's history. The house where he was born on May 9, 1800, was destroyed by fire in 1918, but the site is marked with a stone wall and a small memorial. To find it, follow Route 4 west from Torrington center toward Goshen. Take a right onto University Drive. Follow for about 1 mile before turning left onto John Brown Road. The site is about a half mile down the road on the right.

torringtontrivia

Torrington was once known by the rather odd moniker of "Mast Swamp."

Litchfield

The stark white Congregational church with the towering spire situated on the north side of the **Litchfield Green** is quite possibly the most photographed church in New England. While the world has certainly changed since the green was laid out in the 1770s, there's still an old-time, upscale feel here.

The heart of historic **Litchfield** consists of a block or two of North Street, a few blocks of South Street (Route 63), and a few blocks of West Street immediately off the green. There's plenty of on-street parking, so you can leave your car and take your time to enjoy the history and shopping to be found.

While you can't visit the following privately owned homes, you can stroll by and take a minute to appreciate them. Standing on the green, facing north, look for East Street, on which you'll find **Dr. Reuben Smith's 1781 Apothecary Shop** (9 East St.), the earliest commercial building in the state (this building used to exist next to Dr. Smith's North Street residence but was moved to its present location in 1812 and is now occupied by a doctor's office).

Now turn east and walk toward South Street (Route 202), where you will find the renovated 1812 **Litchfield County Jail** (7 North St.) standing on the corner but looking much different than its past life. This is the oldest public building in town and served as a holding place for prisoners of the War of 1812, making it one of the oldest penal facilities in the state. It served as a jail until the early 1990s, then as a rehabilitation center until 2010. It stood vacant for a while and was offered to the town at no cost, but it was determined to be too big of a project for them to maintain. In the late summer of 2014, a private real estate developer purchased the building for $130,000 and began renovations, not really knowing what they were going to end up with but having a vision of a multi-use venue, with retail, office, and living spaces. Today, you'll find **The Bakehouse of Litchfield** (7 North St.; 860-361-6423; thebakehousect.com), sharing space with other businesses in the renovated building. And since you're there, this bakery is a good place to stop and grab some delicious bread or other portable food to bring with you if you're going to make a stop at the Litchfield Distillery (see below). You'll want some cushion in your stomach if you're going to taste their samples! Open Wed–Sat, 8 a.m.–4 p.m.; Sun 8 a.m.–2 p.m.

Head down the road to the 1816 **First National Bank of Litchfield** (13 North St.). This building has housed a bank since it was built and is the oldest continuously operating business in Litchfield and the oldest nationally chartered bank in the state.

Next up is the 1760 home of **Benjamin Tallmadge** (47 North Street). Once George Washington's spymaster, Tallmadge built the house with the money he made selling land in Connecticut's "Western Reserve"—now northeastern Ohio. Tallmadge and his family lived there until his death in 1835. It was purchased and sold a few times before coming back into the family when Tallmadge's granddaughter, Julia Tallmadge Noyes, and her husband bought the house. They eventually passed it to their daughter, Emily Noyes Vanderpoel, who used it as a summer residence until her death in 1939. In 2009, the house was up for sale again and languished on the market for a couple of years. Around 2011, there was hope that the Litchfield Historical Society could purchase it, but it proved too big a project for them. But by the end of 2011, the house was scooped up by restorers extraordinaire Louise Arroyo and Thomas Callahan. These two have been busy in Connecticut, purchasing and restoring historically significant houses, mainly in the northwest region of the state. In 2014, the 6,840-square-foot home that currently sits on just under 1 acre sold for close to a million dollars and is currently off the market.

A bit farther up North Street, across from each other, you have the **1760 Sheldon Tavern** (73 North St.), where George Washington really did sleep (he visited town five times), and **Dr. Reuben Smith's house** (of apothecary fame, remember the shop used to be here, next to his house before it was moved). This house is notable for having been built in 1770 by the famed builder of churches, **Giles Kilborn**, who lived in nearby Bantam and built the West Church there.

A building you *can* visit is back past the green on South Street. The **Litchfield History Museum** (7 South St.; 860-567-4501; litchfieldhistoricalsociety.org) is located in the Noyes Memorial Building and allows you to trace the history of Litchfield through a variety of exhibits. There's a really nice collection of historic items from the town and surrounding areas, including information on the 1792 Pierce Academy and its founder Sarah Pierce. The groundbreaking academy was the first in the country for girls. Pierce established her innovative program in the family home on North Street in 1792, and it ran successfully until 1833. Today, there is only a marker to indicate the site; the house currently at 133 North Street was built on the site of the former academy. The museum does a good job of displaying what a typical day for the girls attending the academy would have been like.

The museum is open mid-Apr through the end of Nov, Wed through Sun, 11 a.m. to 5 p.m. Admission is free. The lower level of the building is home to the **Helga J. Ingraham Memorial Library**, which is open to researchers year-round Tues through Fri by appointment, except if there is an event. Check calendar.

When you're done here, head to the **Tapping Reeve House & Litchfield Law School**, located a block south of the museum at 82 South St. Founded in 1773, this was America's first law school. Tour the school that trained political conspirator and former vice president **Aaron Burr**. Of course, it also schooled the likes of ***John C. Calhoun*** and some 130 other congressmen and senators, not to mention three Supreme Court justices, six cabinet members, and a dozen governors. Today, the Reeve House exhibits tell the story of students who attended the school. As part of the Litchfield Historical Society, the Tapping Reeve House & Litchfield Law School is also open mid-Apr through the end of Nov, Wed through Sun, 11 a.m. to 5 p.m. Admission is free.

Visitors can also explore the grounds of the house, known as ***Tapping Reeve Meadow***, year-round, dawn to dusk. The grounds have been landscaped with plants and elements that would have been found in this area from the 18th through the 20th centuries. You'll find a small orchard, a chestnut grove, a children's garden, and education pavilion all accented with stonewalls and period fencing. Programs and events are often held here throughout the year. Visit litchfieldhistoricalsociety.org/calendar-list for the latest offerings.

Now that you've done your homework and taxed your brain with all these names and dates, take a little adult time, get back in your car, and head to the ***Litchfield Distillery*** (569 Bantam Rd.; 860-361-6503; litchfielddistillery.com) where you can learn all about the process of distilling spirits and just how much goes into what they call the "Farm to Bottle to Farm process." It is incredibly illuminating to see the science behind creating these delicious concoctions and how the two brothers who own the distillery, David and Jack Baker, truly embody the "spirit of hard work." One of the brothers will take you on a tour through the process, which ends with a tasting of their bourbons and vodkas (and their maple syrup if you're lucky!). Generally open Mon to Fri, 10 a.m.–5:30 p.m.; Sat 11 a.m.–5 p.m.; Sun 11 a.m.–4 p.m. Tours on the hour starting at 11; last tour at 4 (3 on Sunday). If you want to be sure you'll be accommodated at a specific time, call ahead or visit their website or Facebook page and make a reservation. You must be 21 or older to take part in the tasting, although those younger than that can accompany you.

Once you're done imbibing and you have your bottle safely tucked into the trunk of your car for later, head out to walk it all off at the ***White Memorial Foundation and Conservation Center*** (80 Whitehall Rd.; 860-567-0857; whitememorialcc.org). These 4,000 acres constitute one of Connecticut's largest nature centers and wildlife sanctuaries. This privately owned facility administered by the nonprofit ***White Memorial Foundation*** contains bird-feeding stations, numerous picnic areas, camps, several campgrounds, bird-watching platforms, 40 miles of riding and hiking trails (including some on boardwalks through expansive wetlands and one for the blind with Braille signs), more than 70 acres of open water, and more than half of the Bantam Lake shoreline, a marina, and event facilities for rent. The property is open year-round for fishing, canoeing, cross-country skiing, and similar activities.

The Conservation Center's Nature Museum features fluorescent rocks, a working honeybee hive, and a variety of exhibits, including some stunning nature dioramas, as well as live animals. They also offer scavenger hunts (both indoors and outdoors) to keep little ones busy. The center and its gift shop are open year-round, Tues through Sat, 9 a.m. to 5 p.m.; Sun, noon to 5 p.m. Admission for non-members, free for members. Admission for children younger than 12 (accompanied by an adult) is free for 17 weeks of the year. This is made possible through member donations and is continually growing.

White Memorial also features two campgrounds, Point Folly Family Campground and Windmill Hill Family Campground, with links on the main website. The Campground Store (123 North Shore Rd.) is open from early May until mid-Oct.

Not exhausted yet? Head south on Route 63 to **White Flower Farm** (167 Litchfield Rd., Morris; 800-503-9624; whiteflowerfarm.com), a family-owned and -operated mail-order nursery that has been in business since 1950. It was started by two writers from New York City, who purchased land in Litchfield with a barn on it that they converted to their house in 1930. As they say, one thing led to another, and the pair found themselves planting seeds, creating gardens, growing vegetables and wanting to share them with others. The converted barn still stands on the north side of Esther's Road along with the Moon Garden the couple created with all white flowers and from which the company gets its name.

A more recent addition to the farm is the herd of Angus cattle. You can go to the farm and pick your own steer from the herd if you wish, or if you'd rather, you can just order the cuts you wish, though you may have a bit of a wait. The process and prices are outlined on their website with the promise that all the animals are humanely and naturally raised without chemicals or cruelty.

White Flower Farm is open daily 9 a.m. to 5:30 p.m. during the growing season, which is generally mid-Mar through Nov. It's always best to call ahead and be sure they are open.

North of White Flower Farm, back toward the green but to the east on Route 118 (East Street), just past the East Cemetery is the **Lourdes in Litchfield Shrine** (83 Montfort Rd.; 860-567-1041; shrinect.org). For 32 years, Montfort Missionaries have operated this 35-acre shrine, which features a replica of the famous grotto at Lourdes, France. An outdoor Stations of the Cross path winds its way to a spectacular crucifixion scene at the top of the hill. The grounds are open year-round sunrise to sunset daily and include a picnic area and gift shop. In addition, outdoor services are conducted, weather permitting, throughout the pilgrimage season (May 1 to mid-Oct), Tues through Sun, 11:30 a.m. If the weather does not cooperate, Mass is held in the chapel. There is a series of special blessings throughout the year, including an Anointing of the Sick, a Blessing of Animals, a Living Rosary, a Living Nativity, and more. They also offer a summer book reading and lecture series. A cafe is open Thurs through Sun, 10 a.m. to 2 p.m.; gift shop open Tues to Sat, 10:30 a.m.–4:30 p.m.; Sun 11:30 a.m. to 4:30 p.m. Check their website for the latest information.

Wisdom House Retreat & Conference Center (229 E. Litchfield Rd.; 860-567-3163; wisdomhouse.org), formerly a convent for the Sisters of Wisdom, is now the site of Connecticut's only outdoor labyrinth. Don't arrive thinking you'll find a high, boxwood maze like those in England or in Colonial Williamsburg. Walking the low, circular spiral path helps you meditate and heighten your awareness. You'll find a helpful pamphlet at Wisdom House suggesting different meditative approaches to walking the labyrinth. Whichever approach you take, it's a peaceful way to get in touch with your inner self, find some peace in the silence, and shed the cares of 21st-century life. Many visitors use the labyrinth for silent meditation, so it probably isn't a place to visit if you are accompanied by rowdy children or a particularly talkative friend. The center offers all sorts of services on the 70-acre site, including an outdoor swimming pool, overnight accommodations for 140, conferences, and more. Visit their website for the most up-to-date information.

South of Wisdom House Retreat & Conference Center is **Topsmead State Forest** (Buell Road; 860-567-5694), an estate-turned-park that looks as if it belongs in the British midlands. When Waterbury heiress **Edith Morton Chase** came home from a European tour enchanted with English manor houses, she was determined to build herself an authentic Cotswold cottage, complete with leaded-glass casement windows, hand-hewn beams, and buttery stucco exteriors. Here in Litchfield, the cottage of her dreams was designed by architect **Richard Dana**, who shared Miss Edith's love for English cottage architecture.

Topsmead, however, was more than a building. It was also a vast garden and a working farm. Miss Edith was as fond of English country gardens as of English architecture, and she surrounded her home with formal manicured gardens and cutting gardens full of the flowers most beloved by English gardeners: roses, sweet William, and phlox. Even in her late 70s, she reputedly walked a daily mile around these gardens, inspecting, issuing orders, and sipping from an ever-present glass of skim milk. When she died in 1972, she left her 511-acre estate to the State of Connecticut so that everyone could enjoy a touch of England in Litchfield. Topsmead State Forest is open all year for picnicking, sledding, cross-country skiing, and hiking; there's even a letterbox or two. You can tour the house on the second and fourth weekends of each month from June to Oct, noon to 5 p.m. (the last weekend of Oct, it closes at 4 p.m.).

Fifty years after his father sold off the last cow from their family's dairy operation, John Morosani of **Laurel Ridge Grass Fed Beef** had reinstated the cattle on his family's 700-acre farm and developed a thriving business. However, according to Morosani and his business partner, Jim Abbott, this wasn't their original intent. They decided to bring cattle back to the land to help maintain the overgrown fields. They thought they'd raise a few cows, use the meat themselves, and call it a day. But the more they learned about the business, and the more local residents heard about them, well, growth was natural. By starting off slow with seven calves in the spring of 2003, and applying for various government grants to help, Morosani and Abbott built **Laurel Ridge** (66 Wigwam Rd.; 860-567-8122; lrgfb.com) into the successful business it is today.

Laurel Ridge's cattle are entirely pasture fed with their diets not supplemented by "anything but a salt lick." The farm also offers pastured pork, humanely raised on high-quality pig feed and foraged food. Laurel Ridge meat is in such demand now that Morosani and Abbott have a hard time keeping up. They sell their products at various farm markets, farm stands, and stores throughout the area; check their website for details.

Laurel Ridge is known for its beef, but it's really the flowers that make it famous. Daffodils, in fact—thousands of them. It all started back in 1941 with Remy and Virginia Morosani when they first moved to Litchfield and purchased 17 acres of land. The couple was surveying their property and decided that one pasture was just too rocky to be of much use as a crop field, so they planted 10,000 daffodil bulbs. Do you know what daffodil bulbs do every year? They multiply. The Morosanis were diligent in digging up their multiplied flower bulbs and replanting them every fall for more than 20 years. By then, the daffodils had become something of a local legend and people came from miles away to see their beauty. The Morosanis started the **Laurel Ridge Foundation** to be managed and supported by their descendants to ensure the daffodils would be cared for. Lucky for John, hay season for his cows is winding down when the major work for the daffodils begins. To find the daffodils, head south on Wigwam Road for about a half mile. There are walking trails and myriad photo ops when the flowers are in bloom (Apr and May), just please be respectful of the No Parking signs and do not block private drives. For more information on when to visit, please go to litchfielddaffodils.com.

On Route 209, in southwest Litchfield, you'll find the **Bantam Cinema and Arts Center** (115 Bantam Lake Rd.; 860-361-6066 for show times; bantamcinema.com), just south of Route 202. This gem is an old-fashioned movie theater that screens those offbeat, independent, or imported films that never seem to get much play at suburban theaters. Even though the screening rooms and sound systems are modern, it's a wonderfully intimate and kind of old-fashioned way to see a film. Opening in 1927, the cinema is the "oldest continuously operated movie house" in the state. From the era of silent movies, the theater went through a variety of owners until Lisa Hedley purchased it in 1990 and started the "Meet the Film Maker" series. She would invite writers, actors, producers, and directors to come speak about their work. The cinema saw some big names, likely due to its proximity to New York and the fact that more than a few Hollywood names live or lived in the area, including Arthur Miller, Maureen Stapleton, Liza Minnelli, and Mia Farrow. New owners took over in 2007, but the lecture series continued, bringing Rebecca Miller, Joan Rivers, and Daniel Day-Lewis, who came to speak about his part in *Lincoln*. Check the cinema's website for upcoming events. In the meantime, take in a film and enjoy the atmosphere while munching on organic popcorn with real butter.

And since you are in the area, it would be a mistake to bypass the **Bantam Bread Company** (853 Bantam Rd.; 860-567-2737; bantambread.com). This is the type of hearth-baked bread that people line up for in New York and Los Angeles. Holiday Bread is a popular (and vegan) option made with organic white and whole rye flours and seasoned with "cranberries, raisins, pecans, sourdough, rye chops, caraway seeds, and sea salt." Other offerings include a semolina batard, a sunflower and flax seed loaf, a Calamata olive sourdough, and more. If you're looking for something a bit sweeter, try their cakes, tarts, cookies, biscuits, or "Dirt Bombs," nutmeg-scented muffins dipped in butter and rolled in cinnamon sugar. Heaven.

The owners are big proponents of supporting local artisans as well and offer an ever-changing variety of local goods. Some of these include delicious-smelling **Goatboy Soaps** (New Milford), **Winding Drive Jellies and Jams** (Woodbury), greeting cards by local artists, seasonal fruits and vegetables from local farms, oils and vinegars from local importers, regional cheeses and butters, the list goes on and on. The bread is fresh and delicious, and it doesn't stay on the shelves for long. Open Wed to Sat, 9 a.m.–4 p.m.; Sun 9 a.m.–3 p.m.

If you're looking for something sweeter, don't pass **Love Heart's Bakery and Cafe** (583 Bantam Rd.; 860-361-6526; loveheartsbakery.homestead.com), where you'll find a cozy little place that serves up deliciousness. Named after owner Allison Barker-Croce's daughter, the bakery half offers a wonderful assortment of cookies, brownies, baklava, cakes (chocolate, fruit, carrot, cheese), pies, and tarts. On the cafe side you can choose from soups, salads, and/or sandwiches and wraps on fresh-made breads. You never know what is going to be on the menu, so stop in often. Open weekdays 6 a.m.–3 p.m.; Sat 7 a.m.–3 p.m.; Sun 8 a.m.–2 p.m.

ANNUAL EVENTS IN THE LITCHFIELD HILLS

APRIL

Riverton Fishing Derby
Farmington River between Hogback Dam and Pipeline Pool
(860) 379-0811
rivertonct.com

MAY

Annual Sports Car Championships & Royals Car Show
Lime Rock Park
467 Lime Rock Rd., Lakeville
(800) 435-5000
limerock.com

JULY

Litchfield Jazz Festival
116 Old Middle St., Goshen
(860) 361-6285
litchfieldjazz.com

AUGUST

Bridgewater Country Fair
100 Main St. South, Bridgewater
(860) 354-4730
bridgewaterfair.com

Annual Podunk Bluegrass Music Festival
Goshen Fairgrounds
116 Old Middle St, Goshen
(860) 491-3655
podunkbluegrass.com

Sharon on the Green Arts and Crafts Fair
63 Main St., Sharon
(860) 364-1400

Terryville Lions Country Fair
171 Townhill Rd., Terryville
(860) 582-0709
terryvillefair.org

SEPTEMBER

Bethlehem Fair
384 Main St. North, Bethlehem
(203) 266-5350
bethlehemfair.com

Colebrook Fair
562 Colebrook Rd., Colebrook
colebrookfair.weebly.com

Goshen Fair
116 Old Middle St., Goshen
(860) 491-3655
goshenfair.org

OCTOBER

Harvest Bounty Brew Fest
421 Bantam Rd., Litchfield
(860) 567-8302
beerfests.com/events/harvest-bounty-brew-fest/

Harwinton Fair
150 Locust Rd., Harwinton
(860) 485-9066
harwintonfair.com

Riverton Fair
16 Main St., Riverton
(860) 379-0060
rivertonfair.org

DECEMBER

Christmas in Riverton
rivertonct.com

Bethlehem

For most of the year, **Bethlehem** (on Route 61 north of Woodbury) is just another quiet New England country town. During the Christmas holiday season, however, all that changes, and for a few brief weeks, Bethlehem bustles with activity.

The reason, of course, is the name. The local post office doubles its staff each December to accommodate the thousands of folks who want a Bethlehem postmark on their Christmas cards. If you're going to be passing through during early December, bring yours along and they'll be glad to add them to the bin. The **Bethlehem Christmas Town Festival** in mid-December also draws a lot of people to listen to the music, ride hay wagons, and look at holiday arts and crafts and a small festival of lights—a far cry, you will agree, from the days when the Puritans who wrote the colony's stringent blue laws prescribed a 5-shilling fine for "Christmas Keeping." For details call the town clerk's office during the morning at (203) 266-7510, ext. 2.

About 1.5 miles down Flanders Road (off Route 61), is the **Abbey of Regina Laudis** (273 Flanders Rd.; 203-266-7727; abbeyofreginalaudis.org), which operates the Monastic Art Shop, offering items handcrafted on the premises by Benedictine nuns. Among crafts represented are printing, potting, and blacksmithing. You can also buy beauty products, honey, herbs, and postcards showing the abbey grounds. The abbey's holiday decorations include a nativity scene composed of 18th-century Neapolitan figures. Regular hours for the Monastic Art Shop are Fri 10 a.m.–noon; Sat and Sun, 10 a.m.–noon, and 1:30 p.m.–4 p.m. Call ahead or visit their website for hours and information on special events.

If you are in Bethlehem in the warmer months, stop by the **Bellamy-Ferriday House and Garden** (9 Main St. North; 203-266-7596; ctlandmarks.org), a 1754 homestead with beautiful art and lilac-haunted garden. Once called the Bellamy Manse, it was built by Reverend Joseph Bellamy, a preacher who traveled throughout New England preaching the message of the First Great Awakening. His writings were published in New York, Boston, and Scotland throughout the 1700s, and he eventually turned this large house into a theological seminary, where he taught many important people, including future writer of the Constitution, senator, and Chief Justice of the Supreme Court Oliver Ellsworth.

The formal garden was added in the early 20th century by Caroline Ferriday, an actress and philanthropist involved in the civil rights movement. The gardens connect to 2 miles of trails run by the Bethlehem Land Trust called the Bellamy Preserve, with the entrance a few steps away on Munger Lane. The Bellamy-Ferriday House also runs painting workshops at the house throughout the summer, and you could not have a better subject to try your brush on. Open May through June, Wed to Sun, noon–4 p.m.; July to Sept, Thurs to Sun, noon–4 p.m.; October, Sat and Sun, noon–4 p.m.

Woodbury

Situated in the south-central part of Litchfield County on US 6, **Woodbury** was one of the first towns established in inland Connecticut, and today Woodbury's Main Street is nicknamed "***Antique Avenue***." Some travel guides create the impression that unless you roll up in a chauffeured Rolls, you won't get very good treatment at many of the antiques shops in Woodbury. Not so! Even if you show up in faded jeans and scuffed-up sneakers, you can look forward to being treated with great kindness and helpfulness.

It's a pleasure just to walk through **Mill House Antiques & Gardens** (1068 Main St. North [US 6]; 203-263-3446; millhouseantiquesandgardens.com), a restored mill house with imaginative displays of top-quality English and French furniture. Mill House also offers extraordinary gardens full of antique urns and statues. They promise you'll really feel as if you're strolling through Europe. Open Mon through Fri, 10 a.m. to 5 p.m.; Sat and Sun, noon–5 p.m. They ship globally if you find something but can't fit it in your car!

For a taste of the Woodbury that antiquers rarely see, visit the **Canfield Corner Pharmacy** (2 N. Main St.; 203-263-2595). It has an old-fashioned soda fountain and is crammed from floor to rafters with every nostrum and homemaker's convenience on the market. Travel back in time when you step through the doors and "walk on wooden floors older than you!" How can you resist? Open Mon through Fri, 9:30 a.m. to 5 p.m.; Sat, 9:30 a.m. to 3 p.m.

Although they are not antiques, the pewter plates, mugs, lamps, and other accessories at the **Woodbury Pewter Factory Store** (860 Main St. South; 800-648-2014; woodburypewter.com) look as authentic as any antique you would buy in Woodbury. Woodbury Pewter has been around since 1952, when it was a tiny shop tucked into a blacksmith's shop. Today, it's a modern retail operation that features not only its own products but also the pewter work and jewelry of pewterers from across America. Open Mon to Thurs, 10 a.m.–5 p.m.; Fri and Sat, 9 a.m.–5 p.m.; Sun 11 a.m.–5 p.m. Woodbury Pewter also holds several very good sales throughout the year.

A glebe is the parcel of land granted to a clergyman during his tenure of office. The gambrel-roofed **Glebe House Museum and Gertrude Jekyll Garden** (49 Hollow Rd.; 203-263-2855; glebehousemuseum.org), off US 6 in the center of town, has always had ecclesiastical connections. Mere weeks after the start of the American Revolution, a group of clergy secretly assembled in the house to elect the first American bishop of the Episcopal Church, the **Reverend Dr. Samuel Seabury**. His election broke the American connection with the Church of England and laid the foundation for the separation of church and state in America. Today, the old farmhouse is used as a museum and kept much as it was. The original paneling remains, and the rooms are stuffed with period furnishings collected locally. Garden open year-round for self-guided tours dawn to dusk; Glebe House open May through Sept, Fri to Sun, 1 p.m.–4 p.m.; last tour at 3:20. Events scheduled through Oct and off-season tours and group tours by appointment. Admission.

Roxbury

The town of **Roxbury** was home to (among countless other celebrities) *Alexander Calder*, 20th-century sculptor, from 1933 until his death in 1976. Calder has many ties to our state. He is the creator of the city's *Stegosaurus* (see page 13). He was also a favorite of Wadsworth Atheneum director **Chick Austin**, who purchased and exhibited his work. He spent two weeks in 1925 sketching scenes from Bridgeport's Ringling Bros. and Barnum & Bailey Circus, which greatly influenced his life's work.

Calder moved to Roxbury with his wife Louisa James (grandniece of author Henry James) when they purchased an old farmhouse in town, painted it flat black, and converted an old ice house into a studio. They had two daughters, Sandy and Mary. The Calders spent the next years summering in Roxbury and renting studio space in New York in the winter months. Calder met with great success, becoming one of the world's most acclaimed artists. He died in New York on November 11, 1976, at the age of 78. His home can still be seen at 306 Painter Hill Rd., but it is privately owned so please be respectful.

Many of the celebrities who lived in Roxbury have donated land for public use, including playwright Arthur Miller, who wrote *Death of a Salesman* and *The Crucible*, and novelist William Styron, who wrote *Darkness Visible* and *Sophie's Choice*. These properties are walkable through the **Roxbury Land Trust Trails** (7 South St.; 860-350-4148; roxburylandtrust.org). Connecticut has many of these "secret" trail systems that few outside of each town pay attention to. Roxbury Land Trust has created one of the best of these "private" sets of trails. Along with the Miller and Styron preserves, one of the best in Roxbury is Mine Hill, which could easily be a state park, containing the remnants of a huge foundry, roasting ovens, and other ruins. The Land Trust offices are open at the address above during weekday mornings, but the trail maps all can be found online.

After some brisk hikes, why not stop for refreshment at **Mine Hill Distillery** (5 Mine Hill Rd; 860-210-1872; minehilldistillery.com). Mine Hill distills gin and vodka from locally sourced corn, rye, wheat, and malted barley. Owner Elliot Davis raised his children on a farm just down the road and is working with other farmers in the way agriculture is supposed to work—as partners in the craft. Spent grain from the process feeds heritage livestock at the local farms. The distillery's classic dry gin includes eastern white pine and the classic vodka is distilled from their own wheat. Open Mon to Fri, noon–4:30 p.m., but call ahead to make a reservation; Sat and Sun, walk-ins welcome noon–4:30 p.m.

Washington

Lake Waramaug State Park (30 Lake Waramaug Rd.; 860-868-2592; ctparks.com/parks/lake-waramaug-state-park) offers seasonal camping, fishing, swimming, car-top boating, and picnicking. With its surrounding forests and hills, the lake is often likened to Switzerland's Lake Lucerne, and the inns that ring its waters reflect the same alpine charm. The lake is named for **Chief Waramaug**, whose Wyantenock tribe hunted and wintered in the area. One of the best ways to see the area, especially during leaf-peeping season, is to take the almost-1-mile drive around the lake. The burning autumn colors of the surrounding hardwoods, reflected by the cool, crystal-clear lake, make this a picture-postcard setting.

The crossroads village of **New Preston** at the southeast tip of Lake Waramaug contains several shops that are well worth a stop, especially if you like antiques. Open Wed through Mon, 11 a.m. to 5 p.m. ***J. Seitz & Co.*** (9 E. Shore Rd.; 860-868-0119; jseitz.com) handles both Southwestern antiques and reproductions, as well as other home furnishings and decor, apparel

The Legend of Chief Waramaug and His Great Lodge

About the time settlers first arrived in northwestern Connecticut, the Native Americans who lived along the banks of the Housatonic River were led by a great leader, *Chief Waramaug*. Waramaug lived in a lodge high above the west bank of the Housatonic, not far from the beautiful alpine lake that bears his name. The hundred-foot-long lodge was apparently so majestic that it was called Waramaug's Palace and, in its time, was without a doubt the most elegant dwelling in Connecticut. Native American artists from all over New England worked ceaselessly for months to create Waramaug's Palace. Using bark gathered from all over New England, they intricately painted the bark with sumptuous colors distilled from herbs and flowers. Although much of the decoration came from Waramaug's own people and from the Iroquois from nearby New York, the Hurons, the Delaware, and even the fearsome Mohawks all sent their greatest artisans to decorate Waramaug's great lodge.

The interior was as magnificent as the outside. Waramaug's council chamber was decorated with portraits of the great chief, his family, and the elders and wise men of the tribe. Other rooms were alive with pictures of the animals who shared the forests with Waramaug and his people. According to legend, Chief Waramaug died peacefully in his great lodge and was buried nearby. For years after his death, passing warriors would add a stone to his gravesite as a gesture of respect for the great leader.

and accessories for both men and women, jewelry, and gifts. If you're lucky, you'll find yourself in town during the semiannual tent sale. Open every day 11 a.m.–5 p.m. **Privet House** (13 E. Shore Rd.; 860-868-1800; privethouse.com) offers jewelry, table- and kitchenware, soaps, cream, candles, and more. Their website says they are an "An Emporium of Home Goods, Antiques, and Curiosities." Their items certainly are original. Open Wed through Sun, 11 a.m. to 5 p.m.

Southeast of New Preston off Route 199 is the **Institute for American Indian Studies** (38 Curtis Rd.; 860-868-0518; iaismuseum.org). Splendid Indian craft exhibits and authentic re-creations of Indian dwellings are among the features of this museum. The institute attempts, fairly successfully, to cover 10,000 years of Native American life; displays include a 17th-century Algonquian village and garden, a furnished longhouse, a simulated archaeological site, a prehistoric rock shelter, and a variety of nature trails. There's also a museum shop. The institute holds several special events throughout the year. The museum is open Thurs through Sun 11 a.m.–4 p.m. Tours available at 11, 1, and 2:30 when open.

Close by is the **Steep Rock Reservation** (2 Tunnel Rd.; steeprockassoc.org), a nature preserve with hiking trails along the rivers and up to the summit of Steep Rock, where there are views of the Shepaug River below. There are old carriage roads in here, too, which served a hotel, and other vestiges of the past. With nearly 1,000 acres, there's a lot to see, but the do-not-miss spot is the old railroad tunnel just at the bend of the Shepaug's horseshoe bend (they call it the clamshell). This 235-foot tunnel was carved through solid rock by a crew of coal miners from Pennsylvania in 1872. It took them 9 months to complete the project, and it ran for 7 decades before ceasing operation in 1948. Today, the utterly black hole in the hillside beckons hikers. In the winter it ices up, so don't attempt it then without micro spikes or crampons. But in the warmer months, the cool air flowing through chiseled bedrock is incredible.

While you're in town, stop at the **Hickory Stick Bookshop** (2 Green Hill Rd.; 860-868-0525; hickorystickbookshop.com), an independent bookstore at the crossroads of Washington Depot. They are famous for their frequent book signings, even on Sunday afternoons, and have a hand-picked music section, a huge children's section, cards, clothing, Vera Bradley bags, games, and puzzles. They get a lot of local support from some of the exclusive nearby private schools like The Gunnery, and partner with local libraries for events. Overflowing with quality books, this is a community bookstore through and through and makes a great stop during a day of sightseeing.

Warren

The Hopkins Inn (22 Hopkins Rd.; 860-868-7295; thehopkinsinn.com) in ***Warren***, overlooking the northern shore of picture-perfect Lake Waramaug, has welcomed travelers since 1847, and they are good at what they do. The food here is so stellar that people tend to recommend the inn solely for its cuisine and forget that it is a warm and comfortable hostelry in its own right, with 11 guest rooms and 2 private apartments at reasonable rates. The outdoor patio, open for dining spring through fall, provides a spectacular view of the lake. The cuisine is contemporary Austrian, complete with rich desserts. The inn is open year-round; the restaurant is open from late Mar through Jan 1, Tues through Sun 8:30 a.m.–10 a.m.; lunch Tues to Sat noon–2 p.m.; dinner Tues to Fri, 5:30 p.m.–8 p.m.; Sat 5 p.m.–8:30 p.m.; Sun noon–7 p.m. Reservations strongly recommended. When the restaurant is closed, the inn operates as a bed-and-breakfast.

There's no connection between the inn and the **Hopkins Vineyard** (25 Hopkins Rd.; 860-868-7954; hopkinsvineyard.com). But the dairy farm–turned–winery and the inn do share a name and spectacular views of Lake Waramaug and the surrounding countryside. The Hopkins family has farmed the land around the lake since the late 1700s but didn't plant its first grapevine until 1979. The vineyard produces a variety of wines, including a rich Cabernet Franc and a delightful Chardonnay. Try their off-dry cider as an ingredient for autumn recipes or as a celebratory drink before Thanksgiving. You'll find tastings, sales, and a gift shop in the winery's bright red barn. The winery also hosts special events throughout the year. Tasting room hours vary seasonally, and include Nov to Dec weekends only; Jan to Apr Wed to Sun; peak tourist season of May to Oct daily; weekdays 11 a.m.–5 p.m.; Sat 11 a.m.–7 p.m.; Sun 11 a.m.–6 p.m. Event schedule on website.

Places to Stay in the Litchfield Hills

NORFOLK

Manor House
69 Maple Ave.
(860) 542-5690
manorhouse-norfolk.com
Expensive
Beautiful Victorian B&B in the heart of Norfolk

MORRIS

Winvian
155 Alain White Rd.
(860) 567-9600
winvian.com
Expensive
One of the premier places to stay, not just in Connecticut but in America

RIVERTON

Old Riverton Inn and Royal Coachman
463 East River Rd.
(860) 379-8678
rivertoninn.com
Moderate to expensive

WARREN

Hopkins Inn
22 Hopkins Rd.
(860) 868-7295
Thehopkinsinn.com
Moderate to expensive

WASHINGTON

Grace Mayflower Inn & Spa
118 Woodbury Rd.
(Route 47)
(866) 217-0869
aubergeresorts.com/mayflower
Expensive
Located less than 2 hours from New York in the middle of beautiful Washington, the Mayflower offers 5-star accommodations with pool and fitness center.

WOODBURY

1754 House
506 Main St.
(203) 405-3735
1754house.com
Moderate
Connecticut's oldest inn, in operation since 1754 in one way or another. Be sure to ask the owners about the secret entrance, rumored to have been used by the Freemasons once upon a time.

Places to Eat in the Litchfield Hills

BARKHAMSTED

Log House Restaurant
110 New Hartford Rd.
(860) 379-8937
theloghouserestaurant.com
Moderate
Family-owned and -operated since 1973

LITCHFIELD

West Street Grill
43 West St.
(860) 576-3885
weststreetgrill.com
Moderate to expensive

NEW PRESTON

The Smithy Café at 9 Main
9 Main St.
(860) 619-0699
Caféat9main.com
Moderate
Offers bakery items, specialty sandwiches, and salads.

NORFOLK

The Norfolk Pub
3 Station Place
Norfolk, CT 06058
(860) 542-1200
thenorfolkpub.com/
Home of the Wings!
Moderate

Gateway to New England

For most of America, Connecticut's southwestern shore is truly the Gateway to New England, the place where mid-Atlantic names, customs, and speech patterns begin to drop away and we Yankees start to quietly assert our personality. Most visitors to New England form their first impressions of our region from what they see in the busy towns and cities of Fairfield and New Haven Counties.

Many Fairfield County residents commute daily to jobs in the banks, brokerage houses, and corporate headquarters of Manhattan. The wealth they bring back to the state combined with that generated by the dozens of corporations that have headquarters here has earned this area the nickname of the Gold Coast. As you move north and east, the tony quality of the Gold Coast gives way to the working-class atmosphere of cities such as Bridgeport and Norwalk. This transition is complete by the time you cross the line into New Haven County, the bridge between the commuter towns of the southwest and the outlying communities of metro Hartford. New Haven is a mixture of town and gown, famed as the site of Yale University but also revered by the cognoscenti as the home of Louis' Lunch, birthplace of the American hamburger. Across the Quinnipiac River

GATEWAY TO NEW ENGLAND

from New Haven, population density begins to fall away quickly as one moves east, and the eastern townships of New Haven County are more typical of the shore than of the populous southwestern part of the state.

Geographically, the Gateway country is really just one long, lightly wooded coastal plain, with elevations ranging from sea level along the shore to 800 feet inland. The coastline of this low-lying plain is broken by many small bays and inlets and by the mouths of five rivers: the Mianus, Saugatuck, Mill, Housatonic, and Quinnipiac. A few miles inland, numerous lakes and ponds dot the countryside. The neighboring Long Island Sound helps temper the climate, making for pleasant summers and relatively mild winters, with plenty of rain and moderate snowfall.

The Gold Coast

Greenwich

The southernmost of Fairfield County's towns, **Greenwich** is only 28 miles from Times Square and has been one of the most desirable addresses in America since the late 1800s. It is the largest town on the "Gold Coast," and contains two of the wealthiest and most expensive zip codes in the country.

As its mission statement proclaims, Greenwich's newly expanded **Bruce Museum** (1 Museum Dr.; 203-869-0376; brucemuseum.org) "bridges the arts and sciences for people of all ages and cultures to foster learning and to preserve the past for the future." Sounds uplifting, to be sure. Fortunately, it's also fun. For big people, the collection includes works by some of Connecticut's famed impressionists, including **Childe Hassam**, plus a wealth of art honoring diverse cultures. For the youngsters, there are scads of well-thought-out interactive exhibits, from rocks and minerals to Connecticut wildlife. There are also temporary exhibits throughout the year. Open 10 a.m. to 5 p.m. Tues through Sun. Admission; free on Tues. Blue Star Museum.

Little Bethel A.M.E. Church (44 Lake Ave.; 203-661-3099) and **First Baptist Church** (10 Northfield St.; 203-869-7988; firstbaptistgreenwich.com) are the first and second African American churches, respectively, to be established in Greenwich. Before the 19th century, the African-American community really had no defined nucleus; they were not allowed such freedom. But as slaves began to gain their freedom, this started to change. Neighborhoods began to appear, and many turned to religion for comfort and community. Little Bethel A.M.E. Church was

greenwichtrivia

In 1640, European settlers gave Native Americans 25 coats in exchange for the land now occupied by the prosperous town of Greenwich.

AUTHOR'S FAVORITES

Bruce Museum
Stamford Cone
Center Church on the Green

Discovery Museum and Planetarium
Beinecke Library

established in 1883, while First Baptist came along in 1909, although the first official prayer meeting of the congregation occurred in 1897. Both churches are now listed on both the **Connecticut Freedom Trail** and the **National Register of Historic Places**.

When the **Merritt Parkway** was opened in 1938, it was praised for its beauty and efficiency. Today, it is acclaimed as a scenic alternative to the newer, grittier, and truck-laden I-95. The Merritt, which is on the National Register of Historic Places, runs 37 miles, from Greenwich on the state line to Milford's border at the Housatonic River. At that point it becomes the Wilbur Cross Parkway, and the scenery and architecture become less distinguished.

Credit for the Merritt's unique charms goes especially to its landscape architect, **Weld Thayer Chase**, and to **George Dunkelberger**, designer of the 68 distinctive bridges. Watch closely and you will see the Connecticut state seal, an owl, a blue-and-white Yale textbook, and a pair of Nike's wings on the many Art Deco spans that cross the parkway. The grassy median that separates the Merritt's north- and south-bound lanes is also a delight, with its varied landscape of trees and shrubs. Two bonuses: The Merritt is toll-free, and trucks are not allowed. One drawback: The Merritt is a four-lane highway, so if there are traffic issues, there's not a lot of room to maneuver; be prepared to wait.

New Canaan

This tiny village is home to some big celebrities but despite, or maybe because of that, it seems off the beaten path. Since the 1940s, **New Canaan** has been known as a center of the modern design movement, and 40 fascinating homes of that period remain in town, the best known being **Philip Johnson's Glass House** (199 Elm St., #11; 203-594-9884; theglasshouse.org). Sponsored by the National Trust for Historic Preservation, the Glass House is more than a house, actually a 47-acre park dedicated to 20th-century architecture. The iconic Glass House itself was the architect's residence, but other houses are scattered across the idyllic landscape. The on-site art collection includes giants like Frank Stella and Andy Warhol. The site offers a variety of guided tours, and you should buy tickets beforehand. This is one of the most fascinating sites in

Connecticut, a stone-walled farmland that has been transformed by one of the most creative minds of his age. Open Apr to Dec, Thurs to Mon, 9:30 a.m.–5 p.m. Reservations.

If you are there on a Saturday between May and November, stop at the **New Canaan Farmers Market** (244 Elm Street; newcanaanfarmersmarket.net), one of the best in the state. Located near the train station in the Lumberyard Lot on Elm Street, this upscale Farmers Market brings locals fruits and vegetables, fresh flowers and herbs, tasty breads and baked goods, gourmet pasta, soup, cheese, shellfish, meat, and mushrooms. And so much more! Open May through the third week in Nov, Sat 10 a.m.–2 p.m.

Stamford

As you leave Greenwich and enter **Stamford**, watch for the **Stamford Cone** on the corner of N. State Street and Washington Boulevard in its own little park-like area. Stop for a visit and you'll feel like you're standing inside a giant kaleidoscope. This 45-foot-tall structure is made up of 204 panels of glorious stained glass. There's something magical about standing inside and watching the play of light and color. The cone is open to the public from 9 a.m. to 4 p.m. After dark, the cone is lit inside until dawn.

Jackie Robinson Park (Richmond Hill Avenue and W. Main Street), on the city's west side, is dedicated to the baseball Hall of Famer who broke the color barrier on April 15, 1947, when he became the first African American to play major-league baseball. Within the park is a bronze statue of the man who called Stamford his home for nearly 20 years. The statue declares "Courage, Confidence, and Perseverance"—words to live by.

The 22,000-square-foot **Antique and Artisan Center** (69 Jefferson St.; 203-327-6022; theantiqueandartisangallery.com) has been called the best antiques center in the country, and it's easy to see why. The 85 or so booths have a variety of antiques, all handpicked by the owners, Bruce Wylie and Mari Ann Maher. If you are looking to complete your dream house, this is the place to get period furniture, lamps, benches, bars, tables, desks, chairs, and architectural elements. You can also pick up jewelry and vintage couture. There are buttons to press for assistance, and notepads and pens scattered throughout so you can write down your favorite items. Open Mon through Sat 10:30 a.m.–5:30 p.m.; Sun noon–5 p.m.

The **Stamford Museum and Nature Center** (39 Scofieldtown Rd.; 203-977-6521; stamfordmuseum.org) is something of a hybrid attraction, with plenty to appeal to a variety of tastes. For many visitors, the animals on the small working farm are the chief lure. Wheelchair-accessible paths wind gently around pastures and barns with cows, oxen, sheep, goats, pigs, llamas, alpacas, horses, donkeys, and barnyard fowl. One of the neatest exhibits includes a microscope/television system for viewing the mysteries of pond life. The nature center's 118-acre woodland site also includes galleries for interactive exhibits, a planetarium, picnic tables on a meadow overlooking the pond, a state-of-the-art observatory with research telescope, two stores, and a hardwood forest with miles of hiking trails.

Norwalk

During the 1930s, unemployed artists were commissioned under the **Works Progress Administration** (WPA) to paint murals, many portraying the art of everyday life in America, in public buildings. Most of the structures that once housed these underappreciated masterpieces have fallen victim to the wrecking ball, but some of Connecticut's Depression-era buildings, especially post offices, still display these modern wonders. **Norwalk**, however, has retained and restored one of the largest collections of Depression-era murals in the US. Maintained by the **Norwalk Transit District** (275 Wilson Ave.; 203-852-0000; norwalktransit.com), these murals were originally painted on the walls of the old high school. When that building was torn down, the art was carefully preserved, restored, and rehung in municipal buildings throughout the city. You'll find them at the city hall, community college, Maritime Aquarium at Norwalk, the public library, and of course, the transit district.

If you're looking for some on-the-water time, the **Small Boat Shop** (144 Water St.; 203-854-5223; thesmallboatshop.com) offers guided tours of the beautiful and privately owned Norwalk Islands. You must make reservations in advance; the tours carry a fairly hefty per-person price tag. Open 9 a.m. to 5 p.m. daily.

SoNo, shorthand for **South Norwalk**, was once an all-too-common decaying inner-city neighborhood, but that all started to change in 1949 when a man named **Roger Wilcox** and his family built a community. This community, they decreed, would be "a different type of community with a completely democratic character, [with] no discrimination because of race, color, creed or politics." This was a new idea in 1949; it pleased some folks and greatly displeased others. But the community has survived and is officially on the **National Register of Historic Places**, as well as gaining a mention on the Connecticut Freedom Trail. The community known as **Village Creek Historic District** includes Dock Road, Outer Road, and Split Rock Road. Today, the area around Washington and S. Main Streets has pulled itself up by the bootstraps to become a home to artists and artisans, much like Manhattan's trendy SoHo. This restored waterfront is now home to dozens of galleries, specialty shops, and restaurants.

norwalk trivia

At one time, Norwalk was the oyster capital of Connecticut. Severe pollution changed all that for a while. Today, thanks to tough environmental legislation that is cleaning up Long Island Sound, Connecticut is once again one of the country's top oyster producers. And the new home base for Connecticut's oystering industry is, once again, Norwalk.

The centerpiece of the SoNo revival is the ***Maritime Aquarium at Norwalk*** (10 N. Water St.; 203-852-0700; maritimeaquarium.org). At the center, part museum, part aquarium, and part theater, what ties it together is life on (and by) the sea. Don't miss the harbor seal performances, along with the otters and sea turtles, sharks, and jellyfish. You can touch live stingrays, which call out and flap their winglike fins. The building also contains restaurants and a nice gift shop. Open daily 10 a.m. to 5 p.m. Closed Thanksgiving and Christmas. Admission.

The ***SoNo Switch Tower Museum*** (77 Washington St.; 203-246-6958; SoNoTower.org) is an interesting part of the district's thriving cultural scene. Run by the Western Connecticut chapter of the ***National Railroad Historical Society***, the museum was originally the switch tower in the timing building. Now it is a participatory museum. Some memorabilia are on display, but the main attraction is standing above the tracks and watching the trains roar by beneath you. Visitors can also pull the levers that move the switches and signals on the main line. The museum is open May through Oct, Sat and Sun, noon to 4 p.m. Admission is free, but donations are appreciated.

Just a short ferry ride off Norwalk, the historic ***Sheffield Island Lighthouse*** (70 Water St.; 203-838-9444; seaport.org) is a pretty cool place to spend a hot summer day. Sheffield is the outermost of Norwalk's 13 islands and offers scenic views of both Long Island Sound and the Norwalk River. The passenger ferry leaves for the island from Seaport Dock (corner of N. Water and Washington Streets in South Norwalk) twice a day on weekdays and three times on weekends. Weekend and holiday service starts Memorial Day weekend; daily service runs from late June through Labor Day. Dates and times are posted on the website. On the round-trip cruise, the ferry's crew offers lively commentary on Norwalk's oystering past and the island's sometimes racy history and folklore. Island clambakes are held Thurs evening throughout the summer. There are also Haunted Lighthouse and Christmas in July weekends. Whenever they choose to go, visitors can tour the lighthouse, picnic, or walk to the trail of the McKinney Wildlife Refuge. Fee for ferry ride and clambake. The light, which is now on the National Register of Historic Places, was constructed in 1868 and was an active working light until 1902. From May 24 to Aug 31 weekend tours leave at 10 and 2; weekday tours leave on Tues from June 24 to Aug 26 at 10 a.m.; Wed– Fri from June 25–Aug 29 tours leave at 10 and 2; from May to Aug Wed–Sun a sunset tour leaves at 6:30 pm.

Westport

Downtown **Westport**, with its collection of boutique shops, has its own charm, although the streets and stores can get crowded on peak shopping days. The shops come and go, so just park and go where your fancy takes you.

One of the best reasons for visiting Westport even on the busiest days is a place called **Coffee An'** (343 Main St.; 203-227-3808), a world-class doughnut shop. The doughnuts are made from scratch, and they keep coming fresh out of the oven all day. They also serve breakfast, salads, and sandwiches. Open Mon through Sat, 7 a.m. to 3 p.m.

One of the oldest nature centers in Connecticut is a good place to walk off doughnuts from Coffee An'. **Earthplace** (10 Woodside Ln.; 203-557-4400; earthplace.org) offers 2.5 miles of trails (open dawn to dusk) and an excellent display of native plants on this 74-acre sanctuary. On weekends, the hands-on aquarium exposes kids to marine life, and the Discovery Room has many hands-on natural-history activities, puzzles, artifacts, and scientific equipment to use. Since 2005, the exhibit hall has featured activities for kids. There is also an animal rehabilitation center where injured and abandoned animals are cared for. The center also has a wheelchair-accessible trail. The center is open Mon through Sat, 9 a.m. to 5 p.m.; Sun, 11 to 5 p.m. Admission.

The small but mighty **Museum of Contemporary Art Connecticut** (19 Newtown Tpke.; 203-222-7070; mocact.org) is a cultural hub hidden in the north wilds of Westport. As one of the state's newest museums, the MoCA\CT was first called the Westport Arts Center, and then claimed the grander title. Their changing exhibitions of contemporary art punch way above their weight, with immersive and groundbreaking art. Open Thurs noon–8 p.m.; Fri noon–5 p.m.; Sat 10 a.m.–5 p.m.; Sun noon–5 p.m.

And if you linger in the evening, take a dramatic turn at the **Westport Country Playhouse** (25 Powers Ct.; 203-227-4177; westportplayhouse.org). Since 1931, the Playhouse is both a local tradition and a national institution. The building is a restored 1835 cow barn, giving it the name "Country," and the actors who have graced its stage are legendary: Helen Hayes, Ethel Barrymore, Jose Ferrer, Henry Fonda, Alan Alda, Cicely Tyson, Liza Minnelli, and many more. You'll see both new talent and veterans on this stage, so check their website for upcoming shows.

Fairfield

The ***Connecticut Audubon Birdcraft Museum*** (314 Unquowa Rd.; 203-259-0416; ctaudubon.org/birdcraft-museum) is housed in the first privately owned songbird sanctuary in America. It was established in 1914 by **Mabel Osgood Wright**, a pioneer in the American conservation movement and founder of the ***Connecticut Audubon Society***. At the time Wright created this sanctuary, she was fighting the common practice of people killing random birds in their backyard and elsewhere without provocation, something that is hard for us to wrap our minds around today. That alone is a testament to the success of Wright and the rest of the Audubon Society's work. Birdcraft building hours are Mon–Fri 9 a.m.–5 p.m.; Birdcraft museum hours are Tues, Thurs, and Sat 10 a.m.–3 p.m.

fairfieldtrivia

Wiffle ball was invented by David N. Mullaney of Fairfield in 1954. "Wiffle" comes from the sandlot baseball term "whiff" (strike), which is what you usually do when you try to hit that crazy plastic ball with all those holes.

Take Unquowa Road south and turn left on the Old Post Road. In just 2 blocks you will find the ***Fairfield Town Green***. In 1779 300 British and Loyalist troops camped here, taking a short break from burning almost every building in town, including the old Trinity Church. Later, in the 19th century, the green became the center of an almost completely new town, anchored by a beautiful American Gothic mansion, the home of Jonathan Sturges. On the green itself you'll find the 1780 Sun Tavern, visited by George Washington, and a sign marking the site of Trinity Church as the parish for 40 years of Reverend Philo Shelton, first in America to be ordained by Bishop Samuel Seabury. Interestingly, Seabury was actually a fervent Loyalist during the Revolution, though he acquiesced to the new Constitutional government once the "colonials" triumphed.

On the south end of the green is the ***Fairfield Museum and History Center*** (370 Beach Rd.; 203-259-1598; www.fairfieldhs.org). Unlike many of Connecticut's small-town museums, this one has a professionally curated exhibit room, with displays on precolonial Fairfield, children's education in the 19th century, and of course the burning of the town in 1779. Don't miss the cemetery nestled onto Beach Road right next to the museum driveway, with its wonderful old graves. Open Tues to Sun, 10 a.m.–4 p.m.

Bridgeport Area

Bridgeport

Phineas Taylor (P. T.) Barnum is quite possibly the country's most famous entertainment entrepreneur. Born in 1810, in an era when entertainment was pretty much divided along class lines between the cultural and the popular, Barnum revolutionized showbiz by presenting entertainment designed to appeal to people of all classes. Barnum also served as the mayor of **Bridgeport** in 1875, and today that city is repaying him by working hard to rebuild the museum that honors his work and memory. The ***Barnum Museum*** (820 Main St.; 203-331-1104; barnum-museum.org) has met with disaster after disaster. An F1 tornado blew through the city in 2010, hitting the museum and causing serious structural damage along with damaging many of the precious artifacts. In 2011 and 2012, Hurricane Irene and Superstorm Sandy caused additional damage to the museum. The first priority of the museum staff was to save and restore as many artifacts as possible. Once that was done, they turned to the job of stabilizing the museum's building, which is a jewel on its own.

Recovery efforts are still ongoing and day-to-day operations and programming at the museum have been understandably curtailed, and the museum remains closed for renovations in 2025. The museum is otherwise open year-round; check the website before traveling. Admission is free, but donations are welcome. The show must go on!

Bridgeport has another museum that is definitely worth a visit. Someone once described the ***Discovery Museum and Planetarium*** (4450 Park Ave.; 203-416-3521; shudiscovery.org) as "more fun than a basket of puppies." It is indeed a splendid place for kids of all ages, offering permanent and changing exhibits throughout the year. While some museums are "don't touch" places, the Discovery is a "please touch" place. You can make a variety of delightful things happen by simply pulling a lever, turning a crank, or pushing a button. At the Dare to Discover exhibit you can design a structure then see how earthquake vibrations impact it. And the Everbrite exhibit will summon your inner child. Inspired by the Lite-Brite toy, this massive exhibit features 464 adjustable LED dials that rotate through the color spectrum. Visitors are invited to create designs, patterns, pictures, or simply explore. The museum is open year-round Fri to Sun, 10 a.m. to 5 p.m. and Tues to Thurs 10 a.m. to 6 p.m. Admission.

bridgeporttrivia

Famous last words: On his deathbed, P. T. Barnum is reported to have said, "How were the receipts today at Madison Square Garden?" However, he never said the oft-quoted "there's a sucker born every minute"—that was invented by his rivals.

> ### One to Watch
>
> *The Mary & Eliza Freeman Center for History and Community* is still in the planning stages but is already facing serious challenges. The Main Street houses that belonged to Mary and Eliza have fallen into such a state of disrepair that they are in danger of being demolished. Luckily, the houses were recently placed on the National Trust for Historic Preservation's list of America's 11 Most Endangered Historic Places.
>
> The houses, along with the *Walters Memorial A.M.E. Zion Church* (12 Gregory St.), are all that remain of a free Black community referred to as Little Liberia that thrived in the 19th century. Neither Freeman sister ever married, and they were successful and amassed huge real estate portfolios at a time when that was difficult for African American women. We have no doubt Connecticut will rally and save this treasure. Mary and Eliza, we are rooting for you!

The **Henry B. duPont III Planetarium** offers shows starting at 1 p.m. (for children 7 and under) and 3 p.m. (for 8 and older). There are more shows on the weekend, so check the website or call for details. Planetarium admission is included in the general admission.

For 50 years when the Ringling Bros. and Barnum & Bailey Circus wintered in Bridgeport, the animals were taken for walks in Beardsley Park. When **Connecticut's Beardsley Zoo** (1875 Noble Ave.; 203-394-6565; beardsleyzoo.org) was started, they received some of their first animals from the circus. Now, almost 100 years later, the zoo features North and South American animals of all sorts, like ocelots, peccaries, red wolves, buffalo, and otters. The zoo includes a picnic area, snack bar, and gift shop. It is open daily from 9 a.m. to 4 p.m. Admission.

A relic from a different era in our history, the **Famous 50's Diner** (472 Huntington Tpke; 203-572-0777; famous50sdinerct.com) is a destination in itself. When you walk in the door, it's like you literally walked back in time. Memorabilia from the sock-hop era line the walls, furniture is reminiscent of the times, and the food, well, it's diner delicious and reasonably priced. Even the friendly staff is outfitted with Pink Ladies T-shirts. To you from me, Pinky Lee. Open Mon 7 a.m.–4 p.m.; Tues–Thurs 7 a.m.–8 p.m.; Fri and Sat 7 a.m.–1 a.m.; Sun 7 a.m.–8 p.m.

One of the secret, off-the-beaten-path places in Bridgeport was once the most popular—from 1892 to 1958 the island of **Pleasure Beach** (bridgeportct.gov/pleasurebeach) was home to an amusement park. Today, the amusements are gone, but the park remains. During the summer, take the ferry from downtown Bridgeport to visit this deserted beach.

The main beach for Bridgeport is not exactly off the beaten path, but **Seaside Park** (1 Barnum Dyke; 203-367-7917; bridgeportct.gov) has its secret places. The park was designed by Connecticut native Frederick Law Olmsted (who also did Central Park in Manhattan and several others in this book) and today boasts the longest stretch of public shoreline in Fairfield County. Its long beach on the west side of the park gets busy during the summer months. However, the eastern side of the park is worth exploring, with historic carriageways and odd, subtropical trees that house some of Connecticut's mysterious green parrots. Statues here honor showman P. T. Barnum and Elias Howe, whose sewing machines sparked Bridgeport as an industrial powerhouse. The huge, distinctive 1916 arch at the entrance on Park Avenue was built by Henry Bacon, who designed the Lincoln Memorial in DC the same year. But the most secret spot is at the very end of the beach, where a jetty heads out to Fayerweather Island. This island was once much larger, with a house and space for a herd of sheep. The 1823 lighthouse was kept by local hero Catherine Moore for over 60 years, beginning when she was 12 years old. During that time, she saved at least 21 lives, and retired a rich woman, having sold duck decoys, oysters, and wool to the townsfolk of Bridgeport. Watch the oyster boats out in the harbor and think of her lonely vigil here and wonder.

bridgeport trivia

Frisbie Pie Company truck drivers invented the game of Frisbee by tossing back and forth surprisingly aerodynamic empty pie tins from the Bridgeport bakery.

Shelton

The Jones family believes if you are good to the land, the land will be good to you. In fact, those words have been passed down for generations by **Phillip James Jones**, founder of **Jones Family Farms** (606 Walnut Tree Hill Rd.; 203-929-8425; jonesfamilyfarms.com) in **Shelton**. And that was 150 years ago, so they must be doing something right. The family currently farms 400 acres and offers pick-your-own opportunities throughout the year—pumpkins in the fall, strawberries and blueberries in the summer, Christmas trees in the winter. The family also owns and operates *Jones Winery*, and its wine is consistently voted Best Connecticut Wine by *Connecticut Magazine*. A more recent addition to the farm is **The Harvest Kitchen** where they offer small farmhouse cooking classes to teach visitors how to take farm-fresh food and turn it into a healthy, delicious meal.

Special events are offered throughout the year. The farm is closed Jan through Mar but generally open Mon through Sat, 9 a.m. to 5 p.m.; Sun, 8 a.m.

to noon, with longer or shorter hours depending on the season. The winery is open Fri, Sat, and Sun, 11 a.m. to 5:30 p.m., with expanded hours in the warmer months; check the website for times. All activities on the farm are weather-dependent, so be sure to call or check their website before traveling.

On the south side of town, take a walk or cycle trip along the **Shelton Lakes Recreation Path** (Shelton Avenue and Meadow Street; sheltonconservation.org/recreation/shelton_trails). This multi-use path goes from Route 108 just south of the downtown all the way to old Huntington Village over 5 miles away. It is more challenging than the usual canal or railroad bike paths around the state, so maybe get in shape first. The forest here is beautiful, with white pines, oaks, hickories, birches, and maples. At the southern end, stop at one of the bakeries for a snack, then head back over the hills.

Derby

Tucked back from Route 34, hidden unless you are looking at a map, is **Derby**'s **Osbornedale State Park** (555 Roosevelt Dr.; 203-735-4311; stateparks.com/osborndale). Willed to the state in 1956 by businesswoman and investor **Frances Osborne Kellogg**, this rambling forest has numerous trails that wander through forests, meadows, fishing ponds, and stone walls. At the southwest corner of the park, the **Kellogg Environmental Center** provides educational lectures and hands-on learning experiences and the **Osborne Homestead Museum** gives a tour of a restored interior displaying the original contents of the estate, including many antiques and fine arts. The small nature trail by the center is a great starter for kids just learning to hike, and the pond across the street from the center in the park is rich with turtles. Park open dawn to dusk, but the museum is open May through Oct, Thurs, Fri, and Sat 10 a.m.–4 p.m.; Sun noon–4 p.m.

On the east side of the Naugatuck River is the 1698 **General David Humphreys House** (37 Elm St.; 203-735-1908; derbyhistorical.org). This is the birthplace of the Revolutionary War officer and friend of George Washington who later became our nation's first ambassador and who introduced merino wool sheep in America. Today it serves as the headquarters for the Derby Historical Society and is open in the summer, Mon to Fri, 10:30 a.m.–2:30 p.m.

Stratford

Do you have a future pilot in the family? Then the **National Helicopter Museum** (2480 Main St.; 203-375-8857; nationalhelicoptermuseum.org), located in Stratford Eastbound Railroad Station just off I-95, should be on your itinerary. Here your budding aviator can learn all about how these whirlybirds were developed. There are pieces designed by Stratford's own **Dr. Anselm Franz**, inventor of the gas turbine engine in the 1950s. Local inventor **Igor Sikorsky**'s career is chronicled and a model of his first craft is on display. From the dragonfly and hummingbird to today's incredible flying machines, it's all here. Open the end of May through mid-Oct, Wed through Sun, 1 to 4 p.m. or by appointment.

connecticutfreedom trailtrivia

Stratford resident Asa Seymour Curtis was a farmer with a huge heart. His home at 2016 Elm St. was a known stop on the Underground Railroad. Mr. Curtis is buried in Union Cemetery (23 Temple Ct.) in Stratford. See the rest of his story at ctfreedomtrail.org.

Nearby is **Two Roads Brewing** (1700 Stratford Ave.; 203-335-2010; tworoadsbrewing.com), one of the most popular and successful of the Connecticut breweries that have appeared in the past decades. The name is a reference to the Robert Frost poem, and it seems that they took the road less traveled—or was it the other one? Either way, this is one of Connecticut's best places to visit for those of us who enjoy a pint of good beer.

Another place to make a short stop along the I-95 corridor is the **Stratford Antique Center** (400 Honeyspot Rd.; 203-378-7754; stratfordantiquecenter.com). This enormous multi-dealer antiques depot is located in a huge warehouse, with rows of stalls full of ancient signs, paintings, and furniture. A short stop may turn into a few hours of browsing, as you try to decide which fascinating relics of yesteryear to take home. Dig through the piles of treasure and you'll find a fine set of silverware or a vintage movie poster.

At the opposite end of town, by the Merritt Parkway, is the unusual **Boothe Memorial Park and Gardens** (5800 Main St.; 203-381-2046; boothememorialpark.com). This small, 32-acre park was once the estate of the Boothe family, including the site of what is often called the oldest homestead in America, built on the foundation of a 1663 house. But what makes this museum and park unique was that two brothers in the Boothe family, David and Stephen, were avid collectors of buildings, which they had transported to the property. As you stroll around, you'll find a blacksmith shop, icehouse, miniature windmill, trolley station, clock tower museum, carriage house, tollbooth plaza, aviary, a redwood building, and more. Children walk around thinking they're in some sort of Disneyland exhibit, but all these buildings are real. Open dawn to dusk.

Milford

Milford bills itself as the "little city with a big heart." With a population of more than 54,000, Milford has a rich and varied history along with a vibrant beach community. Originally purchased from Paugusset Chief Ansantawae, Milford became home to settlers beginning in 1639. Pirates are said to have roamed the area's waters and rumor is that **buried treasure** is hidden on a small island off the shores of **Silver Sands Beach**. In Revolutionary times, the city hosted George Washington as he made his way across the area. The city saw the ravages of the Civil War and helped slaves to freedom on their way through the Underground Railroad.

Fans of military history should visit the **Soldiers Monument** in Milford Cemetery (Prospect Street), which honors 46 soldiers who contracted smallpox and were abandoned by a British ship on a Milford beach. One of the doctors who volunteered to try to help the men contracted the disease himself and is buried with them in the common grave. The **First Baptist Church** (28 North St.; 203-878-1178) contains a memorial marker honoring six African Americans who fought in the American Revolution.

Milford also has beautiful beaches. **Silver Sands State Park** (203-735-4311) is located off Route 1 and offers free parking (hard to find in this area!). There is a long wooden boardwalk to be enjoyed, and at low tide you can sometimes walk all the way out to **Charles Island** (remember, hidden treasure). Silver Sands and **Walnut Beach** (113 E Broadway) offer the longest stretch of beach in the city. The Walnut Beach community offers some cool events over the summer, including a free concert series sponsored by the local Rotary Club. Held on Sun during July and Aug at 4 p.m. at the Devon Rotary Pavilion at Walnut Beach, the concerts feature local performers playing all genres. Visit the Walnut Beach Association's website (walnutbeachassociation.com/summerconcertseries) for the latest.

New Haven Area

New Haven

New Haven is perhaps best known as the home of **Yale University** (24 Hillhouse Ave; 203-432-4771; yale.edu), one of those American treasures measured in terms of firsts, bests, and similar benchmarks. In 1861, it granted the first doctor of philosophy degree in the US. In 1869, its School of Fine Arts, the first in the country, opened its doors.

Yale boasts some of the most interesting architecture in the country, and if you have a chance to walk through campus, I urge you to do so. Start at **Phelps Gate** on College Street. Beyond the gate is the **Old Campus**, ringed with Gothic buildings. **Dwight Hall** introduced Yale to this type of architecture in 1842. Built as the college library for the then mind-boggling sum of $33,253, it was a strange marriage of spare New England Puritanism with opulent overindulgence. It boasts 32 carved heads of man and beast mounted on turrets on its 90-foot tower. Over the next 70 years, other architects designed additional Gothic buildings for the Old Campus. Bingham and Vanderbilt Halls on Chapel Street and the bridge over High Street all have their own menagerie of mythological beasts. Free student-guided tours of Yale are available through the **Yale Visitor Center** (149 Elm St.; 203-432-2300; visitorcenter.yale.edu). Register for a tour online.

Yale University's **Beinecke Rare Book and Manuscript Library** (121 Wall St.; 203-432-2977; beinecke.library.yale.edu) is like no other building you've ever seen. To protect the fragile documents inside from sun damage, it was built without windows. Instead, the exterior walls are made of wafer-thin marble slabs. When the sun shines, the building's interior has a cloudy amber glow. The library, which is open to the public, has five major collections. The permanent exhibit on the mezzanine features the **Gutenberg Bible**. Printed in about 1455 in Mainz, Germany, it is regarded as the first book printed from movable type in the Western world. *Audubon's Birds of America* is also on display. This is a great place to visit, but maybe not one for toddlers or younger children. Court level is open to registered researchers. The public exhibit hall (ground floor and mezzanine) are open Mon, Tues, and Thurs 9 a.m–7 p.m.; Wed 10 a.m.–7 p.m.; Fri 9 a.m.–5 p.m.; Sat and Sun noon–5 p.m.

If you walk down High Street between Chapel and Elm Streets, you will come across a spooky stone edifice with no windows. This is the **The Tomb** (64 High St.), headquarters of **Skull and Bones**, the infamous secret society at Yale University. Its alumni include George H. W. Bush and his son George W., plus a host of CIA agents and big-shot dignitaries. Skull and Bones had an unwanted national spotlight shined upon its Greco-Egyptian facade during the 2004 presidential campaign, which featured the eerie coincidence of two "Bonesmen" (Bush the younger and US senator John Kerry) running against each other. Neither of them would discuss his membership in this elite group that supposedly practices secret rituals involving coffins. According to folklore, Geronimo's skull is inside the building. If you're contemplating trying to get inside, forget about it. Just walk on and wonder.

Yale is also home to several of America's finest museums. A showcase for British art and life, the **Yale Center for British Art** (1080 Chapel St.; 877-BRIT-ART; britishart.yale.edu) was built around the extensive collection of **Paul Mellon**, a 1929 Yale graduate who spent 40 years amassing works by a host of British artists. Mellon's holdings have been expanded since the center opened in 1977, and the building now houses the largest collection of British art outside of Great Britain. It also houses a 13,000-volume research library. Open Tues, Wed, and Sat 10 a.m.–5 p.m.; Thurs 10 a.m.–8 p.m. (Sept–June);

yale trivia

The *Yale Bowl*, completed in 1914, was the first enclosed football stadium in the US, and while it wasn't quite the Final Four, the first intercollegiate basketball game was played in New Haven in 1896.

and Sun 11 a.m.–5 p.m. Museum closed on Mon and major holidays.

On the opposite corner of Chapel and York Streets is the **Yale University Art Gallery** (1111 Chapel St.; 203-432-0600; artgallery.yale.edu). Founded in 1832, this is the oldest university art museum in the US, and its collection spans various eras, cultures, and art styles. The museum has gone through many changes and expansions over its long history. The museum's most recent expansion promises to enhance visitors' experience and learning. With more than 200,000 objects on display, how can a visit not be enlightening? There's also a sculpture garden, with works by Moore, Nevelson, and others, that makes an awfully nice setting in which to dream away a spring afternoon. Open Tues through Fri, 10 a.m. to 5 p.m.; Thurs (Sept through June), 10 a.m. to 8 p.m.; Sat and Sun, 11 a.m. to 5 p.m.

The **Yale Peabody Museum of Natural History** (170 Whitney Ave.; 203-432-8987; peabody.yale.edu), at the intersection of Whitney Avenue and Sachem Street, is the largest natural history museum in New England. The Peabody has the largest collection of mounted dinosaurs in the world, including the 67-foot Apatosaurus. The Peabody is open Tues through Sat, 10 a.m. to 5 p.m.; Sun, noon to 5 p.m. Admission. Blue Star Museum. There's loads of great info about visiting the museum on their website, including information on how to get in free, so be sure to check it out.

But there's much more to New Haven than Yale University. For starters, there's the crypt under **Center Church on the Green** (250 Temple St.; 203-787-0121; centerchurchonthegreen.org). For tourists who are truly committed to getting off the beaten path, this attraction is hard to beat. The graves in this crypt are believed to be unique to America. Nowhere else, historians say, was a church built over a colonial graveyard, a decision that helped protect the graves from the elements. The original graveyard dates to the 1600s. Here lie the remains of up to 1,700 early New Havenites, including Benedict Arnold's first wife, the family of President Rutherford B. Hayes, and Yale's founder, Rev. James Pierpont, among others. Headstones and tomb "tables" abound in the cold, subterranean expanse. Crypt tours are available on the second Sunday of each month at 10 a.m. The tours are free, but donations are accepted to help preserve the crypt and its remarkable contents. The church is also on the **Connecticut Freedom Trail** for its role in supporting the Mende African *Amistad* captives.

Connecticut pizza lovers claim that ***Frank Pepe Pizzeria Napoletana*** (157 Wooster St.; 203-865-5762; pepespizzeria.com) in New Haven makes the best clam pizza—maybe the best pizza—in the world. There is some reason to accept that claim. Pepe's special white clam pizza, prepared by hand on the premises like everything else here, is topped with fresh littlenecks, olive oil, garlic, oregano, and Romano cheese. For other types of pies, if you want cheese, you have to ask for it; otherwise, you get a marvelous pie crust topped with tomato sauce. The splendiferous pies are baked in a coal-fired oven to emerge as flat, crisp circles of dough with a firm, chewy crust.

Pepe's in New Haven is open Mon through Sun 11 a.m.–10 p.m. (Pepe's now has other locations in Connecticut as well as in New York, Massachusetts, Rhode Island, Maryland, Virginia, and Florida; check the website for details.) If you can't handle the line at Pepe's (and there will be one), you can always try ***Sally's*** (237 Wooster St.; 203-624-5271; sallysapizza.com), but chances are there might be one there, too. You can't go wrong at either place; Sally's rivals Pepe's in the quality of pizza it serves, with (some say) a better sauce, while

newhaventrivia

You probably know that Connecticut inventors produced the submarine and anesthesia, but did you know that the Nutmeg State was also quite possibly the birthplace of the lollipop? Some sources credit New Haven resident George Smith with the creation in 1908. The name (maybe) is a nod to the famous racehorse of the time, Lolly Pop. Who knew?

The Boulevard for Bargains

You'll sometimes hear Nutmeggers whisper, "Oh, I got it at the Boulevard." There will usually be some winking and smiling going on during said conversation. That's because the *Boulevard* (500 Ella T. Grasso Blvd.; 203-772-1447; fleact.com) is a year-round flea market where bargains abound. We caution you, however, to go with your eyes open. While you will find great deals, you will also find cheap knockoffs. Most of the time people are fine with that as long as the knockoff is well made, but you need to know what you are looking for so you don't get bamboozled. The vendors here don't bargain much, but we, of course, encourage you to try—you never know. Bring cash; that's all they deal with. We suspect the Boulevard has been raided a time or two, so any truly name-brand merchandise is often sold quickly and quietly. For a while North Face jackets and UGG boots were hot items, but you might also find MAC makeup, Tiffany jewelry, Coach scarves, and oh so much more.

The flea market is held on an open field, and there is limited paved parking; the rest is on bumpy ground. They open at 7 a.m., but it gets busy fast. Open year-round, Sat and Sun, 7 a.m. to 4 p.m.

Pepe's has a better crust. Open Sun 11 a.m.–9 p.m.; Mon–Thurs 11:30 a.m.–9 p.m.; Fri and Sat 11 a.m.–10 p.m. The third member of the "holy trinity" of *apizza* joints is **Modern Apizza** (874 State St.; 203-776-5306; modernapizza.com), started in 1934 and serving more amazing New Haven Style. Open Tues to Sat, 10:30 a.m.–10 p.m.; Sun 3–10 p.m.

One of the most interesting places to spend an evening is the recording studio and performance space at **Firehouse 12** (45 Crown St.; 203-785-0468; firehouse12.com). Located (obviously) in an old firehouse, the downstairs bar looks like a 1920s speakeasy and serves classic cocktails to prove it. Then, the uniquely designed recording studio upstairs is a soundproof space seating 75 people. You can get tickets for any of the creative, experimental jazz groups (and others) who play here, as they record their live albums and perform. See website for showtimes and tickets.

The **Five-Mile Point Light** (1 Lighthouse Rd.; 203-946-8005), located at the eastern point of New Haven Harbor, was built in 1847. The 65-foot-high stone lighthouse was functional until it was taken out of service in 1877. Now it dominates **Lighthouse Point Park** (2 Lighthouse Rd.; 203-946-8019; newhavenct.gov). The park includes lots of nature trails, a bird sanctuary, a splashpad, and a 1916 carousel that is one of the largest in America (52 feet in diameter) and holds 72 figures: 69 horses, one camel, and two dragons. The parking fee is steep if you're not a resident, and there's a small admission for the carousel. Carousel rides are available noon to 4 p.m. weekends and holidays from Memorial Day through Labor Day.

New Haven is justifiably proud of its role in liberating the captives aboard the ship **Amistad**. In 1839, a group of Africans who had been kidnapped from their homes in Sierra Leone by slave traders mutinied and took over the ship. But they were seized by naval authorities and taken to New Haven for trial.

After being imprisoned in a jail by New Haven Green, where abolitionists took up their cause, the prisoners were acquitted, first in Connecticut courts and then by the US Supreme Court. This amazing and courageous saga received wide attention when Steven Spielberg's movie *Amistad* was released in 1997. Three years later, a reproduction of the *Amistad* was completed in Mystic and arrived at its home port of

newhaventrivia

New Haven is affectionately called the "Elm City" because of the stately elm trees that dotted the New Haven Green and Yale University campus in the late 18th century, creating a leafy canopy over the downtown area. Gradually these majestic trees succumbed to Dutch elm disease, but two survived, and in recent years the seeds from these trees have been nurtured with the hope that this magnificent tree will reign supreme once again.

New Haven in July 2000. The storied ship is available for tours when it is docked at Long Wharf, alongside **New Haven Harbor** (389 Long Wharf Dr.). But during many times of the year, it's on tour at other ports or in winter storage. Today, the *Amistad* is managed by **Discovering Amistad** (860-992-4933; discoveringamistad.org). They treat the ship very much like a floating classroom, bringing it and their programs to ports all over the state and beyond. Check the website to see where she'll be visiting next.

newhaventrivia

Famous New Haven inventions include the meat grinder, the corkscrew, and Isaac Strouse's misogynistic little torture device: the corset.

You can also visit the **Amistad Memorial** (165 Church St.) and read about Joseph Cinque (also known as Sengbe Pieh), one of the ship's passengers. The 11-foot bronze statue was created by Ed Hamilton and was dedicated in 1992. It stands in the location of the New Haven jail at the time of the trials.

East Haven

The **Shore Line Trolley Museum** (17 River St.; 203-467-6927; shorelinetrolley .org) in **East Haven** maintains nearly 100 vintage trolleys and other vehicles. For detailed descriptions of which ones are on display, visit their website; it's a wealth of information. There are also some interpretive displays, including hands-on exhibits and audio-video displays at the museum. We suspect, though, that most people will be drawn by the trolley rides. The museum offers 3-mile round-trip rides in vintage trolley cars on the Branford Electric Railway, the nation's oldest operating suburban transportation line. Hard-core trolley freaks are also welcome to hang around the car barn watching the restoration process. You can picnic on the grounds, and there's also a gift shop. Your ticket entitles you to ride all day on all trolley cars mid-June to Sept 1. The rest of the year, open for special events only. Check the website for current events and times.

Hamden

Traveling north from New Haven, you'll come to suburban **Hamden**. The town's **Eli Whitney Museum** (915 Whitney Ave.; 203-777-1833; eliwhitney .org) includes displays tracing two centuries of industrial growth on the site plus various technology-oriented, interactive, hands-on exhibits. The museum is mainly devoted, however, to the achievements of Eli Whitney, one of the towering figures of the Industrial Revolution. Whitney was a local firearms manufacturer who pioneered the use of interchangeable parts. He also changed the course of American history by inventing the cotton gin, a device that became the foundation of the Southern plantation economy, spurred the spread of slavery, and contributed mightily to the political crisis that ended in America's Civil War. You'll find a waterfall, a covered bridge, and walking trails behind the museum. Open Sat and Sun, 10 a.m. to 3 p.m.

Hamden also contains some great picnic spots, most of them located within the confines of **Sleeping Giant State Park** (200 Mt. Carmel Ave., Route 10; 203-287-5658). According to legend, the basalt mountain where the park is sited is actually an evil giant by the name of Hobbomock, who was put to sleep to prevent him from doing harm to local residents. As you drive up I-91 from New Haven, you can see today the chain of high, wooded hills that make up the park really does resemble a sleeping giant. Today, people climb all over the giant. Many of Sleeping Giant's trails lead to gentle or moderate hikes, so even if you're out of shape you can still get in a good walk. All told, the park's 13,000-plus acres include more than 28 miles of trails, some with spectacular views. Free parking for in-state vehicles; for others parking fees for weekends and holidays Memorial Day through the end of Oct. The park is open 8 a.m. to sunset.

Walk down the sidewalk west of the park entrance and just across the river you'll find the ruins of the stone-walled Axle Works Factory, which used the Mill River for power here in the 19th century. Across the street from this location is the *Jonathan Dickerman House* (105 Mount Carmel Ave.; 203-248-6030; hamdenhistoricalsociety.org), a charming 1792 farmhouse that includes period furnishings and a sweet-smelling herb garden. Jonathan was a member of the storied Dickerman family of Hamden, which includes a Civil War hero, three sisters who started an early private school for girls, several writers, a famous painter, and the founder of one of the earliest commercial vineyards in Connecticut. Open June to Aug, Sat and Sun, 1–4 p.m.

After your hike, visit **Wentworth Homemade Ice Cream Company** (3697 Whitney Ave. [Route 10]; 203-281-7429; wentworthhomemadeicecream.com). Located just down the road from the Sleeping Giant State Park entrance, Wentworth's occupies a yellow-sided house on your right as you're leaving Hamden. Wentworth's makes all of its own ice cream on-site. Incredibly dense and not too sweet, Wentworth's products seem to capture the essence of each of the dozens of flavors in the ever-changing repertoire. Almond amaretto (one of many "adult" flavors that use real liquor) will win you over even if you don't care for sweet liqueurs. The best flavor of all, though, is the peach, a gift of ambrosia lovingly crafted from fresh, tree-ripened fruit. For kids, there are silly flavors such as Cookie Monster, neon-blue vanilla with cookie bits. There's even Canine Crunch for your fur-children. Wentworth's is open Mon through Sat, noon–9 p.m.; closed Sun.

South-Central Connecticut

Cheshire

The ***Farmington Canal Greenway*** is a Connecticut attraction that is quite literally off the beaten path. It's also a marvelous example of recycling on a grand scale. In the early 1800s, New Haven was a thriving port city, but there was a problem: The goods that arrived by boat couldn't be transported easily to the north. So in 1828, a canal was built that ran a total of 83 miles, from the harbor through Hamden, ***Cheshire***, Plainville, and Farmington, and up to Northampton, Massachusetts. The Farmington Canal became the economic lifeline of central Connecticut. But just 20 years later, it was replaced by a railroad that ran adjacent to the canal.

The railroad operated until 1982, when floods washed out a portion of the line. For years the railroad beds lay abandoned and neglected. At best, they became overgrown with grass and weeds. At worst, sections became eyesores, piling up with fast-food packaging, soda cans, old tires, and discarded shopping carts. But as the national rails-to-trails movement gained momentum, a grassroots effort emerged in southern Connecticut to restore this historic rail-canal corridor for recreational use. The result is a linear park for walkers, joggers, cyclists, and cross-country skiers that starts in downtown New Haven and runs into Southington. After a broken section, it continues in Farmington and goes all the way to the Massachusetts border. Find more information about all the entrances and parking areas at fchtrail.org. The trail is also wheelchair accessible and has benches every so often for resting. One more thing, if you're walking or have younger children, be aware of the sometimes numerous bicyclists and in-line skaters on the trail. Most will shout an "On your left" or "On your right" before they come up behind you, so don't be alarmed, but be aware. The trail is open year-round dawn to dusk.

On Route 42 in Cheshire, you'll find a restored section of the canal at ***Lock 12 Historical Park*** (487 N. Brooksvale Rd.; 203-271-6600). In addition to the canal, the grounds contain a museum, a lockkeeper's house, a helicoidal bridge, and a picnic area. The park is open year-round, dawn to dusk. The museum is open by appointment only.

At ***Roaring Brook Falls*** (cheshirelandtrust.org), just off Roaring Brook Road (west of the junction of Route 70 and I-84), you'll find a wonderful hiking trail and overlook—the perfect place for a spring or fall picnic—and the foundation of an old mill to explore. But the draw here is Connecticut's highest single-drop waterfall. The Cheshire Land Trust's website makes the distinction between Roaring Brook Falls's single-foot drop and Kent Falls's 250-foot drop of multiple cascades.

Your kids might think that animation starts with *The Simpsons* and ends with *SpongeBob*, but a visit to the **Barker Character, Comic, and Cartoon Museum** (1188 Highland Ave. [Route 10]; 203-272-2357; barkermuseum.com) will widen their (and your) horizons. Herb and Gloria Barker, the museum's guiding lights, are longtime collectors of 'toon memorabilia, and they've packed a lot of history into this jewel-box museum. You'll find, among other things, many cartoon cells on view, a collection of lunch boxes and pull toys featuring cartoon characters from days gone by, and McDonald's Happy Meal toys, once giveaways, now pricey collectibles. Animators and illustrators such as George Wildman of Popeye fame often visit the museum for talks and special events. The museum is open Wed through Sat, 11 a.m. to 5 p.m. Admission. Blue Star Museum.

Bethany

Tucked away on an idyllic road with only a small sign from Route 69 pointing the way is **Whitlock's Book Barn** (20 Sperry Rd.; 203-393-1240; whitlocks bookbarn.com), surely one of the most off-the-beaten-path places you'll find. In business since 1948, this charming tumbledown pair of barns has plenty of rare and cheap used books for both a casual browser and avid collector. Don't miss the upstairs of the second barn, which has an amazing collection of maps and prints for sale. When you've had your fill of books, take a drive on picture-postcard Sperry Road, or if you're in the mood for a walk, head down the gravel extension just south of Whitlock's, one of the most gorgeous old stone-walled roads in the state. Go left at the turn-off to Sperry Park, on a path that leads past a foundation from **Sperry Farm** (where one of the three judges hid), to a rushing waterfall with the remnants of an old mill.

Naugatuck

Established in 1790, **Gunntown Cemetery** (Gunntown Road) is home to members of both sides of the American Revolution. But even though relatives bid

---

Secret Hiking Trails

Connecticut's Regional Water Supply companies offer recreational opportunities in and around lakes and reservoirs. The South-Central Connecticut RWA (rwater.com/recreation) offers a permit program; for a few dollars you get two years of access to hiking, fishing, and horseback riding trails that few residents take advantage of. Get a permit and try these trails on a busy holiday weekend—when state parks are crowded—and you will find you have the forests to yourself.

their loved ones goodbye with hopes they would rest in peace, there isn't a lot of peace to be found within this cemetery. There have been various claims of people hearing music coming from within its walls, and some claim they have heard children laughing or have seen a young boy playing by the far wall and then disappearing. There are stories of a man riding a horse through the grounds or a man walking with a lantern and leading his horse. Multiple ghost hunters have captured mysterious orbs and mists. Connecticut demonologists Ed and Lorraine Warren even declared the cemetery haunted. We leave it up to you to translate your experience here at Gunntown. As always, please be respectful of the surroundings. Also, parking is on a narrow road and cars go whipping by; you don't want to join the spirits roaming the grounds.

Waterbury

Ten miles or so northwest of Cheshire is the city of **Waterbury**. The brass industry moved into the city in the mid-1800s, and the Brass Capital of the World, as it was then known, was built largely on wealth derived from brass manufacturing. In the years since, this industry has moved elsewhere, but its architectural legacy remains. During the heyday of brass, Waterbury residents erected hundreds of rambling Victorian mansions and imposing public buildings. Entire neighborhoods of these buildings are preserved almost intact and, as part of an ongoing renaissance program, other neighborhoods have been restored to their former glory. As a result, much of modern-day Waterbury is a living museum of 19th- and early 20th-century architecture.

If you're interested in architecture, you'll want to visit the **Hillside Historic District**, once home to Waterbury's captains of industry. Now listed on the National Register of Historic Places, the district includes 310 structures dating from the 19th and early 20th centuries. The center of Waterbury's restoration program, however, is the tree-lined city green, one of the most beautiful greens in any northeastern city. Within a few blocks of the green, you'll find scores of lovingly restored structures. Among the more interesting are a marvelously

waterbury trivia

Preserving food in tin cans was a great idea, but getting the food out of those tins needed another. So when in 1858 Ezra J. Warner of Waterbury found a way to quickly open tins, tummies all across America thanked him.

Unfortunately, his invention looked more like something from a slasher movie than the latest housewife's helper. You stuck a rather intimidatingly big, curved blade into the tin and rammed it around. Since the opener tended to open the user as well as the tin, someone else invented the less dangerous cutting-wheel can opener a decade later.

misplaced railroad station modeled on the Palazzo Pubblico in Siena, Italy. There are also five municipal buildings designed by prominent American architect **Cass Gilbert**.

The modernized and expanded **Masonic Hall** on the northwest corner of Waterbury's green has been transformed into the **Mattatuck Museum** (144 W. Main St.; 203-753-0381; mattmuseum.org). An oddly satisfying combination of industrial museum and art gallery, the Mattatuck includes the works of American masters who have an association with Connecticut, household items and furnishings dating from 1713 to 1940, and local history exhibits about the region's industrial development. Its holdings include collections of 19th-century furniture, novelty clocks and watches, early cameras, and Art Deco tableware. The most curious item might be Charles Goodyear's rubber desk. The museum is open Tues through Sat, 11 a.m. to 5 p.m.; Sun 11 a.m. to 4 p.m. There is a gift shop and cafe on-site.

Meriden

Way before there were golden arches on every street corner, the central Connecticut towns of **Meriden** and Middletown had developed a local specialty called the "steamed cheeseburger." Steaming the burgers makes them incredibly juicy and reduces the sharp Wisconsin cheddar to just the right degree of molten wonderfulness. Locals know to order theirs in the form of a "trilby" (a regional term for anything served up with mustard and onions). You have your choices in the area for steamed cheeseburgers. Perhaps the most well-known is **Ted's Restaurant** (1046 Broad St.; 203-237-6660; tedsrestaurant.com), where they've been serving, and we kid you not, world-famous steamed cheeseburgers since 1959. Open every day, 11 a.m. to 8 p.m.

Then there's **K LaMay's** (690 East Main St.; 203-237-8326; klamays steamedcheeseburgers.com), where Kevin LaMay whips up steamed cheeseburgers just like he learned to do at Ted's. That's right, he used to work there and has now struck out on his own, with his own, secret recipe for some seriously delicious burgers. He started out serving hot sandwiches from a back room in a Meriden pub called Garryowen's. His creations were so well received, he moved his operation into his current location and has been there ever since. K LaMay's is open Mon through Sat, 10:30 a.m. to 8 p.m.; Sun, 10:30 a.m. to 3 p.m. LaMay also serves his style of steamed cheeseburger at the Double Play Café in Wallingford (320 Main St.; 203-265-2599).

Next door to Kevin's restaurant is **Les's Dairy Bar** (654 E. Main St.) where you can get a cool treat to wash down that burger. Choose from flavors such as tiramisu, white cake batter, and cheesecake, as well as Italian ice in flavors such as lemon or blood orange and frozen yogurt. Les's has been an institution since it opened in 1950, and for many people in town, the fun just doesn't start until Les's is open. Open noon to 9 p.m.

Another interesting eatery in the area is **Huxley's Bookmark Café** (1376 East Main St.; 203-237-4087; huxleyscafe.com). Named for English author Aldous Huxley, Huxley's has been in the Klonaras family since 1999 when Gregory Klonaras purchased it. Now his son Dimitrios runs the cafe alongside his dad and mom, Stella. There's definitely a literary theme. The walls are lined with shelves filled with books of all tastes. A painting that hangs on the wall depicts Aldous Huxley in much the same setting. Huxley is the author of a book called *The Doors of Perception,* which is famous not for its literary acclaim but because it's the book from which The Doors took their name. Their book theme carries through to the menu where they offer a Poetic Breakfast and a Literary Lunch. If you're in a hurry, call ahead and they'll have your meal ready for you. Open Sat and Sun, 6:30 a.m. to 2 p.m.; Mon through Fri, 6:30 a.m. to 2:30 p.m.

Call ahead to Huxley's and order a breakfast sandwich and home fries to go, then head over to **Hubbard Park** (199 Notch Rd.; 203-630-4259; cityofmeriden.org), designed by the sons of Frederick Law Olmsted. However, beyond the pleasant little park (which has a nice Christmas light drive in December) the 700-foot cliffs of the volcanic Hanging Hills rise sharply to the sky. On the top a stone tower was built in 1900, and the 360-degree view from the battlements is one of the top five in the state. On a clear day you can see to Long Island Sound and across the northern border into Massachusetts. From Memorial Day to Oct the drive around the reservoir and up to the tower is open, so you can drive up and eat on the cliff. But at other times of year you can enjoy the hiking trails and have the mountains to yourself.

For an even quieter time, try **Black Pond State Park** (1690 East Main St., Middlefield) on the town line, where you can enjoy your breakfast while soaking in the quietude of Black Pond and the surrounding forest. No one is usually there very early in the morning unless they are fishing, and it's always fun to watch the fishermen ply the waters as the steam rises on a cool morning. Ahh, perfection. Enjoy.

Wallingford

Another option for that Connecticut original—steamed cheeseburgers—is the next town over from Meriden. In **Wallingford** you can try **American Steamed Cheeseburgers** (92 Quinnipiac St.; 203-294-8888). Tucked behind the Wallingford Train Station, this establishment has been churning out delicious food since 2013 with owner Jayson Anthony Paul at the helm. You can get veggie burgers, salmon sandwiches, and even an egg and cheese sandwich. If you dare, you can get The Bimmer, which is two double cheeseburgers, two

> ## Trail of Terror
>
> If you're anywhere in the state of Connecticut on a weekend in October and you like to be scared—set your sights for *Wallingford's Trail of Terror* (60 N. Plains Hwy.; 833-600-0054; trailofterror.com). While this wonderful New England town is filled with spooky extravaganzas at this time of the year, this Trail of Terror is *really* scary. (This is *not* a children's activity.)
>
> You travel outdoors through more than 30 "very interactive" fright scenes. Some you'll recognize and love. Some, not so much. *But* it's all for a good cause! This is a volunteer-run operation and they donate all the proceeds to charity. Over the years, the trail has donated $700,000 to the local Red Cross chapter. They also support the Community Revitalization Efforts of Wallingford and other local charities (a complete list is on their website).
>
> The attraction is very popular and they limit the number of tickets each night, so if you don't plan ahead, they may sell out before you arrive! Luckily, there are a few ways you can go about gaining entrance. If you're feeling lucky, head over and wait in line for a $15 general admission ticket. You can also go to their website and purchase a $20 Timed Ticket ($18 if you purchase it before Sept 1). You will be given a time and date at which you are to arrive at the trail for your turn. There are also group discounts.
>
> The trail is weather dependent and will close for heavy rain and/or wind. They keep their Facebook page up to date, so it's best to watch there if you're thinking of heading out. The trail opens Fri, Sat, and Sun at 7 p.m. Last entry is 11 p.m. on Fri and Sat; 10 p.m. on Sun.
>
> Parking can be a little difficult. You can pay $8 to park in the Polish National Alliance parking lot, but everything else is at your own risk. Please respect the No Parking signs, cars *will* be towed. Happy scaring!

steaks, and extra, extra cheese. You can even get a hot dog on a cheeseburger! Open Mon through Thurs, 1 p.m.–1 a.m.; Fri and Sat 1 p.m.–2 a.m.; Sun 1 p.m.–11 p.m.

Wherever you choose to eat, be careful what you say when talking to other Nutmeggers about steamed cheeseburgers. People are about as loyal to their burger joint as they are to their baseball team and will argue until the cows come home on whose is best.

If consignment shops are your thing, don't miss **Cindy's Unique Shop** (32 N. Colony St.; 203-269-9341), where you will find all sorts of treasures. There's the usual brand-name items at greatly reduced prices (Vera Bradley, Longenberger, etc.), but you'll also find refinished farmhouse furniture, handmade wooden signs, jewelry, glassware, holiday decorations (seasonally), and more. Cindy even posts pictures on her Facebook page every week so you can see all the cool new things that have arrived. She'll save things for you if you see it and must have it, but only for a limited time. She also offers great discounts and is always willing to work with her customers. Open Tues through Sat 9:30 a.m.–4:30 p.m.

Near Cindy's is **Redscroll Records** (69 S. Turnpike Rd.; 203-265-7013; redscrollrecords.com). What started as a record label and morphed into a record store is owned by Joshua Carlson and Rick Sinkiewicz. They carry records, CDs, tapes, books, magazines, accessories, and more. They "specialize, but are not limited to, music that is generally off the mainstream radar (underground)." They also buy, sell, and trade, which gives them a nice selection of both new and used items. They are not particularly interested in "most 78s, anything classical, show tunes, crooners," but other than that they are happy to take a look at what you have. They said there's no need for an appointment and there are no set hours to bring your stuff in. "Any time we're open you can come on by." Open Sun 11 a.m.–5 p.m.; Mon–Thurs 11 a.m.–6 p.m.; Fri and Sat 11 a.m.–7 p.m.

How about eating or having a drink in a restaurant that used to be a library? You can, at **The Library Wine Bar and Bistro** (60 North Main St.; 203-678-4656; thelibrarywinebar.com). Formerly Wallingford's town library, this 1889 beautiful building has numerous floors and incredible acoustics. It wasn't always this beautiful; in fact, the Gouveia family put a lot of time and effort into bringing this beauty back to her glamorous self. The food they serve is just as beautiful, which makes the entire thing an amazing experience. Dinner is served Tues–Thurs 4 p.m.–9 p.m.; Fri and Sat 4 p.m.–10 p.m.; Sunday Brunch

OTHER ATTRACTIONS WORTH SEEING

Lockwood-Mathews Mansion Museum
Mathews Park
295 West Ave., Norwalk
(203) 838-9799
lockwoodmathewsmansion.com

Railroad Museum of New England
242 E. Main St., Thomaston
(860) 283-7245
rmne.org

St. James Church
25 West St., Danbury
(203) 748-3561
saintjamesdanbury.org
Established in 1762, used as storage during the Revolutionary War

St. Peter Church
104 Main and Center Streets, Danbury
(203) 743-2707
stpeterdanb.org
Established in 1851, third oldest parish in the diocese

Stepping Stones Museum for Children
Mathews Park
303 West Ave., Norwalk
(203) 899-0606
steppingstonesmuseum.org
Focusing on the arts, science and technology, and culture and heritage

10 a.m.–2 p.m.; Happy hour in the loft, patio, and bar is Tues–Fri 4 p.m.–6:30 p.m. Reservations are recommended.

And if you like their restaurant, you're going to love their winery with its beautiful stone house, stunning views, and lip-smacking wine. **Gouveia Vineyards** (1339 Whirlwind Hill Rd.; 203-265-5526; gouveiavineyards.com) sits on 140 acres of beauty. Seriously, the views from up there are incredible and worth the trip alone. Joe Gouveia purchased the Wallingford property in 1999; the tasting room followed in 2004. The winery has since become a destination and produces 90,000 bottles of wine a year, such as Chardonnay Oak, Seyval Blanc, Whirlwind Rose, Stone House White, Cabernet Franc, and more. Wine tastings are available and you get an etched souvenir wine glass to keep. Come for the wine, stay for the views. Open daily Mon–Sat 11 a.m.–8 p.m.; Sun 11 a.m.–6 p.m.

Danbury Area

Weston

Weston is an especially pretty town smack-dab in the middle of Fairfield County, thanks to tough zoning regulations and restrictions on development. According to folklore, old Mr. Scratch himself left some hoofprints on the rocks thereabouts. Lucifer's purported stomping grounds are now the site of the ***Lucius Pond Ordway/Devil's Den Preserve*** (203-226-4991) on Pent Road (take Godfrey Road, which is off either Route 53 or 57, to Pent Road). Owned by the Nature Conservancy, Devil's Den consists of more than 1,756 acres with 20 miles of hiking trails. This is a great place to scout out examples of rare or unusual plant species, including hog peanut and Indian cucumber root. Or you can just have a pleasant hike. If you plan to do so, be sure for your own safety that you pick up a map at the Pent Road entrance and sign in. Special programs and guided walks are held on some weekends, with attendance by reservation only. The park is open from dawn to dusk daily. There are no restrooms, and dogs and bicycles are not allowed.

Wilton

When ***J. Alden Weir*** saw his first impressionist painting in a Paris gallery, it gave him a headache, but by 1881 the American artist was honing his own distinctively impressionistic style. Today, his **Wilton** home, **Weir Farm** (735 Nod Hill Rd.; 203-834-1896; nps.gov/wefa/index.htm), is a National Historic Site. Weir designed his farm as he would a painting, mixing and matching visual elements until everything was perfect.

The farm, which he called "the Land of Nod," provided inspiration for his own paintings of late 19th-century family life and for the works of fellow artists Childe Hassam, John Twachtman, and John Singer Sargent. The self-guided **Painting Sites Trail** is a living landscape. It's well marked to highlight a series of views from Weir's paintings, including Weir Pond, which he built with the prize money from his 1895 painting *The Truants*. Admission is free, as are ranger-led tours. All buildings are closed from Nov–Apr, but grounds are open dawn to dusk; seasonal hours are May–Oct. Visitor center open Sat and Sun 10 a.m.–4 p.m.; starting in June, Wed–Sun 10 a.m.–4 p.m.; Weir house and studio tours in May, Sat and Sun; June–Oct, Wed–Sun house and studio tours start at 11, 1, 2, and 3 p.m.

Ridgefield

Nearby **Ridgefield** was the site of a minor 1777 skirmish known as (what else?) the **Battle of Ridgefield**, in which Benedict Arnold led the colonists against General William Tryon's British. The historic 1733 **Keeler Tavern** still carries a legacy of the battle in the form of a British cannonball embedded in the wall. Now the **Keeler Tavern Museum** (132 Main St.; 203-438-5485; keelertavernmuseum.org), the inn has been restored and furnished with authentic 18th-century furniture, appointments, and artifacts. Guides in colonial dress conduct 45-minute tours of the tavern Mar through Dec. Hours in Mar–May and Nov–Dec are Thurs–Sun 11 a.m.–4 p.m.; hours June–Oct Thurs–Sun 11 a.m.–5 p.m. Admission. There is a garden that bursts with color in the spring, summer, and fall, and is free and open to visitors from dawn to dusk.

A short distance down Main Street is the **Aldrich Contemporary Art Museum** (258 Main St.; 203-438-4519; thealdrich.org), the only large museum in our state dedicated to contemporary art. This close to New York, it tends to get works from the best of America's young artists. Often the artists represented are relative unknowns whose first important exposure comes at the Aldrich. Behind the museum is a broad green lawn dotted with several dozen pieces of modern sculpture. Most are massive, towering over the art aficionados in their midst.

You can tour the museum and its grounds on your own if you wish, but there are also guided tours for a per-person fee or a curator-led tour for about double the price per person. These guides know their stuff and can make your visit a true experience. The Aldrich is open Mon and Wed–Fri, and Sun noon–5 p.m.; Sat 10 a.m.–5 p.m. The garden is always open, even when the museum is closed. Admission, but military families, teachers, and children 12 and under are admitted free. There is also free admission on the third Sat of each month.

Walk from the museum down the long sidewalks into the charming center of Ridgefield, where there are shops of all sorts to tempt your consumerist heart. Make sure to stop at **Books on the Common** (404 Main St.; 203-431-9100; booksonthecommon.com), selling books to tourists and locals alike since 1984. Open Mon to Fri, 10 a.m.–5:30 p.m.; Sat 10 a.m.–5 p.m.; Sun 11 a.m.–4 p.m.

Down the road you can find **No. 109 Cheese & Wine** (109 Danbury Rd.; 203-438-5757; 109cheeseandwine.com), where the husband and wife owners Monica and Todd Brown combine the best of all worlds—cheese and fresh, gourmet snacks in one of their small shops and wine and craft beer in the other. The Browns carefully choose their stock so that they easily pair with each other and they often have guest pourers come in and share their wares. The two work well together, with Monica offering private pairing classes and tastings and Todd spearheading the picnic basket program, offering packaged meals much as he does for the Aldrich. Open Tues through Thurs, 10 a.m. to 6 p.m.; Fri and Sat, 9 a.m. to 6 p.m.; Sun, 10 a.m. to 4 p.m. They also own a shop in Kent (6 Kent Green Blvd; 860-592-0366), with hours Wed–Sat 10 a.m.–5 p.m., Sun 11 a.m.–4 p.m.

In the evening, head to **Ridgefield Playhouse** (80 East Ridge Rd.; 203-438-5795; ridgefieldplayhouse.org). This restored, Cass Gilbert Jr.-designed theater hosts plays, musical acts, question-and-answer sessions with film industry people, stand-up comedy, and speakers and lecturers from around the world. Nearly every seat in the 500-seat theater has a good view, and you can eat real buttered popcorn while you watch. Check the website for events and tickets.

Redding

When Washington's Northern Army went into winter quarters at the end of November 1778, it was dispersed in an arc from New Jersey to Connecticut to ring the British garrison in New York. Three of the army's brigades had their winter encampment at **Redding**, where they were strategically positioned to defend the region from British raiders. Their commander was Major General Israel ("Old Put") Putnam, a larger-than-life hero, who is often called Connecticut's Paul Bunyan. There is a memorial to Old Put on Hartford's Bushnell Park and more about the man in that section of the book.

That winter was relatively mild, but the harvest had been poor, and supplies were scarce. The men, many of whom had been through the hell of Valley Forge the previous year, began to mutter about a similar privation winter in Connecticut. Then in December the state experienced one of the worst winter storms in New England history. Two days after it ended, the men of one brigade mutinied and prepared to march on the colonial assembly in Hartford to

ANNUAL EVENTS IN GATEWAY TO NEW ENGLAND

MAY

Dogwood Festival
Greenfield Hill Congregational Church
1045 Old Academy Rd., Fairfield
(203) 259-5596
greenfieldhillchurch.com

JUNE

International Festival of Arts and Ideas
New Haven
(888) ARTIDEA (278-4332)
artidea.org

AUGUST

Milford Oyster Festival
downtown Milford
milfordoysterfestival.org

SoNo Arts Celebration
Washington and S. Main St., Norwalk
sonoartsfest.com
(518) 852-6478

Good Vibes Only Festival
McLevy Green
102 Bank St., Bridgeport
infobridgeport.com/event/good-vibes-only-festival-on-mclevy-green

SEPTEMBER

Fall Festival and Hawk Watch
Audubon Center
613 Riversville Rd., Greenwich
(203) 869-5272
greenwich.audubon.org

Connecticut Folk Festival and Green Expo
Edgerton Park
75 Cliff St., New Haven
ctfolk.com

Norwalk Oyster Festival
42 Seaview Ave., Norwalk
(203) 866-8810
seaport.org/Oyster-Festival

North Haven Fair
290 Washington Ave., North Haven
(203) 239-3700
northhaven-fair.com

Orange County Fair
525 Orange Center Rd., Orange
(203) 430-6044
orangectfair.com

West Haven Apple Fest
West Haven Green
1 Church St., West Haven
westhavenapplefest.com

Wolcott Country Fair
245 Wolcott Rd., Wolcott
(203) 879-5466
wolcottfair.com

OCTOBER

Pumpkins on the Pier
Walnut Beach
113 Bdwy., Milford
boysandgirlsclubofmilford.com/pumpkinsonthepier

Scare Fair
Weston Historical Society
104 Weston Rd., Weston
westonhistoricalsociety.org

DECEMBER

Brookfield Craft Center Holiday Exhibition and Sale
Rte 25, Brookfield
(203) 775-4526
brookfieldcraft.org/holidays

Fantasy of Lights
Lighthouse Point Park
2 Lighthouse Rd., New Haven
(203) 777-2000
goodwillsne.org

demand overdue supplies and wages. Putnam was able to break up the protest only with the greatest difficulty. Thus began the winter encampment at Redding that came to be known as Connecticut's Valley Forge.

The original encampment is now the site of **Putnam Memorial State Park** (499 Black Rock Tpke.; 203-938-2357; putnampark.org), Connecticut's oldest state park, at the junction of Routes 58 and 107 in Redding. These days the 12-man huts are just piles of stone where their chimneys stood, and the old magazine is only a stone-lined pit. The officers' barracks have been rebuilt, though, and there is a museum containing exhibits dealing with the Redding encampment. There's also a great statue by the front gate showing Old Put riding his horse down a flight of stairs to escape capture during a British raid in February 1779. Open daily, 8 a.m. to sunset. Visitor Center and museum open Memorial Day to Veterans Day, Thurs–Sun 10 a.m.–5 p.m.

Bethel

Greenwood Features (269 Greenwood Ave.; 475-256-1130; greenwoodfeatures.com) screens art and independent films, attracting a large audience wanting more than the latest blockbuster sequel. The two-screen theater is known for showing films long before the rest of the world hops on the bandwagon. Generally two films are shown during a run, and mainstream movies are shown as well. The matinees are kind to tight budgets, and local restaurants offer discount deals. The theater publishes a newsletter with information about upcoming features and film-related lectures.

Further down Greenwood Avenue is another cultural hub, **Byrd's Books** (178 Greenwood Ave.; 203-730-2973; byrdsbooks.com). Owner Alice Hutchinson has decades of experience in the fields of bookselling and business and runs a professional but homelike bookstore that carries new titles, with a special focus on Bethel authors, Connecticut authors, poets, publishers and illustrators. Along with books for adults and children, you can find greeting cards, gifts, and puzzles. The store fronts Bethel's main street, but there is plenty of parking across the street at the library. Don't miss the statues of Abraham Lincoln riding a horse and reading, and of hometown hero P. T. Barnum. Open Tues to Sat, 10 a.m.–6 p.m.; Sun noon–4 p.m.

Readers of a certain age might have spent their teen years hanging out at drive-in restaurants where the uniformed carhops roller-skated out to your car and delivered the food on steel trays that clipped to the window (others may have heard stories from parents and grandparents). At the *Sycamore* (282 Greenwood Ave.; 203-748-2716; sycamoredrivein.com), those readers can relive those memories (or introduce them to younger generations). In continuous operation since 1948, the Sycamore is an old-fashioned drive-in restaurant that has become a Bethel landmark. Carhop service is available spring, summer, and fall. Just pull in and flash your lights. Order a burger and brewed-there root beer (the recipe is a deep, dark secret), which can taste sweet and full or sparkly and dry, depending on its age. The malts are made with real malt powder. The Sycamore hosts Cruise Nights throughout the summer, but you might see a vintage car pull in at any time (with Sunday often having a regular traffic in these vehicles). Open Mon through Fri, 11 a.m. to 8 p.m.; Sat, 7 a.m. to 8 p.m.; Sun, 7 a.m. to 7 p.m.

Danbury

There was a time when a good hat was an essential wardrobe item, and you weren't really dressed without a good topper. In those days, Connecticut was hatmaker to America, and **Danbury** was the center of the hat making business. Today the glory days of hat making are remembered along with other Danbury history in the **Danbury Museum and Historical Society** (43 Main St.; 203-743-5200; danburymuseum.org). There are actually several buildings at this address, and exhibits are scattered among them. The oldest building, the Rider House, was saved from demolition in 1941, thanks to the efforts of Danbury's citizens, and is now part of the museum. Exhibits deal with early American life, the Revolutionary War, and the history of Danbury. Another highlight is the recording studio of opera singer Marian Anderson, who was a Danbury native and the first African American to perform at the Metropolitan Opera in New York. One year before she and her husband purchased their house in Danbury in 1940, Anderson performed her famous concert on the steps of the Lincoln Memorial after being denied permission to sing at Constitution Hall. An astounding 75,000 people watched. The studio is a stop on the Connecticut Freedom Trail and houses many artifacts from her career and life. Museum hours are Tues through Sat, 12 p.m. to 4 p.m.

Danbury is also home to the natural beauty that is **Tarrywile Park** (70 Southern Blvd.; 203-744-3130; danbury-ct.gov). This 722-acre town-owned park offers 21 miles of hiking trails through meadows and forest, along streams and ponds, up steep climbs among granite outcroppings. There are picnic areas, too, for those less inclined to hike (or for refueling after). Don't be surprised if you see a bunch of kids running in groups; several high schools in the area use the park for cross-country meets. The park is open from dawn until dusk.

Within Tarrywile Park are two beautiful structures, one in its heyday, the **Tarrywile Mansion**, and one that has seen better days, Hearthstone Castle. Both are listed on the National Register for Historic Preservation, but only the mansion is in current use. Surrounded by beautiful gardens, an orchard, and manicured lawns, the mansion is a popular spot for weddings

danbury trivia

Zadoc Benedict founded the nation's first hat factory in Danbury in 1780. It produced a dizzying three hats a day! By the mid-1800s, the Hat City led the world in hat production, and by 1949 more than 66 percent of the nation's hats carried a "made in Connecticut" label. From 1949 to 1977, Connecticut honored the hat industry with Hat Day, and both houses of Connecticut's legislature would be filled with examples of the hatmaker's art, from tough-guy fedoras to Miss Porter's–perfect pillboxes.

and other social events. There's even a children's garden on the front lawn for the littles to explore. In 1910, Charles Darling Parks bought Tarrywile Mansion from Dr. William C. Wiles and had a modern (for the time) dairy operation there. Mr. Parks was a very successful businessman as president of C.D. Parks Company and held many interests in Danbury.

Hearthstone Castle (tarrywile.com/hearthstone-castle) was originally designed as a summer estate for Danbury native Elias Starr Sanford and his wife Emma. The magnificent 3-story, 16-room mansion was designed by Ernest G. W. Dietrich; it took 4 years to complete, from the fall of 1895 until the summer of 1899. Today, the castle lies in ruins and is currently fighting for its life as once again people try to save a piece of our state's history. If you want to get involved, see how you can contribute the campaign to save this wonderful piece of history.

Adults commuting into Manhattan may think of trains as something to be endured, but some of us will always see trains as romantic and vaguely magical. At the **Danbury Railway Museum** (120 White St.; 203-778-8337; danburyrailwaymuseum.org), housed in a restored 1903 train station and adjoining a 6-acre rail yard at Danbury's Union Station, a group of dedicated volunteers is doing its part to keep that magic alive. They've transformed the old station into a museum of train paraphernalia and restored trains.

The museum holds some neat events, such as Easter, Christmas, and Halloween trips, and rides in the rail yard, including the opportunity to experience the turntable. Near the front of the museum is a small but interesting gift shop. If Union Station looks familiar, it might be because Alfred Hitchcock used it in *Strangers on a Train* as the setting for his own cameo appearance. Open Sat and Sun 10 a.m. to 4 p.m. Admission.

Brookfield

Looking for a one-of-a-kind gift for that special someone? Head to the **Brookfield Craft Center** (286 Whisconier Rd.; 203-775-4526; brookfieldcraft.org) north of Danbury on Route 25, which houses a school of contemporary arts and crafts within six colonial buildings (including a 1780 gristmill) set on the banks of Still River. The associated arts-and-crafts gallery and retail shop offers unique hand-crafted items from the artists themselves. From woodcrafts to fused glass to jewelry to pottery and cloth, you're sure to find something you just have to have, and that no one else will! Open Tues through Fri, noon to 5 p.m.; Sat, 11 a.m. to 5 p.m.; Sun, noon to 4 p.m. Closed major holidays.

Newtown

East of Danbury is **Newtown,** where the **Second Company of the Governor's Horse Guards** (4 Wildlife Dr.; 203-426-9046; thehorseguard.org) practice, usually in full uniform. A horse guard practice is something no horse- or animal-loving kid can resist. Chartered in 1808, the Second Company of the Governor's Horse Guards escorted the governor and distinguished visitors on ceremonial occasions, and it is one of the oldest cavalry units in continuous service in the country. Today, the troop is an all-volunteer cavalry militia designated by the governor to serve the people of southwestern Connecticut. Weekly practice drills take place Nov to Apr, Sun at 10 a.m., and Apr to Nov, Thurs at 7 p.m. You can also see them at their July horse show and Fall Open House. Check their website for details and call or email ahead and let them know you're coming if you want to watch.

And if you like horses, why not llamas? At **Rowanwood Farms** (175 Huntingtown Rd.; 203-270-8346; rowanwoodfarm.com) you can hike with Peruvian, Bolivian, Chilean, and Argentinian mini llamas, letting them escort you through rural Newtown. Hikes include a brief "Llamas 101" session and an opportunity to connect with your new buddy, before heading off on a guided trek. These walks are suitable for beginners ages 8 and up, and last 1.5 hours with plenty of time for photos. For those llama experts out there, or returning visitors, a 2-hour hike over moderate to challenging terrain is another option. Reservations required.

After this delightful walk, stop at **Ferris Acres Creamery** (144 Sugar St.; 203-426-8803; ferrisacrescreamery.com) for some of the best ice cream in the state. This dairy farm was founded in 1864 by William Ferris and remains owned by the family today. The ice cream shop with its line of customers in front of the silo and barn offers dozens of flavors of ice cream, milk shakes, floats, sundaes, and sorbet, including vegan options. Try the "Campfire" ice cream (vanilla with fudge swirls, graham cracker pieces, and mini marshmallows) in a waffle bowl. This is a working family farm that hires specifically for the shop, and it is open from spring through fall, Mon through Sat 11 a.m.–8 p.m.; Sun 11 a.m.–5 p.m.

Monroe

Connecticut's most famous ghost, the "***White Lady***," is said to haunt the ***Stepney Cemetery*** (Pepper Street) in ***Monroe*** and the ***Union Cemetery*** (Sport Hill Road) down the road in nearby Easton. Visitors to the cemeteries report that the apparition wears a white nightgown and a bonnet. Others say they've seen not only the White Lady but also shadowy specters who try to grab her. The late Ed Warren of Monroe, a legendary ghostbuster who, incidentally, is also buried in Stepney Cemetery, believed her name was Mrs. Knot, and her husband was murdered near Easton in the 1940s. Mrs. Knot is said to have met the same fate as her husband shortly after his unfortunate demise. As with any cemetery, visit with respect and only during its operating hours.

Southbury

Not so long ago, your chances of seeing eagles hunting and soaring in the wilds of New England were somewhere between slim and none. Today, thanks to the Endangered Species Act, the American eagle population is itself soaring, and we need to continue to protect them. One way we can do that is to increase awareness of and educate the public about these majestic birds. In winter, Connecticut bald eagles find the ***Southbury*** area much to their taste. In fact, it's such a popular place that their eagle buddies from as far away as Canada and Maine flock there, too. The ***Shepaug Dam Bald Eagle Observation Area*** (2150 River Rd.; 860-895-6468; shepaugeagles.info) is a wonderful place to watch for these majestic birds. Supported by First Light Power Resources, this observation area is staffed by knowledgeable guides to coach you in observing these beautiful birds—some of whom have a wingspan of 7 feet—while they fish, hunt, and soar. Eagle observations are held mid-Dec through mid-Mar on Wed, Sat, and Sun, 9 a.m. to 1 p.m., although the season can vary. Please check the website for current conditions. It also has a page with essential tips for planning your visit and a place to make the required online reservations.

When you have your fill of the eagles (is that even possible?), you'll want to bring your camera with you to ***Southford Falls*** (175 Quaker Farms Rd.; 203-264-5169), where you'll find the lovely cascade of Eight Mile Brook as it rushes to meet the Housatonic River. The park also includes the remains of the Diamond Match factory, which was destroyed by fire in 1923. The ruins include an old steam engine foundation, a grinding stone, and some of the sluice pipe. The little covered bridge, built by carpenter Ed Palmer with the help of

southburytrivia

Kettletown State Park in Southbury gets its name from the story that settlers paid the Native Americans, who originally lived on the spot, one brass kettle for the land.

author/artist **Eric Sloane**, is based on an 18th-century arch design. There are picnic tables by the bridge, just the place for a romantic spring picnic, or you can perch on a rock by the falls and spend some time just listening to the water or reading. The park also includes a lookout tower, great for viewing fall foliage. Southford Falls State Park is located just south of Southbury on Route 188, south of I-84.

Oxford

Rich Farm Ice Cream Shop (691 Oxford Rd.; 203-881-1040; richfarmicecream.com) on Route 67 has been serving up delicious, creamy concoctions made with milk from Dave and Dawn Rich's own herd of Holsteins since 1994, but the farm has been in Dave's family for five generations. In summer, the place is packed, and you might wait in line a good 15 to 20 minutes, while you enjoy real farm sights and real farm smells. At haying time during the summer, just a whiff of the fresh-cut hay distills summer. As for the ice cream, you can choose from among 25 everyday flavors with additional seasonal favorites, such as pumpkin, and kid flavors, such as Cookie Monster. Or keep things simple and stick with a good old-fashioned chocolate cone. The shop also makes ice cream cakes and seasonal treats, such as ice cream Yule logs. They also now serve lunch Mon through Fri. Bring cash—they don't accept plastic—and please leave Fido in the car so he doesn't scare the cows. Open daily Apr through Oct, 11:30 a.m. to 9 p.m.

Places to Stay in Gateway to New England

GREENWICH

Stanton House Inn
76 Maple Ave.
(203) 869-2110
stantonhouseinn.com
Expensive
Built by architect Stanford White, the inn was named for the owner's grandmother, Elizabeth Cady Stanton, pioneer for women's right to vote.

NEW HAVEN

The Study
1157 Chapel St.
(203) 503-3900
studyhotels.com
Moderate
This unique boutique hotel in New Haven set a new standard for the city.

RIDGEFIELD

West Lane Inn
22 West Ln.
(203) 438-7323
www.westlaneinn.com
Expensive
This elegant, pale yellow 1849 Victorian house has oodles of charming village appeal.

WESTPORT

Inn at Longshore
260 Compo Rd. South
(203) 226-3316
Innatlongshore.com
Expensive
Elegant inn that once hosted President Roosevelt, J. D. Rockefeller, and F. Scott and Zelda Fitzgerald

Places to Eat in Gateway to New England

CHESHIRE

Blackie's Hot Dog Stand
2200 Waterbury Rd.
(203) 699-1819
www.blackieshotdogs.com
Opened in 1928, this classic road-food stand serves the best hot dogs in the state, or at least the best relish.

FAIRFIELD

Mecha Noodle Bar
1215 Post Rd.
(203) 292-8222
Mechanoodlebar.com
Moderate

MILFORD

Rainbow Gardens Restaurant and Bar
117 N. Broad St.
(203) 693-2912
rainbowgardens.org
Moderate to expensive
New American cuisine served in a lovingly restored Victorian on the Milford Green

NEW HAVEN

Claire's Corner Copia
1000 Chapel St.
(203) 562-3888
clairescornercopia.com
Moderate
Vegetarian, organic, sustainable, kosher, and gluten-free

Louis' Lunch
263 Crown St.
(203) 562-5507
louislunch.com
Inexpensive
Oldest hamburger joint in America

Marjolaine Pastry Shop
961 State St.
(203) 789-8589
marjolainepastry.com
Inexpensive
Great place to stop to satisfy your sweet tooth

STAMFORD

Colony Grill
172 Myrtle St.
(203) 359-2184
www.colonygrill.com
Inexpensive
Serving pizza (including its famous hot oil pizza) since 1935

WALLINGFORD

Neil's Donuts
83 N. Turnpike Rd.
(203) 269-4255
www.neilsdonuts.com
Inexpensive
Best doughnuts in the state

WATERBURY

Nardelli's
540 Plank Rd.
(203) 754-5600
nardellis.com
Inexpensive
Best grinders (subs) in the state

Coast & Country

Connecticut has 253 miles of shoreline, all of it bordering the Long Island Sound. This coastline was settled shortly after the first towns were built in the Connecticut River Valley. Today the southwestern portion of the state's coastal plain has been largely urbanized, while much of the eastern portion has been given over to tourism. It is the less densely populated portion of this coastline (between New Haven and Rhode Island) that most people envision as the Connecticut shore. Home to clam shacks and posh inns, popular sandy beaches and lonely old lighthouses, modern submarines and ancient whalers, riverboats and coastal mail packets, the Connecticut shore reflects the romance of the sea like few other places on Earth.

Even if you're not a big fan of the sea, this part of Connecticut has much to offer. The inland portion of the coastal plain and the lower reaches of the Thames and Connecticut Rivers that comprise New London and Middlesex Counties and the easternmost part of New Haven County are all part of what we call "the Shoreline." Here you'll find attractions as disparate as the glorious wedding-cake architecture of the Goodspeed Opera House and the Gothic extravagance of Gillette Castle, or the famous hunt breakfasts at the Griswold Inn and the pastries at Two Wrasslin' Cats.

COAST & COUNTRY

The Western Shore

Branford

According to legend, **Captain William Kidd** was a black-hearted pirate and bloody-handed murderer who savagely preyed upon America's eastern coast. Well, not exactly. As a matter of public record, the real Captain Kidd was a Scottish-born merchant transplanted to America who was commissioned in 1695 to hunt down the pirate Thomas Tew (of Newport) in the Indian Ocean. While pursuing Tew, Kidd stretched the limits of his commission, which embarrassed his prominent British backers (including the Crown). When he returned home, Kidd was seized and, after a rigged trial in which evidence of his innocence was suppressed, convicted of murder and piracy and hanged in 1701.

Whether your view of Captain Kidd leans toward the mythical or the historical, it's hard to resist the tantalizing legends of pirate gold and buried treasure. Many of these tales are linked to Connecticut's **Thimble Islands**, just off the coast of **Branford's Stony Creek**, and local residents have long nurtured the Kidd mythology.

The Thimble Islands were discovered in 1614 by Adrien Block, but were known to Native Americans before that as "the beautiful sea rocks," or *Kuttomquosh*. The islands hung around being pretty rocks for a few decades before a man named William Bryan decided to build a hotel on his island. And what legend helped sell those rooms and attract tourists? You got it, Captain Kidd.

After the Civil War, summer homes, private residences, and more hotels were built on the islands, and boating companies adjusted their routes to include stops there. Life was good until September 21, 1938, when a hurricane hit the area without warning. Long Island Sound saw waves as high as 40 feet and the Thimble Islands were severely damaged. Entire houses were swept out to sea and seven residents lost their lives.

The storm was the beginning of permanent change for the archipelago. Today, only 23 of the 365 "islands" (some are merely rocks jutting out of the water) are inhabited, only six have electricity. However, you can still get a closer look at the islands on a Thimble Island Cruise. Take your pick of several different-sized boats run by the three companies who cooperatively run the tours. There's the 40-foot *Volsunga IV*, captained by

thimbleislandstrivia

While some of the Thimble Islands are admittedly not more than a rock occasionally peeking above the water's surface, the name comes not from their small size, but from a type of wild blackberry—thimbleberries—that once grew there.

> **AUTHOR'S** FAVORITES
>
> Gillette Castle
> Goodspeed Opera House
> Ledge Lighthouse
>
> Two Wrasslin' Cats Coffee House
> Thimble Islands

Anna Milne (4 Indian Point Rd.; 203-481-3345; volsunga4.com). Captain Milne took over captain duties from her dad, the well-known Captain Bob Milne, after he suffered life-changing injuries in a motorcycle accident in 2015. Anna proceeded to earn her captain's license, raise money to purchase the business, and learn what she needed to know. Today you'll find Anna confidently captaining her boat, giving tours and providing a running commentary to make her father proud. Forty-five-minute tours are offered Tues through Sun (closed Mon) and generally leave the dock on the hour. You'll need cash or a check to purchase your tickets though; no plastic is accepted. They generally operate early May through Oct, weather permitting, but check the website for the latest days and times.

Captain Mike Infantino runs his own business with the 44-foot *Sea Mist* (4 Indian Point Rd.; 203-488-8905; thimbleislandcruise.com) along with his sons Justin and Bryan. They offer a variety of tours showcasing the region's geography and wildlife, with lively stories about the area in which they grew up. Their Thimble Island tours run Fri through Sun in May, Sept, and Oct; daily June to Aug. Cash or check; they don't accept credit cards.

Your third option for cruising the islands is the catamaran *Island Time* (99 Block Island Rd; 203-488-8905; islandtimect.com). This 40-foot Catamaran is powered by twin 300HP Suzuki Outboards and features perimeter seating for 28 passengers. They even have a bar on board. Along with public cruises, *Island Time* features a variety of private cruise options, from office parties to bridal cruises, which range from 75 minutes to all day long.

One note about The Thimbles: All the islands are privately owned. Unless you're an invited guest, don't plan on getting off the boat to explore; uninvited guests are understandably not welcome.

The Thimble Islands are not Stony Creek's only claim to fame. The **Stony Creek Quarry** (99 Quarry Rd; 203-488-3904; stonycreekquarry.com) has also made its mark in American history. You could say it made several. Most notably in New York City where the quarry's pink granite can be found in the pedestal of the Statue of Liberty (not the base upon which she stands, but the granite holding the pedestal itself), in parts of Grand Central Station, Jacob Javits

Federal Building Plaza, and the Brooklyn Bridge, as well as in numerous city parks and walkways. First quarried in 1858, Stony Creek granite continues to be used throughout the US. Here in the state, you can find its beautiful pink color in the lobby of Naugatuck Valley Community College, in New Haven as the rock on which Yale Peabody Museum's *torosaurus latus* dinosaur sits, in the steps of Woolsey Hall, in the jetties in many of our state's beaches, and, of course, at Stony Creek's Willoughby Wallace Memorial Library (more on that below).

If you'd like to appreciate the granite in its natural state and learn more about the art of cutting it, you can take a hike through the 450-plus-acre **Stony Creek Quarry Preserve** (35 Buena Vista Rd.), which will take you to a spot high on the yellow trail where you can see the working quarry from afar and will also take you on trails past the abandoned part of the quarry. There are numerous interconnecting trails, and we encourage you to explore them all. Thanks to the efforts of the Branford Land Trust, these lands are preserved and saved for our enjoyment when some of them could have very well become a garbage dump. You can hike **The Branford Trail** and look for the **Selectman's Stones**, explore the more than 100 acres of the **Van Wie Preserve**, which was made possible through donations from the Van Wie family and is maintained by the Trust, and the smaller **Kelley Preserve**, a 10-acre parcel of land purchased through a gift from Brooks M. Kelley in memory of his son Brooks R. Kelley who loved to spend time on these trails. See the website for numerous parking options for these trails and detailed directions. Properties are open during daylight hours; please be respectful, follow the rules, stay on the trails, and leave no trace.

Another place to see granite in use is the **Willoughby Wallace Memorial Library** (146 Thimble Island Rd.; 203-488-8702; wwml.org), a library that almost wasn't. You see, when Stony Creek resident **Willoughby Adelbert Wallace** died in the autumn of 1946, he left much of his life's treasures to the town of Branford with instructions to build a free public library in Stony Creek. Probably knowing how slow things can sometimes move, he gave the town a deadline of 10 years in which to act on his bequest. Should they not take action during that time, then the money would be appropriated to the Congregational Church of Christ to be used as it wished. Old Willoughby knew whereof he spoke, apparently, because it did indeed take the town a decade to make a decision regarding the library, and it was only a few months before the deadline that a town meeting was held in which the issue was heatedly debated. By then, the trust had grown substantially and everyone had ideas of how it should be best spent. Cooler heads prevailed, and it was decided to accept Mr. Wallace's money and build the library. Local architect David Orr agreed to design the building for free and the Castellucci Brothers of Rhode Island, owners of the quarry in town at the time, donated all the granite used in the construction. So should you have the opportunity to drop by Willoughby's library, send up a silent thank you to the generous miser who made it possible. Open Mon through Thurs, 10 a.m. to 8 p.m.; Fri and Sat, 10 a.m. to 5 p.m. (until 2 p.m. on Sat during July and Aug); and Sun (Nov through May) 1 to 4 p.m.

A short walk up Thimble Island Road will take you to the Stony Creek Puppet House Theater now known as ***The Legacy Theater*** (128 Thimble Island Rd; 203-315-1901; legacytheatrect.org). In the early days, the glamorous theater was home to a silent movie theater, Orson Welles and his Mercury Players, a repertory house, and a summer stock house. It then saw life as a World War II parachute factory, then a puppet house that was home to a world-renowned marionette collection. When the puppet house went out of business, however, the building fell into disrepair and was actually slated for demolition in 2008. It was in sad shape with numerous safety concerns. The Legacy Theater Company purchased the building in 2012 with big restoration plans. They were ultimately successful and for the past five seasons have brought a little piece of Broadway to Branford, Connecticut.

Continuing on Thimble Island Road for a half mile you'll come to ***Stony Creek Museum*** (84 Thimble Island Rd.; 203-488-4014; stonycreekmuseum.org). Inside, you'll find exhibits on the marionette collection from the former and aforementioned Stony Creek Puppet House Theater; the town's long history with the quarry and how it shaped its community; an old apothecary store complete with original drugs; and, of course, information on the Stony Creek Fife and Drum Corps, and more. The museum is open only Fri through Sun, 1 to 4 p.m., but you can call ahead and make an appointment to visit at any time.

If it's later in the day, why not head to one of the local breweries? ***New England Brewing Company*** (5 Indian Neck Ave., 203-208-4525; newenglandbrewing.com) is located on the water and serves beers that complement their laid-back atmosphere. They offer a beautiful and spacious indoor/outdoor taproom with views of their canning and bottling process; there's dock access and a game pit. What's not to love? Their beers include lagers such as the Raising Helles and Mr. Lucky's; seasonals such as the Stegosaurus double IPA, Kewl Beans coffee oatmeal stout, and Schnitzengiggles

stonycreektrivia

People from Stony Creek like to call themselves "Creekers," probably to distinguish themselves from the "Yorkers" who swarm the place in summer. We also have it on good authority that residents of the Indian Neck section of Branford are referred to as "Neckers." We're seeing a trend here.

German-style festbier; and more. Their beer names are almost as good as the beers themselves. Open Sun through Thurs 11 a.m.–9 p.m.; Fri and Sat 11 a.m.–11 p.m.

With all that beer floating around in your system, you might find yourself a bit contemplative. Why are we here? What does it all mean? Who are we, really? There's no better place in the area to contemplate than at the ***James Blackstone Memorial Library*** (758 Main St.; 203-488-1441) in downtown Branford; breathtaking in design and decor, it's been lovingly restored, reflecting the justifiable pride town residents take in this unique building.

The Blackstone Library was built in 1896 at a cost of $300,000. The centerpiece is the octagonal rotunda, paved with a marble and mosaic floor. The 50-foot dome is illuminated by an ornamental skylight and decorated with large murals that provide a pictorial history of bookmaking, from *Gathering the Papyrus* to *First Proof of the Gutenberg Bible*. The whole building is studded with elegant period detail, including wide marble staircases leading to the second floor and a large, inviting fireplace in the main reading room. Open year-round Mon through Thurs, 9 a.m. to 8 p.m.; Fri and Sat, 9 a.m. to 5 p.m.; Sun (Sept through mid-May), 1 to 4 p.m. Closed Sun May 27 through Sept 2.

North Branford

Northford is a neighborhood located in the town of ***North Branford***. Its center, known as Northford Center, is listed on the Register of Historic Places. Yes, a whole village is on the list. Cool, right? And one of those reasons is the historic buildings that dot the area. The beautiful brownstone ***Northford Congregational Church*** (4 Old Post Rd.; 203-484-0795; northfordcongregational.church) is one of those buildings. Built in 1846, this church was gutted by a Christmas Eve fire in 1906 but was rebuilt and rededicated 3 years later. You can learn more about this building and others by visiting ***Totoket Historical Society*** (1740 Foxon Rd.; 203-980-9828; totokethistoricalsociety.org), which maintains several properties in the area and works to preserve the town's history. Open Sun 9:30 a.m.–noon; Mon and Tues 9 a.m.–1 p.m.; closed Wed to Sat.

Van Wilgen's Garden Center (51 Valley Rd.; 203-488-2110; vanwilgens.com) might seem like a large operation to those who don't know, but it has always been a family-run farm with deep ties to the community. It all started in 1920 when William C. Van Wilgen immigrated to the US from Holland. Settling in

branfordtrivia

The Connecticut Hospice was the first of its kind in the US. Established in 1874 in Branford, the organization continues to this day offering end-of-life care to patients and support for their families.

the coastal town of Branford, he farmed there for a few years. In 1936, he purchased a larger parcel of land in North Branford. William and his brother, Aart, worked together propagating plants and bushes. The rhododendron called "Wilgen's Ruby" is still available today. In 1960, William's son Cornelius joined the business, which had grown to include landscaping and tree work. Van Wilgen's Garden Center opened in 1977, offering landscaping services and still keeping the retail portion. In 2008, Ryan Van Wilgen, William's great-grandson, joined the business full time, and he continues to run things the family way. The business now has two other locations but hasn't forgotten its roots, always supporting local organizations with donations and sponsorships. Open daily, 8 a.m. to 6 p.m., Van Wilgen's offers everything you need for a beautiful garden, including pink granite from Stony Creek Quarry in Branford.

Guilford

Guilford is a shoreline town steeped in history. Purchased from Native Americans in 1639, Guilford is packed with 17th-, 18th-, and 19th-century homes. You'll also find remnants of a strong Native American history reflected in the town's names and stories.

Route 77, otherwise known as Durham Road, travels from Durham all the way down to Guilford, where it turns into Church Street and takes you to the Guilford Green. While the route is mostly residential, a few restaurants and farm stands are scattered along the route as it meanders through farm land and past Quonnipaug Lake (aka Guilford Lake).

A little more than 3 miles past the lake, you'll find **The Dudley Farm** (2351 Durham Rd.; 203-457-0770; dudleyfarm.com). Built by Erastus Dudley in 1844, the farm's future was uncertain in 1991 with the passing of the farm's last owner, David Dudley. But concerned citizens took action; working together with the North Guilford Congregational Church and the Guilford Probate Court, they helped the North Guilford Volunteer Fire Company obtain ownership of the property. From this collaboration came the **Dudley Foundation**, a not-for-profit organization that now oversees and maintains the **Dudley Farm Museum**. Visitors can explore the farmhouse, barns, and grounds, which have been restored to their 19th-century charm. Even the resident farm animals are representative of those that would have lived on a farm in that century.

The Dudley Foundation offers a Farmers Market, giving local artisans and farmers the chance to showcase and sell their products. They want people to return often, to stop and visit with each other, to enjoy the farm and gardens, to slow down and enjoy the life right in front of them. Not much to argue about there. The market opens June through Oct (check website for times), and the museum is open Thurs to Sat 10 a.m.–2 p.m. You'll find organic baked items, naturally raised meats, honey, jams, jellies, salsa, dried fruits and herbs, and so much more.

There are also multiple opportunities to hike from Route 77, including access to two Guilford Land Trust properties: **Braemore Preserve** (ci.guilford.ct.us), a small part of the Northwoods Trail network managed by the land trust; and **Bluff Head Trails** (guilfordlandtrust.org), a pretty strenuous hike that can be made easier by leaving a car at either end of the trail. Check out their website for details on parking. **Bittner Park** (1390 Durham Rd.; 203-453-8068; guilfordparkrec.com), where there are 136 acres, ball fields, a playground, as well as hiking trails to explore, is also located off Route 77.

For more stops in Guilford, head down Route 77 to **Guilford Green**, with its eclectic collection of boutiques, eateries, and historic properties. Surrounded by Boston, Park, Broad, and Whitfield Streets, the green is a fun place to spend an afternoon or even a day. You will most likely find street parking along the green, even if you have to park a little bit away from the main collection of stores. The Park Street side of the green is home to a bank, a church, town offices, and the Guilford Free Library, all fine to visit, but not as fun as Whitfield Street, where we suggest you start your trip at the **Marketplace at Guilford Food Center** (77 Whitfield St.; 203-453-4849; marketplaceguilford.com). Grab a cup of tea or coffee from Madison's Savvy Tea Gourmet, including Hibiscus Peach, Orange Sunset, Goji Green, Madagascar Black, Lavender Mint and more; many served hot or cold according to your desire. The Marketplace also offers a selection of hot or iced coffee from Branford's Willoughby's Coffee. Choose from mochas, cappuccinos, espressos, and lattes, among others. Many choices coincide with the season, so the menu varies. What the menu always offers, though, are fresh, locally sourced baked goods to go with those drinks. Choose from all-natural breakfast muffins, doughnuts, croissants, breads, scones, and so much more. You can choose to eat in or take your treats with you as you stroll the green. If it's lunch time, you can choose from a variety of fresh-made soups and sandwiches. Make it a picnic! Don't forget the smoothies and juices. The possibilities are endless, but there is no wrong choice. Open Sun to Wed 7 a.m.–3 p.m.; Thurs 7 a.m.–9 p.m.; Fri and Sat 7 a.m.–4 p.m.

Then head next door to **The Village Chocolatier** (79 Whitfield St; 203-453-5226; thevillagechocolatierguilford.com) to choose some chocolates to take home with you. You may have to make some difficult choices with this wide array of fudge and specialty chocolates. Did we mention there's ice cream, too? Yup. Open Mon through Sat, 10 a.m. to 6 p.m.; Sun, noon to 5 p.m.

Nothing goes better with rich chocolate than an equally tasty hot beverage. Stop in at **The Spice & Tea Exchange** (80 Whitfield St; 203-453-0022; spiceandtea.com), a small shop set up like an 18th-century trading post, loaded with spices, herbs, and gourmet teas. Actually a franchise, Spice & Tea Exchanges can be found in 26 states and the District of Columbia, but that doesn't make them any less special. There is one other Connecticut location in Mystic (6 West Main St.; 860-245-4153).

Booklovers will want to head to **Breakwater Books** (81 Whitfield St; 203-453-4141; breakwaterbooks.net). Truly one of the last of a dying breed, this independent bookstore exudes a love of books. There is a lovely collection of local books alongside *NY Times* bestsellers and classics. The children's room is comfortable, welcoming, unrushed, and extensive. They accept online orders as well, so you could have your favorite books waiting for you to pick up and enjoy. Open Mon through Sat, 10 a.m. to 6 p.m.; Sun, 11 a.m. to 5 p.m. Breakwater Books also hosts author signings throughout the year, so be sure to check their website for the latest events scheduled. Don't forget to ask about their Book Lover's card, which will entitle you to $10 off after ten $15 purchases.

With your bags packed with books, head back up Whitfield Street the way you came and stop in at **Flutterby** (55 Whitfield St; 203-458-1941; flutterby-ct.com), where you'll find a wonderful assortment of local, handmade, and definitely unique gifts and clothing.

For more history in the area (it truly abounds here), drive back past the green and farther south on Whitfield Street where you will find the **Henry Whitfield State Museum** (248 Old Whitfield St.; 203-453-2457). Built in 1639 as a combination minister's home, stronghold, and meeting hall, the Henry Whitfield House is the oldest house in the state and the oldest stone house in New England. Today, it's a museum where visitors can take self-guided tours through the three floors of 17th-, 18th-, and 19th-century furnishings and artifacts from the town's history. Parking is free; admission is not. There are also interesting events planned here, including a Firelight Festival the weekend following Thanksgiving, a Night Before Christmas story time in Dec, and others throughout the year. The museum's Facebook page is a great place to check for upcoming happening and available hours. The museum is open May through Oct, Wed through Sun, 10 a.m. to 4 p.m. Admission. Blue Star Museum.

For a beautiful water view, follow Whitfield Street south to **Guilford Harbor** (Whitfield Street and Old Whitfield Street diverge and then converge again and both head to the harbor, so you can choose your way). There's parking available at Guilford Point and some large rocks just right for sitting a spell.

If you like old houses or antique furnishings and you haven't overdosed on history yet, there's another little side trip you can take. Head back up Whitfield toward the green. At the intersection before the green, take a right onto Boston Street to the 1690 **Hyland House Museum** (84 Boston

St.; 203-453-9477; hylandhouse.org), a classic colonial saltbox noted for its unusual woodwork and for no less than 3 walk-in fireplaces. The house and property has a 500-year history, which is explained in fascinating detail on their website. Today the museum hosts special events throughout the year, including a special tour of the museum's quilts and textiles collection, a class on the basics of hearth cooking, beekeeping demonstrations, and more. Museum hours are June through Sept, Sat 11 a.m.–4 p.m.; Sun noon–4 p.m. unless a program is scheduled. It's always best to check ahead, as the house is sometimes closed for private events.

If the family is getting antsy from the museum tours, perhaps a trip to the **Guilford Salt Meadows Sanctuary** (Meadowlands Road; 203-264-5098; ct.audubon.org/Guilford-salt-meadows-sanctuary) is in order. Here you will find the 1-mile **Anne Conover Nature Education Trail**, which sits amid 235 acres of tidal wetlands and is a family-friendly outing and popular bird-watching location. Many educational displays are located along the trail, and guides are available at the trail kiosk. Keep your eyes peeled for the saltmarsh sparrow, which is increasingly in danger of becoming extinct. These sparrows nest only in certain coastal salt marshes from Maine to North Carolina, and lower Guilford saltmarshes seem to be a favorite stop as, according to the Audubon's website, they "support one of the highest density populations of nesting Saltmarsh Sparrows found anywhere in the world." To find your way to the sanctuary, follow Meadowlands Road from Clapboard Hill Road in Guilford. In about a quarter of a mile you'll see an open grass field and a parking area on your right. The sanctuary is open daily from sunrise to sunset.

For more hiking, Guilford's extensive **WestWoods Trail System** (Sam Hill Road; 203-457-9253; guilfordlandtrust.org) is located across town from the Salt Meadows Sanctuary and maintained by the **Guilford Land Conservation**

Sam Who?

Did you notice the name of the road you traveled to reach the WestWoods Trail System (see above)? Did it sound familiar to you? While looking for something lost, have you ever heard your parents or grandparents mutter, "Now where in the Sam Hill is it?" And did you ever wonder who *Sam Hill* was and why he'd have a road named after him? Well, he was a real guy who lived in Guilford (1678–1752). Old Sam was the town clerk for 35 years, judge of the probate court for 12 years, and deputy to the general court for at least 22 sessions. He ran for so many offices that people used to say "running like Sam Hill" when they meant someone was persistent. Poor Sam's name—which had become known throughout the country and sounds so much like the common name for the nether regions—eventually lost that connotation and became a polite euphemism for "hell."

Trust. You can get detailed maps from various locations in town, including the aforementioned Breakwater Books, Bishop's Orchards, and the town hall. This trail system started with 7 miles in 1996; today there are more than 20 miles of mapped trails on 1,200 acres that include cave structures, waterfalls, salt marshes, and an inland tidal lake. Visit their website before you go to map out your route.

Another town treasure in the area of WestWoods is the **Medad Stone Tavern Museum** (171 Three Mile Course; 203-453-2263; guilfordkeeping society.org), which is not a stone tavern at all but a tavern built by a man named Medad Stone. Located farther away from the green and the town's center of activity, Stone chose this spot in 1803 because he believed the main thoroughfare through town would be routed through here; it wasn't, and Stone never opened his tavern. The land and dwelling were occupied by the Davis family for nearly two centuries, however, as they farmed and maintained the property. Leonard Davis Hubbard lived in the tavern for more than 90 years and even wrote about it in a book titled *Old Tavern Tales*. Upon his death in 2001, Hubbard bequeathed the property to the Guilford Keeping Society, which restored the tavern to much as it was when Stone built it. They like to bill it as "the museum that opened 200 years late." We're sure Medad Stone would be happy to see his dream being appreciated and put to good use.

The Medad Stone Tavern Museum is open by appointment June through Sept, Sat 11 a.m. to 4 p.m.; Sun, noon to 4 p.m. Admission is free. Blue Star Museum.

If you're of a mind to see more beautiful scenery, follow Sam Hill Road south to Water Street. Head northeast on Water Street and watch for Mulberry Point Road on your right. Follow Mulberry all the way to its end. You can't park at Mulberry Point, but in the distance you can see **Faulkner's Island Lighthouse**, built in 1802. If it weren't for the determination of the **Faulkner's Light Brigade** (Faulknerslightbrigade.com; 203-215-3559), the Faulkner's Island Lighthouse might have been lost forever. In the early 1990s, this historic lighthouse seemed doomed as a series of storms had worn away the island on which it stood. The structure was on the brink of toppling into the sea until a coalition of local volunteers lobbied their legislators. Eventually, Congress allocated more than $4 million to stabilize the island and save the lighthouse.

The island is part of the **Stewart McKinney National Wildlife Refuge** (see Westbrook entry) and is a sanctuary for the rare roseate and common terns that end their long flight from winter homes in South America and the Caribbean to nest and breed there. This means that usually Faulkner's is off-limits to the public, except for the annual open house in September coordinated by the brigade. Ferry service is offered to the island from the Guilford Town Marina, or visitors can use their own watercraft.

After all this sight-seeing and history appreciation, you may be ready to refuel. If you head back to Route 1 on your way back home, we suggest a stop at **Bishop's Orchards Farm Market & Winery** (1355 Boston Post Rd. [Route 1]; 203-453-2338; bishopsorchards.com). Started in 1910 as a produce stand, Bishop's has grown to become a sizable cider mill and pick-your-own/cut-your-own farm with sidelines in Vermont cheeses, local honey and eggs, and fresh herbs. There's a very old-time farmers' market encased in a more modern supermarket vibe about this place. With fresh baked goods and local produce, you can feed the family from breakfast to dessert here.

The farm market is open year-round, Mon through Sat, 8 a.m. to 7 p.m.; Sun, 9 a.m. to 6 p.m. Closed major holidays. Check the website for the most up-to-date pick-your-own offerings and hours or call (203) 458-PICK.

While you're at the Farm Market, why not stroll across the parking lot to **Bishop's Orchards Winery** (355 Boston Post Rd. [Route 1]; 203-453-2338; bishopsorchards.com), which offers daily wine tastings of their own fruit wines and hard ciders. They also supply wines from other farms and wineries across the state. Winemaker Keith Bishop is a fifth-generation Bishop as well as being co-owner and co-CEO—that's more than enough hats for one person to wear. He's good at what he does, though, turning his farm's apples, peaches, pears, strawberries, raspberries, blueberries, and blackberries into unique and delicious wines. The many awards listed on their web page attests to the fact that Bishop knows his trade. The wine bar is open year-round, Mon through Sat, 8 a.m. to 6:30 p.m.; Sun, 10 a.m. to 5:30 p.m. You don't need a reservation for a tasting unless there are more than nine people in your group, in which case they respectfully request you call ahead. Tasting hours are every day from noon to 5 p.m., and tours are offered Sat and Sun at 2 p.m. There is a cost for both tastings and tours; check the website for the latest information.

Madison

Heading east on Route 1, you'll come to the town of **Madison**, an upscale shoreline community with a great main street and great beaches. But there's history here, too. The 1785 **Allis-Bushnell House** (853 Boston Post Rd.; 203-245-4567; madisonhistory.org) in Madison is noted for the unusual corner fireplaces and original paneling that grace its period rooms. The **Madison Historical Society** maintains the house and its collections of toys, dolls, costumes, kitchenware, and china. The museum is organized in such a way to allow visitors to travel through time from the colonial period, through the Revolution, into the Civil War, and then on to the colonial revival era. What a neat idea. The grounds to the museum, including the herb garden in the back, are open to the public year-round sunup to sundown at no cost. The house is open by appointment and for special events and open houses throughout the year. More information is posted on the website.

Another historic home in Madison comes complete with a family ghost. The 1685 **Deacon John Grave House** (581 Boston Post Rd.; deaconjohngrave.org), located at Tunxis Farm, was owned and occupied for 300 years by the descendants of Deacon John Grave. Throughout its history, it has served as an inn, a tavern, a military hospital, and even a courthouse, but it is the military hospital where this house's ghost story originates. During that time, Anne Grave lived in the house and helped nurse wounded soldiers back to health. She fell in love with one of these soldiers, and when he was well and had to leave, he promised to return but never did. Every once in a while, someone will report seeing the form of a woman walking through the house, items will not be where they were originally placed, a presence will be felt, noises heard. Some speculate that Anne still roams the house waiting for her love to return. Do you believe the ghostly tale? Visit and see for yourself. Tours are available by appointment.

While visiting these homes along Main Street, don't miss the **Madison Mile of Outdoor Art** (Main Street; 203-421-3039; hollycroft.org). Along the path that runs parallel to Route 1, you'll find about 40 pieces of world-class art. The exhibits change every 6 months, so you'll see new entries in this open-air art gallery managed by the Hollycroft Foundation. And be sure to stop in at **R. J. Julia Bookseller** (768 Boston Post Rd.; 203-245-3959; rjjulia.com), the most famous independently owned bookstore in the state. You will probably see an author while you're there; the bookstore has 300 events every year and is the premier place for readings and signings in the state. On the walls are photos of some (but not all!) of those authors, including Martha Stewart, Toni Morrison, and Salman Rushdie. Open Mon to Sat, 10 a.m.–8 p.m.; Sun 10 a.m.–6 p.m.

hammonasset trivia

According to the DEEP website, "Hammonasset" means "where we dig holes in the ground."

During World War II, the Hammonasset Beach was closed to the public and loaned to the US government as an army reservation. Meigs Point was used as an aircraft range. Planes flew over Clinton Harbor, fired at the range, and then flew out over Long Island Sound.

Down the road at the shore is **Hammonasset Beach State Park** (1288 Boston Post Rd.; 203-245-2785), Madison's crown jewel and Connecticut's largest public beach park. With 2 miles of beach along Long Island Sound, this beach has been opened to the public since 1920, drawing 75,000 visitors its first year. Today, more than a million beachgoers flock to its sandy beaches and walking trails. There's also a campground that fills up quickly once it opens for the season. Personally, we like the beach at sunset when the crowds are gone and the peace settles in.

Hammonasset Beach State Park is also home to the **Meigs Point Nature Center** (1288 Boston Post Rd.; 203-245-2785; ctparks.com). The center gives visitors an introduction to the sea life found in Long Island Sound, including horseshoe crabs, lobsters, and a variety of fish. It also has some reptiles found in Connecticut, as well as some mounted animals, including a deer and a black bear. The staff is knowledgeable and dedicated; everyone in your party is sure to learn something. A calendar of family and children's activities is offered. Nature walks are almost always on the calendar along with other special activities; be sure to check it out. The park is open daily 8 a.m.–sunset; open 24 hours Memorial Day–Columbus Day for camping or fishing. Hammonasset can get busy during the summer season, so if you can visit in the off-season, we highly recommend it.

Clinton

At the south end of Commercial Street in **Clinton**, there are two authentic seafood experiences. The first is considered one of the top places to get a lobster roll in America, **Lobster Landing** (152 Commerce St.; 860-669-2005; lobsterlandingct.com). This fascinating little shack is literally on the dock by the marina. The white building with red borders and a simple wooden sign leads you to a place to buy live lobsters, or steamed ones for a little more cash. These lobsters are literally fresh off the boat; at the right time of day you can see fishermen bringing in their traps and nets. But what most people come here for is the hot lobster rolls, now called Connecticut Lobster Rolls, perhaps the perfect way to eat lobster meat, poached with butter and lemon on a grinder roll. Open Apr through Dec, Wed through Sun, 11 a.m. to 6 p.m.

Newer to the scene on the far side of the dock, **Shanks Waterfront Dining** (131 Grove St.; 860-669-4224; shanksclinton.com) is a restaurant housed in a 1974 Bruno & Stillman commercial lobster boat. Don't let the outside fool you, this boat—er restaurant—has state-of-the-art equipment and churns out some serious New England fry (yes, you *can* get a burger if you must; we don't know why you would). Not only is the food wonderful, but the views out over the Clinton Harbor from the picnic tables on the attached deck are second to none, especially at sunset. You can also enjoy misty weekend mornings on the water, when the restaurant is open for breakfast. Open in the summer Mon through Thurs, 11 a.m. to 8 p.m.; Fri, 11 a.m. to 9 p.m.; Sat, 8 a.m. to 9 p.m.; Sun, 8 a.m. to 8 p.m.

It's not a boat, but **Chamard Vineyards** (115 Cow Hill Rd.; 860-664-0299; chamard.com) is still one of the shoreline's hidden jewels. Owned by famed geneticist **Dr. Jonathan Rothberg**, Chamard produces 6,000 cases of wine a year. The vineyard grounds are beautiful and the lodge rustic and charming. They also have a barn where they host live music and other events, and a bistro where they serve "simple, wholesome, classic food influenced by products readily available from the property and in the region." For a fee, you can also create your own wine, from choosing the grapes to fermentation to corking—the process is up to you. The vineyard and wine bar are open Wed through Sat noon–9 p.m.; Sun 11 a.m.–5 p.m.

Westbrook

The Salt Meadow section of the **Stewart B. McKinney National Wildlife Refuge** (Old Clinton Rd.; 860-399-2513; www.fws.gov/northeast.mckinney) was donated in 1972 by Esther Lape in order to save a piece of shoreline from development. In the decades since, more sections of the coastline have been preserved, but this original piece is one of the best. During the fall and spring migrations, the marsh provides resting, feeding, and nesting habitat for 280 species. Bring your binoculars and on a good day you might spot brants, scoters, black ducks, kingfishers, woodcock, bluebirds, red-tailed hawks, ibis, tree swallows, egrets, ospreys, and endangered roseate terns. Spring and fall are best, but during the summer you can still enjoy the permanent avian residents. Open daily, 7 a.m.–7:30 p.m.

The Connecticut River Valley

Old Saybrook

If you're a hardy New Englander, then you know that the best time to visit the beach is in the winter—no crowds, no traffic, no fees. Unfortunately, most of the clam shacks and ice cream stands close in the off-season. That's why it's good to know that **Johnny Ad's** (910 Boston Post Rd.; 860-388-4032; johnnyads.com) is open year-round. Johnny Ad's is a popular destination for tourists; in the winter the locals have it all to themselves.

Depending on the season, you can eat inside or take your food outdoors to the picnic tables and fight the seagulls for it. The **lobster roll** is the genuine, butter-drenched shore favorite, and the fried whole-belly clams are crunchy and briny. Open Sun to Thurs 11 a.m.–7 p.m.; Fri and Sat 11 a.m.–8 p.m.

If you follow Main Street its southernmost distance, you'll come to **Saybrook Point,** where the Connecticut River flows into Long Island Sound. This is ecologically protected National Conservancy topography and the perfect place for lodgings that rank among coastal New England's best—namely, **Saybrook Point Inn, Marina, & Spa** (2 Bridge St.; 860-395-2000; saybrook.com). The layout includes a dock and marina (large enough for 125 moorings) as well as a spa for fitness workouts, massages, a whole menu of sophisticated beauty treatments, and indoor/outdoor swimming pool plunges. All 82 guest rooms are tastefully furnished (Chippendale and Queen Anne styles predominate), with sizable bathrooms, fluffy robes, and ample storage space. If you'd like romantic intimacy, choose one of the 2 suites nestled in the marina's mini-lighthouse. The inn also has 2 historic buildings, Three Stories and Tall Tales, with more rooms. Details are on the website. **Fresh Salt** is the on-site restaurant here, serving breakfast, lunch, and dinner with a beautiful waterfront view. Brunch, served Sun 10:30 a.m. to 2 p.m., is legendary.

old saybrook trivia

It is said that General de Lafayette stopped by the James Pharmacy in 1824 to purchase either socks or soap—the facts are uncertain. What is certain is that Katharine Hepburn was a frequent visitor while she lived at Fenwick.

Essex

With one of the best anchorages on the Connecticut River, **Essex** still looks very much like it did in the 18th century. Clapboard houses, fan-shaped windows, and fences abound, and in the shops that line the street, purveyors of antiques, clothing, and gifts ply their trade to tourists from around the world.

There used to be two shipyards in the town, and from 1754 there was a West Indies warehouse next to the town dock where goods from Africa and the Indies were unloaded for redistribution across the state. It was next to that warehouse at the Hayden Shipyards that America built its first warship, *Oliver Cromwell*, in 1776.

It is therefore fitting that the Connecticut River Foundation's **Connecticut River Museum** (67 Main St.; 860-767-8269; ctrivermuseum.org) is located at Steamboat Dock. The museum chronicles the history of Connecticut by tracing the evolution of the Connecticut River and of steam power. Among the exhibits is a full-scale working replica of David Bushnell's 1775 *American Turtle*. This is the first submarine ever constructed. The museum also contains nautical paintings, shipbuilding tools, and memorabilia. Special events are held here throughout the year, including an annual holiday model train show, and foliage and other sightseeing cruises. The museum itself is open Columbus Day through Memorial Day, Tues–Sun 10 a.m.–5 p.m.; closed Mon and major holidays. Gift shop. Admission. The research archive is open by appointment only.

essextrivia

David Bushnell, designer of the *American Turtle*, coined the word "submarine" to describe his invention.

If you've never visited the 1776 **Griswold Inn** (36 Main St.; 860-767-1776; griswoldinn.com), don't leave Essex without doing so. People who know and love this place often call it the "Gris" (pronounced "grizz"). The inn offers 33 guest rooms, a full-service restaurant, and a taproom with a mouth-watering menu and delicious brews.

The Gris is open daily for lunch and dinner, plus a Sunday brunch in the form of the justly famous Hunt Breakfast. This tradition goes back to the War of 1812, when officers of the British army, which was then occupying Essex, forcefully suggested that the establishment start serving a regular Sunday hunt breakfast. Today, the Hunt Breakfast table groans with an array of food that includes fried chicken, lamb kidneys and mushrooms, and creamed ham and eggs over English muffins. It's almost, but not quite, enough to make you forgive the British for burning the rest of the town after their meal.

Several of the inn's downstairs rooms have been turned into dining rooms. You can, for example, eat in the book-lined library or in the Steamboat Room, with its lifelike mural of steamboating on the river. The owners hold art tours and talks about the amazing collection of art that makes this place seem more museum than restaurant. Visit the website for available dates; reservations are required. The Gris is open throughout the year except for Christmas Day with historic dining hours Sun 11 a.m.–8 p.m.; Mon to Thurs 11:30 a.m.–8 p.m.; Fri and Sat 11:30 a.m.–9 p.m.

If the river formed Essex's early history, the railroad had much to do with its later development. The **Essex Steam Train and Riverboat** (1 Railroad Ave.; 860-767-0103 or 800-277-3987; essexsteamtrain.com) off Route 154 was chartered in 1868. It still runs a steam train, with an optional riverboat ride, along the Connecticut River. Four or more trains per day make the 12-mile round trip from Essex to Deep River, and all but the last train connect with the riverboat. Boats make a round trip from Deep River to Gillette Castle and East Haddam. Before or after the excursion, guests can tour a variety of vintage train cars and visit the gift and snack shops (both in old railroad cars). The railroad runs a varying schedule from May through Oct, and from Thanksgiving through Christmas. Tickets can be purchased at the station in Essex. Special trains like The North Pole Express and Thomas the Tank Engine require reservations and sell out fast.

Essex used to be famous for manufacturing piano keys, and nearby **Ivoryton** was the center of the ivory trade that supported that industry. In fact the town's name derives from the fact that it used to import "ivory by the ton."

Both the legal ivory trade of olden days and the local piano works have ceased to be. But a salute to music of a different sort can be found at the **Museum of Fife & Drum** (62 N. Main St.; 860-767-2237; companyoffifeanddrum.org), where the Company of Fifers and Drummers is headquartered. Exhibits trace the development of military parades in America from the Revolutionary War to the present day and include many uniforms and musical instruments, including drums dating from 1793. There's a special display of Civil War–era musical instruments. This museum is truly unique. Open by appointment. Admission.

The **Ivoryton Playhouse** (103 Main St.; 860-767-7318; ivorytonplayhouse.org) was the first self-supporting summer theater in the nation. Although cozy and unpretentious, the Ivoryton can boast some of the most famous names in American theater: Marlon Brando, Ginger Rogers, Groucho Marx, Helen Hayes, Mary Astor, and Gene Hackman all graced the playhouse's stage. Katharine Hepburn, who was born in Hartford and lived nearby in the Fenwick section of Old Saybrook, launched her career at the Ivoryton. Today the theater offers a full schedule of great plays—musicals, comedies, and dramas, as well as a wonderful children's summer program of theatrical entertainment.

Deep River

Settled in 1635 as part of Old Saybrook, the sleepy village of **Deep River** is known throughout the state as the site of the **Deep River Ancient Muster**, "the oldest and largest gathering of fife and drum participants and enthusiasts in the world," according to Deep River's website. Held annually the third Sat of July, this is truly a family-friendly event. The muster is preceded by a parade that starts at 11 a.m. at the corner of Main and Kirtland Streets, proceeds down Main Street, and ends at Devitt's Field, where the muster commences. Roads close at 10:30 a.m., and people arrive early to claim spots along the route. Visit deepriverct.com for more information.

Connecticut Freedom Trail

Daniel Fisher was a slave. William Winters was a free man. And somewhere in between the two was a trip from North Carolina to Philadelphia to New York to New Haven and eventually to Deep River. On this journey, Daniel was helped by numerous people, including Deacon George Read of Deep River, along the Underground Railroad. During this journey, Daniel became William. He lived a good life with friends and family in Deep River along Winter Avenue, which was eventually named for him. William Winters died in 1900 at the age of 92. He is buried in Fountain Hill Cemetery on High Street.

Down the road from Fountain Hill Cemetery, you'll find the 1840 **Stone House** (245 Main St.; 860-526-1449), where the local historical society maintains a small museum filled with such items as 19th-century furnishings, maritime memorabilia, locally made cut glass, and Native American artifacts. Open June to Sept Thurs 10 a.m.–noon; Sun 2 p.m.–4 p.m.; or call to make an appointment. Donations requested.

Killingworth

Hugh Lofting, the man who gave the world the character **Dr. Dolittle**, rests in a little cemetery in rural **Killingworth**, unseen by virtually all who pass by. Lofting was a native of England but moved to tiny Killingworth in 1928 at the height of his popularity as the author of a series of books about a kindly, eccentric veterinarian who could talk to animals. According to a town historian, Lofting wrote some of his books while living here, in a house on River Road. Lofting died in 1947 and was buried in ***Evergreen Cemetery***, across the street from his house, now privately owned. The cemetery is on Green Hill Road, and Lofting's tombstone is in the back right-hand corner.

Just north of Green Hill Road on Route 80 is ***Chatfield Hollow State Park*** (381 Route 80; 860-345-8521; ct.gov/dep). Set in a large glacial valley between hills, the park includes Schreeder Pond, created by an earth and stone dam in 1934 by the Civilian Conservation Corps. This is a popular place to swim, complete with lifeguards, and the ridges around the lake offer many opportunities for rock climbers. However, few leave the pond to walk the pine-needle trails that loop around the Monson Gneiss ledges. Near the parking lot at the main entrance, a side trail leads to the left to what are called "Indian caves," where many artifacts were found. Of course, Native Americans did not actually live in these caves but probably stopped here on hunting and camping expeditions. You can find more caves on the south side of Route 80 along the Chatfield Trail.

Haddam

Right near the iconic East Haddam Swing Bridge you'll find ***Goodspeed's Station Country Store*** (22 Bridge Rd.; 860-345-7322; goodspeedsstation.com). Walking through the doors is like walking into another world full of beautiful and unique items to discover—books;

haddamtrivia

Heading south from Middletown toward Haddam, taking Route 9 to Route 154, you'll come upon a large rock set well back from the road. This is *Bible Rock* and its cleft marks the line between Middletown and Haddam. Look carefully because the rock is well back from the road and easy to miss when leaves cover the trees.

gifts; cards; local and international food; old-fashioned candy; farm, shabby chic, and primitive decorations; and so much more! Kris and Ann Marie Pszczolkowski carefully choose their products and do their best to support local artisans, but Kris also imports incredible items from Poland. You'll find tea from **Haddam's Whole Harmony 4 U** alongside authentic Polish pickles and so much more. They are normally open Tues to Sun 11 a.m–4 p.m.

Durham

Durham is one of those New England treasures tucked almost exactly halfway between New Haven and Hartford, with its main street being Route 17, which then splits into Routes 79 and 77 and points to the shore (Madison and Guilford, respectively). Durham is a small town with a little more than 6,500 residents.

The spirit of this small town and its traditions is epitomized in the ***Durham Market*** (238 Main St.; 860-788-3335). The market building has been a fixture on Durham's Main Street since 1835 when Leverett W. Leach opened a store here that eventually became known as L. W. Leach & Sons as his children grew and assisted him in the business. When Leverett died in 1866, his sons continued the business as L. M. & O. Leach until selling it to brothers Fred L. and Jesse B. Atwell in 1897. The Atwells expanded the business to include a post office and enjoyed the business until 1934 when John C. Otte and Perley S. Morse purchased the business and ran it as Morse & Otte. The store stayed in

The Bridge Below

In 1994, the state enacted plans to repair the 1920s' bridge that carries Route 17 across Allyn Brook in Durham when they uncovered something unexpected at the construction site—a long-forgotten bridge buried beneath the existing structure.

With the help of the Connecticut Historic Preservation Office, as well as the state archaeologist, local historians discovered that the bridge was most likely the work of East Haddam stonemason Silas Brainerd, who was hired to build the brownstone arch bridge in 1823. Local officials requested that the state reevaluate their original plans and try to incorporate the historic bridge into the design of the new. Amazingly, the state agreed and delayed construction, eventually deciding to carefully excavate the historic bridge and build the new one over the old.

If you want to see the bridge for yourself, park on the side of Old Cemetery Road on the west side of Route 17 on the north side of the bridge. (It's across from the Hill Hollow condominium complex.) Or park at Durham Dari Serv and walk up Route 17 on the sidewalk, cross at the crosswalk and down to see the bridge. There are stairs that lead down to a walkway where you can view the historic bridge that is essentially under the road.

the Otte family (John and Perley were brothers-in-law), passed down through the generations, for 60 years until new owners Chet and Jackie Mounts took over in 1994. The Mounts changed the name to Durham Market and operated it for 23 years before selling it to new owners late in 2017.

The new owners have given the store a complete overhaul, adding a smoothie machine and a local merchant corner where local artisans can showcase and sell their wares. Fresh produce is always available along with fresh meat from local farms. There's organic ice cream, fresh-baked bread, and standard groceries as well; they even offer fresh sushi. Stop in and see what they have to offer; you won't be disappointed. Open Mon to Sat 8 a.m.–7 p.m.; Sun 8 a.m.–6 p.m.

Driving down Durham's Main Street is like driving into the past. The 18th- and 19th-century homes that line the Historic District have been lovingly restored and maintained. In the short 2-mile span, you'll find 25 historic buildings, including the 1763 **Reverend Elizur Goodrich House** (81 Main St.), home to Rev. Goodrich, a Yale University graduate who mentored students, including Eli Whitney, and worked with the likes of Ezra Stiles, president of Yale (1778 to 1795). The house is privately owned. The 1772 **Cook-Fowler House** (119 Main Street) was once home to William Chauncey Fowler, son-in-law of Noah Webster. It is now privately owned. The 1806 **Lemuel Camp Tavern** (199 Main Street) served as a tavern, a boarding house, a summer residence to Wedworth Wadsworth and his wife, and is now restored as an office building. The 1745 **Elias Austin House** (256 Main St.), also known as the Moses Austin House, is the birthplace of Moses Austin, who founded a settlement in Texas. Unfortunately, Moses died before his dream of a state could be realized, but his son Stephen F. stayed on and became known as the "Father of Texas." The house is now privately owned. These are just some of the stories behind the houses. To learn more, visit historicbuildingsct.com/towns/durham.

A Sweet Treat on the Way to the Beach

So many travelers use Route 17 to Route 79 to get from points inland to Hammonasset Beach State Park. It's become a tradition to stop on the way back for an ice cream at *Durham Dari Serv* (13 Main St.; 860-349-3367). It can get busy on a summer night, so be prepared to wait a little bit. It's worth every minute, though. There's no indoor seating; it's walk-up window only with a few benches available outside. Most people just hang out on the tailgates of their trucks and enjoy their ice cream. Open mid-May to about mid-Oct daily, noon to 9 p.m. When the "gone fishin'" sign goes in the window they have closed for the season.

Another hidden gem in Durham is **Deerfield Farm** (337 Parmelee Hill Rd.; 860-301-7828; deerfieldfarm.org), a small dairy farm that processes its own milk and makes its own cheese and yogurt. There is a small self-service farm store in the barn where you are on the honor system. The farm is also open for tours, but you should call ahead. Open daily 10 a.m. to 5:30 p.m.

Middlefield

Middlefield is home to ***Indian Springs Golf Course*** (123 Mack Rd.; 860-349-8109; indiansprings-golf.com), which offers not only a challenging nine-hole, par 36 public golf course but also a family-run, welcoming sort of atmosphere that makes being in a small town so wonderful. They offer a clubhouse, driving range, short-game practice area, and putting green as well as the **Fair Weather Café** with its bar and patio overlooking incredible views. Even if you're not a golfer, it's a great place to stop and get a quick or relaxing lunch and/or dinner. Their menu is fresh and innovative.

While in Middlefield, be sure to check out ***New Guida's Restaurant*** (484 Meriden Rd.; 860-349-9039; newguidasrestaurant.com), home of the famous 10-inch pedigreed hot dog. Guida's has been serving up these delicious dogs since 1946. You can order them plain (but why would you?) or with "everything" (mustard, relish, and onions). Or if you are a true diner aficionado, you can order a chili and cheese dog. They also have all the diner staples—wonderful breakfasts that are popular with the locals, ice cream, fried clams, and more. Open Wed to Sun 11 a.m.–7 p.m. This place can get wicked busy on summer days during lunch, so please plan accordingly.

If you've eaten one too many hot dogs (is that possible?) and need to burn them off, head down the road just over 2 miles (northeast on Route 66, actually), where you'll find the headquarters of **Connecticut Forest and Park Association** (16 Meriden Rd.; 860-346-TREE; ctwoodlands.org). Commonly known as CFPA, this association of wonderful staff and a huge network of volunteers manages and maintains more than 800 miles of hiking trails throughout the state. Yes, these are the folks responsible for all those blue-blazed hiking trails we talk about in this book. The Blue-Blazed Hiking Trail System was created in 1929, a long-term objective to protect land (both public and private) for public enjoyment. Since its first members organized in 1895, CFPA has helped secure more than 100 state parks and forests for the use and enjoyment of outdoor enthusiasts.

One of those uses is right in CFPA's backyard. ***Camille's Way*** is an easy 2-mile loop through 280-acre Highlawn Forest with numerous smaller loops radiating out from it. You can park in the headquarters' spacious parking lot and pick up the trail in the back by the kiosk, following wide, gravel paths before dipping into the forest. This area is used as a demonstration forest and outdoor classroom, which explains the observation platform with stairs leading down to a vernal pool and the large amphitheater. The trail then winds through the former Christmas tree farm where trees have overtaken what used to be open farm fields. The land is protected by a conservation easement, just one example of how the CFPA works to protect and share our land. You will see more evidence of this as you travel throughout the state, spotting CFPA's signposts and parking lots to access points to the blue trails. To see in advance where these are, visit their website for an interactive map, or, better yet, stop into the headquarters and pick up a copy of their *Connecticut Walk Book*. The office is open Mon through Thurs, 9 a.m. to 3:30 p.m.

The organization also hosts a variety of workshops throughout the year. You can also join a volunteer group or purchase some of the nifty swag they offer. That way, when you're on the trails, you'll look like a professional! Sounds like a win-win.

If you're looking for that special gift, be sure to visit **Perrotti's Country Barn** (288 Baileyville Rd.; 860-349-0082), where you'll find a large selection of gifts and collectibles. This family-owned and -operated shop is packed full of the latest trends with such lines as Mantra Bands, Chamilia Beads, Jim Shore, Scout Bags, Vera Bradley, Natural Life, and more. They also offer ice cream seasonally at the **Caboose Ice Cream Stand**, which is next door. Open Mon through Fri 10:30 a.m. to 6 p.m.; Sat 10 a.m. to 6 p.m.; Sun 11 a.m. to 5 p.m.

Middletown

Once a bustling seaport on the Connecticut River, **Middletown** boasts many historic houses and a varied history. The **Middlesex County Historical Society** (151 Main St.; 860-346-0746; mchsct.org) sponsors the **Middletown Heritage Trail**, which features 20 historic sites. Included among these is **Indian Hill Cemetery** (383 Washington St.; 860-346-0452; indian-hill.org), where General Joseph Mansfield is buried. General Mansfield was born in 1803 in New Haven and lived with his family in Middletown. He entered the military academy at the tender age of 14 and ascended the military ranks until he reached the office of Inspector General in 1853. He had married Louisa M. Mather on September 25, 1838, and they had three children.

In 1862, General Mansfield found himself ducking gunfire in Sharpsburg, Maryland, in the Battle of Antietam. He was desperately trying to stop his troops from firing into what he believed was a line of Union soldiers when he was fatally shot. It turns out, however, that his troops were right and had been shooting at members of the Confederacy. Mansfield succumbed to his injuries and his body was transported home to Connecticut and buried in Indian Hill.

After his death, Louisa and the children stayed in Middletown. In fact, the family house at 151 Main Street stayed in the family until 1959, at which time it was acquired by the historical society and remains their headquarters today. Open Tues and Thurs 10 a.m.–3 p.m. or by appointment.

The tour continues at the **Middletown Police Station** (222 Main St.) and can be done at your leisure. Free brochures, which include a map of the trail, are available at the police department, at the society's offices, at **Russell Library** (123 Broad St.), and at the **Middlesex County Chamber of Commerce** (393 Main St.). All but two sites are wheelchair accessible.

Just south of these sites on the southeast corner of the Wesleyan campus is **Union Park**. This oddly shaped piece of land is the center of a large historic district that includes Gothic Revival, Italianate, and Second Empire houses. In the center of the park sits a strange monument, a large bust of a forgotten musician named Henry Clay Work. Born in Middletown in 1832, Work became a fervent abolitionist; his family home was a stop on the Underground Railroad. A self-taught musician, he composed songs that became popular throughout New England, with his most famous and best songs written during the Civil War, including "Marching Through Georgia," about General Sherman's attack through the state near the end of the war. It sold a million copies of sheet music, a record at the time, and was sung by various armies around the world, from the British in India to the Japanese in Russia. It was not as popular in the American South.

Middletown has no shortage of cool little places to eat and shop. Take, for instance, **Perk on Main** (386 Main St.; 860-788-2287; perkonmain.com). Owner Katie Hughes-Nelson has made a commitment not only to the community to which her business belongs, but to the world in which we live. Her mission statement hangs on the wall in the restaurant and proclaims that it is their goal "to help bring forth an environmentally sustainable & socially just human presence on Earth." And she puts her money where her mouth is by buying only fairly traded organic coffee; local products when possible; and using recyclable materials that can be composted, including encouraging customers to bring in their travel mugs for their coffee instead of using paper products that will only end up in a landfill. They even donate the used coffee grounds to local gardens and farms instead of throwing them out.

But recycling isn't even what they do best. Their food is delicious. Choose from berry or veggie smoothies; crepes filled with fresh fruit, or maybe Nutella, if that's your thing; omelets dripping with cheese and meat or vegetables and served with homemade home fries and your choice of many different kinds of bread for toast. For lunch, there are salads that hit the spot, soups, sandwiches, and more—all made fresh. You can't help but feel as if you're doing a good deed when you purchase a meal from Perk on Main and help Katie help our environment.

Another place we highly recommend is **Pocketful of Posies** (386 Main St.; 860-343-0123), the creative and eclectic shop in **Main Street Market**. Voted Best Gift Shop in Connecticut in 2020 and 2023, this store is the creation of Dottie Smith, formerly of Favorite Things in Durham and Pocketful of Posies in Essex and on Martha's Vineyard. Middletown is her sole focus these days, and what she and her staff create is amazing. From handmade floral wreaths and arrangements to the selection of clothing and home décor; to meaningful jewelry to organic candles, soaps, and creams; to items for your pet or garden, this is the perfect place to find that special gift for someone or maybe even for yourself. Open Wed to Sat 11 a.m.–4 p.m.; Sun 11 a.m.–3 p.m.

If you have the littles with you, don't pass up the chance to visit **Kidcity** (119 Washington St.; 860-347-0495; kidcitymuseum.com), where kids (ages 1 to 7) will enter a world just their size. Toddlers can crawl through sea caves (and stay dry) on the lower level; the first floor offers a Space Age Roadtrip, a fishery, a farm, and a Main Street, and more for children a little older to explore. Every room has easily visible entrances and exits so you can relax while you let your children explore; you'll know where they are at all times. This place really is built for them.

There is admission, and we highly recommend if you're going to be traveling the state anyway that you purchase a membership to the museum. This will provide you reduced admission to other kid-friendly museums across Connecticut and also allows you access to members-only hours. It is a great bargain if you think you'll have time to visit them all (or revisit one multiple times). The museum requests that one adult accompany up to four children. Open every day by reservation only 9 a.m.–4 p.m. Blue Star Museum.

If you're in the area on a July evening, be sure to stop by the **Wadsworth Mansion** (421 Wadsworth St.; 860-347-1064; wadsworthmansion.com) for their Music at the Mansion series. The beautiful back lawn of this historic mansion opens at 5:30 p.m. for a 6:30 p.m. concert every Wed evening in July. The concerts are free and open to the public, but donations are accepted and appreciated. Guests are encouraged to picnic, bringing their own food or purchasing from visiting food trucks. They list the schedule on their website along with other events, including tours, teas, outdoor markets, and more. There are also walking trails around the beautiful grounds that are open when an event is not ongoing. Tours of the mansion are available on Wed 2 p.m.–4 p.m. by appointment.

Adventure seekers won't want to pass up a visit to **Empower Leadership Sports & Adventure Center** (6 Countryside Ln.; 860-652-5690;

leadwithempower.com/ct), a 30-acre adventure center founded by Joe DeRing and run with the help of president Dan Jaskot. Individuals and families or groups can zip line through the trees and take part in other team-building and empowering adventures such as a ropes course, rappelling, scavenger hunts, and tree climbing. The idea behind DeRing's operation is to build confidence with experience, but most of all, it's fun! Reservations are required and can be made online. There are some limitations as to who can participate, and they do close if there's too much wind and/or lightning, so be sure to check their website for information and cancellation policy.

Portland

Brownstone Exploration & Discovery Park (161 Brownstone Ave.; 866-860-0208; brownstonepark.com) is located in a former **Portland** brownstone quarry less than 30 minutes from Hartford, New Haven, and Waterbury. Here you'll find challenges for even the most hard-core adventurer in your group. They offer rock climbing up steep walls of brownstone, zip lining, cliff diving, rope swings, scuba diving, wakeboarding, kayaking, a play area for smaller kids to play and swim, and more. Some activities require an additional fee, and some are included with your admission. Visitors are required to wear a life jacket (provided) at all times. You can bring in your own food and beverages, and there is plenty of space to spread out for a picnic. You might even be able to snag one of the floating gazebos (extra charge), which are pretty cool. Open weekends only from Memorial Day to mid-June; after mid-June open 7 days a week; call for reservations.

Another opportunity for adventure begins in Portland and stretches for 50 miles all the way to Thompson. The ***Airline State Park Trail*** (860-295-9523; ctparks.com/parks/air-line-state-park-trail) was once a railway completed in the 1870s. In the 1880s fancy train cars with white-suited porters ran the line to Boston until 1902, when freights took over until the 1960s. Today you can hike or ride the Connecticut section of this wonderful path, though some sections remain gravel and difficult to bike. The section from Portland to Willimantic often rises up above the surrounding swamps and woodlands on a causeway, while the northern section cuts through the surrounding rock. Along the way there are numerous state parks and sanctuaries, including the 168-acre ***Trail Wood Sanctuary*** (93 Kenyon Rd., Hampton; 860-928-4948; ctaudubon.org), once the home of Pulitzer-Prize-winning Edwin Way Teale, who wrote popular books about nature and animals, now run by Connecticut Audubon Society. They also run the 700-acre ***Bafflin Sanctuary*** (218 Day Rd., Hampton; 860-928-4948; ctaudubon.org), a former dairy farm along the Airline now home to hundreds of bird species.

portland trivia

Portland supplied so much brownstone for Manhattan town houses that it was called the "city that changed the face of New York City."

Author Rudyard Kipling rode the Airline often, and wrote, "Without a jar, or roll, or antic / Without a stop to Willimantic / Rain nor snow ne'er stops its flight / It makes New York at nine each night." You can no longer take that fancy but fast train, but you can still ride (or walk) this incredible linear path and see the natural wonders of Connecticut.

If you'd like a more relaxing time, stop in at the ***Arrigoni Winery*** (1287 Portland Cobalt Rd.; 860-342-1999; arrigoniwinery.com), where you can enjoy live local music on the patio while sipping wine made from the grapes grown on the farm's 200 acres. Named for the bridge that spans the Connecticut River between Portland and Middletown, this winery was made possible by boxing champion John "Jack LaSalle" Gherlone, who passed his love of winemaking on to his grandson, who is the current owner of the winery. Sadly, Gherlone passed away before the winery opened, but we think he'd be proud to see what his grandson—and now his great-granddaughter—have accomplished. They also host events, and a calendar is listed on their website. Just look for the animal statues on the front lawn, head in, and get ready to enjoy a New England evening on the farm. Open Fri 11 a.m. to 9 p.m.; Sat and Sun 11 a.m. to 6 p.m.

East Haddam

East Haddam is the only town in the state to occupy both sides of the Connecticut River, and as you approach the eastern part of the township from across the river, you pass over the longest **swinging bridge** in New England.

This uncommon bridge actually pivots sideways to open a path for passing boats. The first thing you see on the other side is a glorious 3-story American Gothic palace that looks like a wedding cake and dominates the East Haddam skyline. This symphony in gingerbread is the ***Goodspeed Opera House*** (6 Main St.; 860-873-8668; goodspeed.org). Founded by William Goodspeed more than a century ago, the Goodspeed is widely known as "the birthplace of the American musical," thanks to the number of Broadway hits that received their first tryouts there. The opera house has a fascinating history, including being used as a town garage for years before being saved by a community action group and restored to its former glory. Goodspeed Musicals' regular season typically begins in early Apr and runs through Nov or Dec depending on extensions and holiday programming. They also offer Festival of New Musicals every Jan and additional programming Feb and Mar, so there's always something going on. Be sure to check the website for the latest information.

Right outside the entrance to the Goodspeed, you'll find the **Gelston House** (8 Main St.; 860-873-1411; gelstonhouse.com), a beautiful waterfront restaurant and lodging. The food is wonderful, and the rooms are gorgeous. It's a perfect accompaniment to a show at the Goodspeed, and the two make for a wonderful weekend away. Apparently we aren't the only ones who think so. East Haddam oldtimers whisper that the Gelston House, built in 1853, was once a hideout for rumrunners during Prohibition. The restaurant can get busy on show nights. Open Wed to Sat 11:30 a.m.–9 p.m.; Sun 10:30 a.m.–8 p.m. Open for all extra Goodspeed performances on special dates, even Mon or Tues.

goodspeedtrivia

Man of La Mancha, *Annie*, and *Shenandoah* all had their debuts at the Goodspeed Opera House.

During World War I, a militia unit was posted in the Goodspeed to guard the East Haddam swinging bridge against possible U-boat attacks.

On opening night, October 24, 1877, the premier production at the Goodspeed Opera House comprised a comedy, *Charles II*, and two farces, *Box and Cox* and *Turn Him Out*.

While you're in East Haddam, stop by the **Nathan Hale Schoolhouse** (29 Main St.; 860-334-2858; sarconnecticut.org), a one-room establishment where Hale taught in 1773–1774. Originally called Union School, it was renamed for Hale after he became an acknowledged American hero. Today, the schoolhouse is a museum containing Hale possessions and displays of artifacts relating to local history. Open June to end of Sept, Sat and Sun noon–4 p.m.; check the docent schedule because the museum is open only if a docent is available. Admission. Blue Star Museum.

Up the road and around the bend a bit is a place unto itself. You can't miss the bright blue and green building with the two large wooden cats at the top. This is **Two Wrasslin' Cats Coffee House** (374 Town St.; 860-891-8446; twowrasslincats.com), where everyone is welcome and the food is fresh and delicious. You won't find burgers and hot dogs here, but you will find fresh roasted coffee, smoothies, fresh bagels, and a variety of sandwiches and salads. Oh, and there's ice cream, too. The seating is in backrooms of the house with couches or tables, or out on the deck on nice days. Either way, you'll feel comfortable and relaxed and able to do your own thing. Don't be fooled by the size of the building from the outside; there's lots of seating inside, around the corner, and up the ramp. Open Wed to Mon 9 a.m.–3 p.m.

Turn north on Route 151 for a quick stop at the impressive 1794 **First Church of Christ**. In the adjoining cemetery, you will find the grave of former slave and author Venture Smith. Smith was born in West Africa, bought "for four gallons of rum, and a piece of calico," sent to Barbados, then to Rhode Island. In 1737 at age 8, he was taken to Fisher's Island. After many years of servitude, he married, made escape attempts, and was sold to a slave-owner in Stonington. Finally, he was able to buy his freedom in 1765 for 71 pounds and 2 shillings. He moved to East Haddam, where he purchased his own land on Haddam Neck. In his memoir, he reflected, "My freedom is a privilege which nothing else can equal…I am now possessed of more than one hundred acres of land, and three habitable dwelling houses. It gives me joy to think that I have and that I deserve so good a character, especially for truth and integrity." He died in 1805, a landowner who had successfully secured his own freedom and that of his family.

Head south on Route 151 to visit the incredible granite structure that is East Haddam's **Gillette Castle** (67 River Rd.; 860-526-2336), built over a 5-year period from 1914 to 1919 as the retirement home of the famous actor William Gillette, who designed the edifice, including its unique, hand-carved interior furnishings and appointments. Built on 122 acres, the 24-room mansion is now a museum, kept almost exactly as it was when Gillette lived there. Among the actor's possessions on display: his collection of more than 100 scrapbooks filled with pictures of cats. Gillette's best-known stage role was as British detective Sherlock Holmes, and Gillette Castle also houses the largest collection of Holmesiana in the world, including a complete re-creation of Holmes's sitting room at 221B Baker Street.

Gillette specified in his will that the property not "fall into the hands of some blithering saphead who has no conception of where he is or with what he is surrounded," thus Gillette Castle is now owned by the State of Connecticut. While there is ample parking, the facilities are generally modest, and the rustic beauty of this spot has been well preserved. Walk around the large pond

Chester–Hadlyme Ferry

A cool way to visit Gillette Castle is to take the *Chester–Hadlyme Ferry* (Route 148) from across the Connecticut River in Chester. This is the second-oldest continuously operating ferry in the US (the Glastonbury–Rocky Hill Ferry is the oldest). The views of the castle from the water are great. On the east side of the river, the privately owned neocolonial house by the dock was once owned by Alice Hamilton, a pioneer of occupational medicine, who is buried just down Ferry Road in a small cemetery on the south side. The ferry runs Mon through Fri, 7 a.m. to 6:45 p.m.; and weekends Apr through Nov, 10:30 a.m. to 5 p.m. The ferry can accommodate up to eight cars at a time. There's a minimal charge for this fun little ride. Tickets can be purchased onboard, cash or check accepted. Exact change is preferred.

> ## Do You Hear What I Hear?
>
> The small village of *Moodus* in East Haddam is the site of a curious phenomenon steeped in legend. At more or less regular intervals, loud noises like the voices of the damned can be heard throughout the town. These are the famous "Moodus Noises."
>
> Native Americans said these noises were the voice of an evil spirit who lived on nearby *Mount Tom*. Early colonists believed the noises were the result of an ongoing battle between the Good Witches of East Haddam and the feared Black Witches of Haddam. According to this myth, when the battle between good and evil goes on too long, a benevolent spirit, Old Machemoodus (for whom Moodus is named) awakes and waves his sapphire wand, clearing away the evil witches and ending the battle. The Black Witches of Haddam then gather their powers once again, and the battle is rejoined, causing more Moodus Noises.
>
> According to geologists, the true cause of the noises is the rubbing of tectonic plates against each other along a fault line, a phenomenon known to generate earthquakes. In fact, in 1791, Moodus was shaken by two quakes that were felt as far away as New York and Boston. In March 2011, the area was shaken again by a 1.3-magnitude earthquake. At first residents feared something had exploded, and firefighters and police searched for a cause before they were alerted that there had been a geological disturbance. Another quake is expected sometime during the next few centuries, and there have been predictions that someday Moodus will be swallowed up by the fault and disappear into the earth forever.

near the entrance where you'll find some of the largest frogs you've ever seen sunning themselves on lily pads. On the west side of the house, the view over the Connecticut River from the castle's broad terraces is one of the best in the state. In late winter and early spring, before the facility opens for the season, you can stand on the main terrace in splendid isolation and watch eagles soar above the river.

Gillette Castle is open from 10 a.m. to 5 p.m. (last tour leaves at 4:30 p.m.) from the Sat of Memorial Day weekend through Labor Day. There is a modest admission fee for the castle tour, but none to picnic or walk the grounds, which are open year-round from 8 a.m. until sunset. A snack bar and gift shop are also located on the grounds.

Allegra Farm (69 Town Road; 860-537-8861; allegrafarm.com) calls itself a "living history museum." Home to the **Horse Drawn Carriage and Sleigh Museum of New England**, the farm is located on Lake Hayward, where the owners work hard to keep the past alive. Horses and carriages from the farm have been featured in movies such as *Amistad*, *Time Machine*, and *Kate and Leopold*. The museum, located in a post-and-beam carriage house and livery stables, is chock-full of carriages, sleighs, coaches, and any other horse-drawn vehicle you can imagine. Horse-drawn carriage rides, sleigh rides, or hayrides are available on reservation. All the horse-drawn rides provide refreshments that vary with the seasons, from iced mint tea to hot chocolate served by a campfire. In the spring and summer, carriages from Allegra Farm are a familiar sight carrying wedding parties throughout the Connecticut River Valley. The museum is open by appointment.

Historians don't agree on how the **Devil's Hopyard** (366 Hopyard Rd.; 860-424-3200) in East Haddam got its name, but they do agree that a lot of fascinating legends surround the 860-acre state park outside the town. The most lurid one has Satan himself playing in the house band while the locally renowned Black Witches of Haddam held sabbath in the area. According to this legend, Mr. Scratch would sit on a rock near the 60-foot cascade of Chapman Falls in the center of the park and play while his minions cavorted.

Nutmeggers' Yankee forbearers were kind of obsessed with Satan, and the sabbath origin certainly seems reasonable. Sadly, the origin of the park's strange name is probably more commonplace than legend admits. There are those who maintain that a local farmer and noted bootlegger named Dibble once cultivated a hopyard along Eight Mile River and brewed his harvest into a particularly potent moonshine. According to this version, the park's name began as Dibble's Hopyard, which later evolved into Devil's Hopyard.

Whatever the true origin of its name, there is no denying that this isolated, heavily forested, and reputedly haunted park is a truly spooky place at night. During daylight, though, Devil's Hopyard is a great picnic spot, and the big rocks around Chapman Falls are especially nice for spreading a blanket and whiling away a summer's afternoon. There are picnic shelters scattered around the park, but most people just lay out a spread near the falls. The park is open from 8 a.m. until sunset.

Lyme

Sankow's Beaver Brook Farm (139 Beaver Brook Rd.; 860-434-2843; beaverbrookfarm.com) has been in the same family since 1917 and is a wonderful place to visit. The 175-acre property was originally a working dairy farm, but in the early 1980s, owners Stan and Suzanne Sankow tried their hands at sheep farming. Successful at that for nearly 20 years, they then reintroduced cattle. They produce and sell high-quality products such as all-natural woolen scarves, hats, and cute sweaters finished with pewter farm-animal buttons; yarn from their own wool; artisanal cheeses, yogurt, milk, and more—all made from the farm's own herds. If you're interested, they also offer fresh lamb meats and homemade white bean chili and lamb curry stew. If you're partial to making your own, you can take one of the cooking or knitting classes offered.

The farm is open daily from 9 a.m. to 4 p.m. Farm tours are available by reservation. You can also find this farm's products at various farm markets around the area. If you're in the area the weekend after Thanksgiving, check out Farm Day at Beaver Brook Farm for sheepshearing and spinning demonstrations, hayrides, and free samples of the farm's delicious products.

Head east on Beaver Brook Road and take a left on Gungy Road, traveling about a mile to find the parking lot for **Hartman Park** (Gungy Road; www.lymelandtrust.org). This truly off-the-beaten-track park contains some of the most interesting ruins in the state. Study the map carefully and follow the painted metal disks to your destination. The orange-blazed Heritage Trail has a collection of mysterious barn and house foundations, piles of stones from various farm buildings, and the most impressive feature, the Three Chimneys "fort" on a ridge. This unusual ruin may be one of the original Puritan forts that Lyonel Gardiner was commissioned to build in 1634, but archaeologists are not sure. You'll have to decide for yourself. Along the paths here and there you will also find charcoal kiln remnants, a mill site, and an ancient cemetery just past the power line clearing. Turn off the orange trail onto the yellow connector trail and the small stones will be on your right at the top of a small hump of earth.

Old Lyme

The **Florence Griswold Museum** (96 Lyme St.; 860-434-5542; florencegriswoldmuseum.org) is housed in Florence Griswold's ship-captain father's 1841 house, which she turned into a boarding house and salon for painters in the 19th century. The light is supposed to be particularly good in this part of the state, due to its proximity to large bodies of reflective water; the shore is near, and the Lieutenant River runs behind the house. Anyway, a community of artists ended up boarding at the Griswold home, where they worked, played, and inspired one another to greater efforts for decades.

The doors and woodwork throughout Florence Griswold's home came to be decorated with original paintings by the likes of Willard Metcalf, Henry Ward Ranger, and Childe Hassam. The vast Griswold collection, including the works of local artists, is on public display inside. Open Tues to Sun 10 a.m.–5 p.m. Admission. Blue Star Museum.

On either side of the museum are two other attractions that are often missed by those dedicated to stamping their Connecticut Art Trail passport. The first is also an art museum of sorts, the **Lyme Art Association** (90 Lyme St.; 860-434-7802; lymeartassociation.org), with changing exhibitions of local artists. Many towns in the state have these sorts of art associations, but this is one of the best. Browse the landscapes and portraits on the walls of this

> ### Connecticut Art Trail
>
> The word *impressionism* generally conjures the revolutionary work of French masters Monet, Renoir, and Degas, but Connecticut was where American impressionism began. From 1885 to 1930, American painters were drawn to Connecticut's picturesque landscape. They painted scenes of bucolic beauty and community life in a distinctive style characterized by vivid colors and broken brushstrokes.
>
> Connecticut is home to 10 museums, including the Florence Griswold Museum, that display the work of some of the artists who played leading roles in the American Impressionist movement. These museums, along with 11 other museums and historic sites, compose the *Connecticut Art Trail*, a self-guided tour of the diverse art collections within the state. For a complete list of the museums and more information about the trail, visit ctarttrail.org.

museum—and if you find something you like, take it home! All this art is for sale. Open Tues to Sun, 10 a.m.–5 p.m.

On the north side of the FloGris is the **Roger Tory Peterson Estuary Center** (100 Lyme St.; 860-598-4218; ctaudubon.org/rtp-estuary-home). Known for his iconic bird identification books, Peterson made his home in the Connecticut River estuary here in Old Lyme for many years. Connecticut Audubon acquired this property as the home for its Roger Tory Peterson Estuary Center in 2020, with the goal of restoring native nesting, foraging, and stopover habitat for birds in Old Lyme. Check the website for events and updates.

Ferry Landing Park is home to the **Connecticut Department of Energy and Environmental Protection Marine Fisheries Headquarters and Boating Division** (333 Ferry Rd.; 860-424-3000) and offers a way-cool boardwalk with the added allure of that universal kid (and adult) favorite, trains. This is a wonderful, out-of-the-way destination for parents and kids. (Don't be put off by the dead-end sign on Ferry Road. Just go all the way to the end, and turn into DEEP marine headquarters; the parking lot is beyond the main building.)

The boardwalk meanders along the river and ends at a marsh. At the marsh you'll find an elevated platform, ideal for bird-watching or just watching the river flow. The fisherfolk who congregate along the river are more than willing to tell tales to anyone who stops to listen of the big one that got away. The boardwalk also rambles under a railway bridge and includes markers identifying local animals. The best time of year to visit is spring through fall. Trains cross the bridge mornings (about 9:30 a.m. to 1 p.m.) and afternoons (around 4 to 6:30 p.m.). The site offers free parking, is wheelchair accessible, and has well-maintained picnic tables. The park closes at sunset.

Niantic

You don't have to be a book lover to spend many contented hours at the **Book Barn** (41 W. Main St.; 860-739-5715; bookbarnniantic.com) in the village of *Niantic*. To call this place a used bookstore is like calling the Grand Canyon a neighborhood park. The Book Barn is a compound of six buildings, each overflowing with volumes and, luckily, meticulously arranged by subject. The proprietors want you to stay as long as possible, so chairs, benches, and couches are strategically placed throughout the complex to entice you to linger. There are also picnic tables, beautiful gardens, and a play area for children. A dozen cats also live here and truly believe everyone works for them. There are a few goats, too, that you can feed.

If all that doesn't convince you to make an afternoon of it, there's also free coffee, doughnuts, biscuits, and juice. Checkers and chessboards are set up for anyone who has the time and urge to play. Paperbacks cost $1, and hardcover novels run about $4 to $5. The Book Barn also purchases books between the hours of 11 a.m. and 6 p.m. Their buying policy is on the website.

The Book Barn's inventory grew so massive that the owners opened additional locations: the **Book Barn Downtown** (65 Pennsylvania Ave.; 860-691-8078), and **Chapter Three** (55 West Main St.; 860-739-0277). We wonder where they'll go next! All stores are open daily 9 a.m. to 9 p.m.

Also nestled in Niantic is the **Children's Museum of Southeastern Connecticut** (409 Main St.; 860-691-1111; nianticchildrensmuseum.org). Frequently children's museums overflow with activities for kids over 5, but fall short for those younger than that, so this interactive educational center is a real discovery. The exhibits and activities are designed to appeal to, but never talk down to, kids and are engaging enough to capture the attention of adults, too. Imagination Station features a lighthouse, fishing boat, and village, encouraging kids to make their own fun. The Discovery Room introduces visitors to the museum's live animals, including a bearded dragon, a tortoise, tree frogs, gecko, and crabs. Did we mention the bee hive you can watch? Need more hands-on activities? Head to Creation Station and build sculptures, learn about magnets, and play a pipe organ!

Throughout the year, the museum hosts a number of special events and classes, including a respected summer camp program that focuses on the environment, science, and the arts. Open Tues through Sat, 9:30 a.m. to 4:30 p.m. Picnic area is available. Admission; kids under 2 free.

Rocky Neck State Park (exit 72 off I-95 in Niantic) is a great location for outdoor recreation, but one that consistently fills up on hot summer days. Luckily, it can also be enjoyed in the off-season. If you like things historical, be sure to check out the pavilion, constructed as a Works Progress Administration project. For picnics, though, walk out to the end of the rocky point, where you have the waters of Long Island Sound on three sides. This is a beautiful and peaceful place to pitch a blanket and share a meal. Be sure to bring some stale bread or a couple of anchovy pizzas for the gulls; they seem to expect it. The park has a picnic area and a place to cook. Open daily from 8 a.m. to sunset.

Salem

Salem Valley Farms (20 Darling Rd.; 860-859-2980; salemvalleyfarmsicecream.com) near the junction of Routes 11 and 85 in **Salem** is another great ice cream stop. "Rich" is one word for Salem Valley Farms' ice cream—rich and, well, eccentric. How else would you describe an establishment that peddles outrageous flavors like ginger and espresso fudge? Actually, the menu features plenty of familiar flavors, as well as an ever-changing menu of innovative items. Everything is made on the premises, and they can have close to 80 flavors at any one time in the summer (a little less in the colder months). If you want to know what you'll find, check their Facebook page, as they usually list them there along with any updates on hours.

Also in Salem is **Gardner State Park** (126 Old Colchester Rd.; 203-526-2336; ctparks.com), a wonderful 528-acre lake for fishing, boating, or swimming. But for the adventurous, it is also the only place to get boat-only access to **Minnie Island State Park**, Connecticut's smallest state park at less than an acre. With a canoe or kayak, it is an easy paddle from the beach. When you reach this tiny gem of an island, you will find yourself likely alone in the middle of a tiny paradise. Open up the picnic lunch and enjoy this "mini" Garden of Eden.

Mohegan Country

Colchester

Located off Route 16, the 1872 **Comstock Bridge** (now honorably retired) is one of Connecticut's three remaining covered bridges. It is now used mainly by fishermen and folks just watching the river flow. The wheelchair-accessible area was designed by Peter Reneson, a polio victim who grew up in **Colchester**.

Lyman Trumbull, a US senator from Illinois, one of the founders of the Republican Party and coauthor of the Thirteenth Amendment, was born and raised in Colchester in the home of his grandfather, historian Benjamin Trumbull, at 80 Broadway St. The house still stands today but is private and not open to the public.

Don't forget to stop by **Cato Corner Farm** (178 Cato Corner Rd; 860-537-3884; catocornerfarm.com) to try Elizabeth MacAlister's amazing artisanal cheeses. These cheeses have been praised across America, and even across the ocean in France. The cows are subjected to no hormones, herbicides, or chemical fertilizers, and Elizabeth built an underground cave to keep the raw milk cheeses at the proper temperature. Try the creamy Brigid's Abbey, popular Bloomsday, or aged Jeremy River cheddar, all spectacular examples of their kinds. The farm shop is open Fri and Sat 10 a.m.–4 p.m.; Sun 11 a.m.–4 p.m.

Lebanon

The sprawling town green in **Lebanon** is over a mile long and one of the historic centers of the American Revolution. It first became an important supply depot during the French and Indian War when merchant and storekeeper Jonathan Trumbull helped to supply the troops fighting in Canada. Fifteen years later as governor of Connecticut during the Revolution he held over 900 meetings of his Council of Safety here, using the green as a staging area for the supplies that saved Washington's army numerous times. Far enough inland, it was safe from British troops for the entire war and became, along with places like Morristown and West Point, one of the most important nodes of American resistance to British tyranny. Supplies were sent from here to save the troops at Valley Forge from starvation, and French troops under the Duc de Lauzun billeted here at the height of the war effort.

Around the green itself (which has a nice walking path circling it) are many historic homes, mostly thanks to **Jonathan Trumbull**, the only colonial governor (1769–1784) to support the American War of Independence. Today at least three buildings in Lebanon are associated with the Trumbulls and the governor's historic efforts to support the Revolution. Two are located near each other on W. Town Street (Route 87) on the green.

The ***Jonathan Trumbull House*** (169 W. Town St.; 860-642-7558; govtrumbullhousedar.org) was once the governor's home. It was built by Governor Trumbull's father between 1735 and 1740. Today it is furnished with period furniture and administered by the Daughters of the American Revolution. Also on this site is ***Wadsworth Stable***. Originally located in Hartford, this stable was saved from demolition due largely to the efforts of Katherine Seymour Day, who raised enough funds to have it relocated. In 1954, the Daughters assumed ownership, dismantled the stable, and moved it to Lebanon. Today it serves as a museum and holds numerous antique wagons and farm implements. While we can't say George Washington slept here, we're pretty sure his horse did. Both the museum and stables are open the second Sat of the month from spring to Nov, noon–4 p.m. or by appointment.

The third Trumbull property, the 1769 ***Jonathan Trumbull Jr. House*** (780 Trumbull Hwy.; 860-642-6579; historyoflebanon.org), is a center-chimney farmhouse with 8 intricately carved corner fireplaces and a gorgeous original cherry staircase with a molded rail. George Washington really did sleep here, on March 4, 1781. Today it is furnished with both reproductions and period antiques. Open mid-May through Columbus Day, Sat and Sun, noon to 4 p.m.

Built in 1727 as the Trumbull Family Store, the **Revolutionary War Office** (149 W. Town St.; 860-873-3399; sarconnecticut.org) was where the Council of Safety met to plan the logistical effort that kept Washington's army in the field during the Revolutionary War. Today the building is owned by the Sons of the American Revolution and is open June 1 to end of Sept; Sat and Sun noon to 4 p.m.; check docent schedule to make sure a docent volunteer will be there. Donations accepted.

The home of **Dr. William Beaumont**, the "father of gastric physiology," is also located in Lebanon. The **Beaumont home** (844 Trumbull Hwy; 860-642-6579; historyoflebanon.org) is maintained by the **Lebanon Historical Society** and houses a display of surgical instruments and a re-created exam room. Open mid-May through Columbus Day, Sat noon to 4 p.m. or by appointment.

Franklin

Tiny **Franklin** offers the **Blue Slope Country Museum** (138 Blue Hill Rd.; 860-460-9877; blueslope.com), where city slickers can get acquainted with farm implements and tools housed in a Pennsylvania Dutch–style Amish barn on a 380-acre working dairy farm. The museum offers educational programs and demonstrations about the importance of farming in this country. Special events in Oct.

Norwich

Located at the confluence of the Yantic and Shetucket Rivers, **Norwich** was founded in the second half of the 17th century. By 1776, it was the second-largest city in Connecticut. Because of that, Norwich is an important historical cornucopia that was often overlooked. A group of representatives from organizations across the city decided to change all that and formed **The Norwich Heritage Groups** with the goal of finding the best ways to promote tourism while preserving and protecting the city's resources. In 2015, in collaboration with the **Norwich Historical Society**, the group opened the **Norwich Heritage and Regional Visitors Center** (69 East Town St.; 860-886-1776) as a center of operations.

A large part of Norwich's history comes from the fact that it was a major Patriot stronghold during the Revolutionary War. Among Norwich's sons who fought in that war was **Benedict Arnold**, the infamous American general who tried to turn West Point over to the British and who later burned New London. And although Arnold was a traitor to his country, he is Norwich's traitor and they celebrate this and what it had to teach us. In fact, the center is located in the historic 1787 **Daniel Lathrop School House**, a school made possible and dedicated to Benedict Arnold's mentor Daniel Lathrop. The school house is usually open from the end of Apr to Oct, Wed through Sun, 10 a.m. to 4 p.m. It's always best to check ahead to be sure someone will be there.

Other Arnold sites can be found on the **Benedict Arnold Walking Trail of Colonial Norwichtown** (walknorwich.org/benedict-arnold-trail). This 2-mile trail starts at the site of the **Arnold Family Homestead** (corner of Washington Street and Arnold Place) and ends at the grave site of Arnold's mother, Hannah Waterman Arnold, who some say died of a broken heart. The website has an amazing narration of the tour, which you can listen to on your phone as you walk the trail. There are 22 stops on the trail which takes an estimated 40 minutes to complete, depending on how fast you walk.

There are three other walking trails created by Heritage Groups with trail maps and information, all contained on their website (walknorwich.org/walk-norwich-trails) and future trails in the works. There's even some cool swag to be had to show your support of this great organization. Free trail brochures are also available at the visitors center, city hall, chamber of commerce, Otis Library, Slater Memorial Museum, and Leffingwell House Museum.

The **Slater Memorial Museum and Converse Art Gallery** (108 Crescent St.; 860-425-5563; slatermuseum.org), on the campus of the Norwich Free Academy, is well worth a visit, especially if you've never been able to get to the Louvre or any of the other great European sculpture galleries. This imposing 3-story Romanesque structure was built in 1888 to house a truly impressive collection of plaster casts of famous Greek, Roman, and Renaissance sculpture. The casts are still the main attraction, but in addition to that collection (one of the three finest in the US), the museum also has displays of antique American and European furniture, Native American artifacts, textiles, and various fine art, including one of the best collections of Hudson River School art in America. Open Mon 10 a.m.–4 p.m.; Wed to Sat 10 a.m.–4 p.m. Admission, although Sat in July and Aug are free.

New England's old, hallowed cemeteries are among the best places to visit during the fall (or any time of year, really). The headstone inscriptions tell us much about rich and poor families as well as entire social histories. Travelers with proper doses of curiosity can easily get lost in the past. **Old Norwichtown Burial Ground** (Old Cemetery Lane) off Town Street reveals a rich colonial history. You'll find the graves of Mrs. Arnold and other Arnold family members, as well as the final resting place of Samuel Hunter, signer of the Declaration of Independence. Open every day until dusk. Brochures are available at the cemetery entrance for self-guided tours.

Early in the 17th century, a Pequot subchief and political visionary named **Uncas** formed a new tribe, the **Mohegans**. During the Pequot Wars of 1638, Uncas and his people sided with the British, beginning a century of intimate involvement in the affairs of European settlers. The Mohegans and Pequots eventually united under Uncas's leadership, and they became a powerful force in southwestern Connecticut. The first major American novelist, *James Fenimore Cooper*, recounted a fictionalized version of their story in his 1826 sensation, *The Last of the Mohicans,* one of his famous Leatherstocking Tales.

In the northern section of Norwich you'll find the village of Yantic, perhaps best known for the **Yantic Falls** (210 Yantic St.) on the Yantic River. The area around the falls was once a favored campsite of the Mohegans in the 1640s. When Uncas led his people into a battle in the area against their rival the **Narragansetts**, the legend goes that the Mohegan warriors chased the Narragansetts to the edge of the falls, where the Narragansetts chose the deadly leap into Yantic River over surrendering to the Mohegans.

Despite the violent legend, today the falls are beautiful to see. A pedestrian bridge offers photo-worthy views of the falls as they cascade 40 feet over rocks to the river below. A train bridge also crosses the river but does not detract from the view. Exercise caution when exploring the falls, as the volume of water is one of the most powerful in the state.

Chief Uncas died in 1682 and is buried in the **Indian Burial Grounds** on Sachem Street in Norwich. **President Andrew Jackson** laid the cornerstone of Uncas's monument in 1833.

Montville

In 1931, *John Tantaquidgeon*, a direct descendant of Chief Uncas, founded the **Tantaquidgeon Museum** (1819 Norwich–New London Rd. [Rte. 32]; 860-235-8057; mohegan.nsn.us) in the Uncasville section of **Montville**. Here the culture and history of the Mohegans and other New England Indians are presented in a series of displays featuring artifacts of stone, wood, and bone made by Indian craftspeople throughout the years. Artifacts from other tribes of the Southeast, Southwest, and Plains are housed in their own sections. Open year-round, Tues through Fri, 10 a.m. to 4 p.m. Tours are given by members of the Mohegan Tribe. It's best to call ahead to check their availability.

Just 200 yards from the Tantaquidgeon Museum is the **Mohegan Congregational Church** (27 Church Ln.; 860-848-2029; mohegancongregationalchurch.synthasite.com), a 1831 meetinghouse founded by three members of the Tantaquidgeon family a century before their descendent would create the

Tantaquidgeon Museum. The three women, Lucy Occom Tantaquidgeon, her daughter Lucy Tantaquidgeon Teecomwas, and her granddaughter Cynthia Teecomas Hoscoat had the foresight to know that identifying themselves as Christian would help them keep their land. They gave this piece of land on Mohegan Hill to the tribe for the purpose of erecting a church for the community. Their strategy worked, and the church is still in use today. Services are every Sun at 9:30 and all are welcome to participate.

Farther north, near the village of Mohegan and across the street from **Mohegan Sun Casino** is **Shantok, Village of Uncas** (Fort Shantok Rd.), formerly known as Fort Shantok State Park. The land on which this park sits was an early settlement of the Mohegan tribe under their Sachem Uncas. They lived on this land from the mid- to late 17th century. During that time, Uncas allied with the English, which didn't make him popular with the other tribes. In 1645, the Sachem used the fort here as a stronghold against members of the warring Narragansett Tribe. Uncas may just have succumbed to the Narragansetts if Thomas Leffingwell had not come to his aid. Today, there is a memorial to Lieutenant Leffingwell acknowledging his help. The history of the land is murky, with the general truth being that the state of Connecticut seized the land through eminent domain in the early 20th century. In 1994, the Mohegan Tribe was allowed to regain their land from the state through the 1983 Land Claims Settlement act, at the cost of $3 million. In 1998, the tribe began to restore the land, resulting in the beautiful setting that exists today, which includes a playground, walking trails, ball fields, barbecue pits and grills, and an outdoor amphitheater. The area, however, is still sacred ground, containing more than 100 graves and a Mohegan tribal cemetery. So while they urge people to enjoy the area, they also ask that sacred areas be respected.

A small stand of pines known as **Freedom Forest** can also be found in the Shantok village. This tiny forest is dedicated to those who fought in **Operation Desert Storm**. Open daily, dawn to dusk.

Montville also offers an attraction of a different sort from an earlier time in our history. **The Dinosaur Place at Nature's Art Village** (1650 Hartford–New London Tpke.; 860-437-0194; naturesartvillage.com) features a 40-foot-tall brachiosaurus and more than 40 of his friends who roamed the earth millions of years ago. There are 1.5 miles of trails through the woods where visitors encounter life-size prehistoric surprises. There is also a splash pad, children's playground, a replica silver mine, minigolf, outdoor picnic area, and ice cream shop. Open daily Apr through Labor Day, 10 a.m. to 6 p.m.; reduced hours before and after the peak season. Last ticket to the park is sold 1 hour before closing. Admission.

The Eastern Shore

Ledyard

In **Ledyard,** on Route 214, you'll find the 11-acre property on which sits the **Ledyard Up-Down Sawmill** (Iron Street; 860-464-2575; ledyardsawmill.org), an unusual restored 1860 water-powered vertical sawmill. The park also has a working blacksmith shop, a 2-acre mill pond, an 1878 "Lane" shingle mill, ice-harvesting equipment, and a picnic area. The park is staffed by volunteers, and the saw operates when the water level is sufficient, usually Apr, May, and mid-Oct to Nov; open to the public Sat 1 to 4 p.m. during those times.

At the west end of Route 214, turn north and you'll find **Holmberg Orchards** (12 Orchard Ln.; 860-464-7305; holmbergorchards.com), with a farm market full of fresh pies, muffins, pastries, farm-fresh fruits, and vegetables, including lavender in the summer and pumpkins in the autumn. Established in 1896, Holmberg's farm and orchards also include seasonally available pick-your-own fruits, with raspberries available in late June, while their orchard trees bear apples, peaches, nectarines, and pears. You'll also find their Pinot Blanc and Gewürztraminer wines, as well as a selection of their delicious ciders. Open 7 days a week, 9 a.m.–6 p.m.

New London

Between 1784 and 1907, **New London** was home port to 196 whaling vessels, more than twice as many as ventured from all other Connecticut ports combined. The industry peaked in 1846 and died off rapidly thereafter.

This history is reflected in the city's **Whale Oil Row** (105–119 Huntington St.), a series of four Greek Revival houses built by **Charles Henry Boebe** between 1835 and 1845. Originally built for Ezra Chappel, the homes were the private residences of leading businessmen of the time until they were turned into commercial office space in the mid-20th century. The four buildings were listed on the National Register of Historic Places in 1970. They are still beautiful to behold, a piece of history that carries some of the aura of those days when Connecticut whale oil helped light the lamps of America.

New London's 26-block **Historic Waterfront District** (City Pier behind Union Train Station) has so many great things to see and do. To follow in the footsteps of such figures as Nathan Hale, Benedict Arnold, and Eugene O'Neill is an experience in itself, but there's also shopping and dining galore.

If you're more of a water fan than a land lubber, visit the granite-walled 1833 **Custom House Maritime Museum** (150 Bank St.; 860-447-2501; nlmaritimesociety.org), the oldest operating custom house in America, where you can book a variety of cruises and peruse centuries of maritime history. There may be a wait for some of these cruises after you purchase your tickets. It can be hot during the summer, and your spot in line isn't in the shade. Just be prepared.

Be sure to check out the museum's front doors, which were assembled from planks taken from the frigate USS *Constitution* (Old Ironsides). Open Jan through Mar, Thurs to Sun, 1 to 5 p.m.; Apr through Dec, Wed to Sun, 1 to 5 p.m. Admission.

As a way to highlight the history that is New London, the Copp family and the staff at the **Avery-Copp House** in Groton (see write-up below) put the wheels in motion to create the **Thames River Heritage Park** (1 Waterfront Park; thamesriverheritagepark.org). Billed as "a new kind of state park" the Thames River Heritage Park pulls together a way for people to visit 18 national and historic sites along both shores of the Thames River. It includes sites in both New London and Groton and includes four centuries of our nation's history.

Opened in 2016, the Thames River Heritage Park is the only heritage park in the state. Perhaps the coolest part of the park is that it's all tied together by water taxi. Boarding and disembarking is available at three of the sites: Fort Trumbull State Park in New London (on the hour), City Pier in New London (20 minutes after the hour), and Thames River Landing in Groton (40 minutes after the hour). Parking is available at these locations as well.

This is a relaxing way to explore these sites. Visitors travel at their leisure between stops, spending as much time as they'd like at each. The taxi runs in a continuous loop, and people hop on and hop off on their way to and from the sites. Each ride takes about 15 minutes.

A complete list of the sites and their history is on the park's website. You can choose to visit them all, or just a few. There is so much history in this one area, it will be a tough decision to make! You can purchase round-trip tickets online or on the boat. The taxis are not handicapped accessible at this time and there are no restrooms aboard. Bikes are allowed if there is room. Dogs are welcome but must be carried or able to navigate the ramp onto and off the boat.

The taxi runs Fri, noon to 10 p.m.; Sat, 10 a.m. to 10 p.m.; Sun, 10 a.m. to 9 p.m. Holidays follow a Sun schedule. After a last stop at Fort Trumbull at 7 p.m., the taxi runs between City Pier, New London, and Thames River Landing, Groton, every 20 minutes beginning at 7:20 at City Pier. Operation is contingent on the weather, so be sure to check the website before heading out.

Some of the New London sites you can reach by water taxi (or by other means) include:

- ***Nathan Hale Schoolhouse*** (19 Atlantic Street; 860-334-2858; connecticutsar.org/sites/nl-schoolhouse.htm) where Nathan Hale taught from 1774 to 1775, before joining the army and heading off to death and glory.

- ***The Shaw Mansion*** (11 Blinman St.; 860-443-1209; nlchs.org), home of the **New London Historical Society**, as it has been since 1907. No, that's not a typo. Founded in 1870, this society is the oldest historical organization in eastern Connecticut. Considered the cradle of the American Navy, the Shaw Mansion was built in 1756 by Captain Nathaniel Shaw and served as Connecticut's naval office during the Revolutionary War (we're not sure if George Washington slept here, but he definitely visited). This is one of the few structures to survive Benedict Arnold's burning of the city. Five generations of Captain Shaw's family lived here until it was turned over to the historical society. Today the mansion is home to an impressive collection of items.

- The 1678 ***Joshua Hempsted House*** (11 Hempsted St.; 860-443-7949) also survived Arnold's burning in 1781. This home of the famous Connecticut diarist, Joshua Hempsted, is now the oldest surviving house in New London. One of the interesting features of this home is that it is insulated with seaweed. Owned by Connecticut Landmarks, it houses a collection of abolitionist papers. Hempsted's diary can be seen at the museum at the Shaw Mansion.

- ***Fort Trumbull*** (90 Walbach St.; 860-444-7591) was originally built to protect the harbor from the British, but the structure that stands today was constructed sometime between 1839 and 1852. The views from the fort over the harbor are second to none. You can walk the grounds and the interior of the fort. There are multimedia exhibits showing the movement of Benedict Arnold's troops in 1781. The fort also has great fishing for striped bass, bluefish, weakfish, and tautog.

- ***Monte Cristo Cottage*** (325 Pequot Ave.; 860-443-5378; theoneill.org/mcc) is the boyhood home of Nobel Prize winner **Eugene O'Neill**, arguably America's greatest playwright. Named for O'Neill's actor-father's best-known stage role, Monte Cristo Cottage is a pretty gingerbread structure that looks like it should be filled with light and laughter. Alas, the years O'Neill and his brother Jamie spent there were more like one of the Grimms' darker fairy tales. Both father James and brother Jamie were heavy drinkers. O'Neill's mother, Ella, addicted to morphine from O'Neill's birth, battled her own demons throughout his childhood, portrayed in O'Neill's classic play, *Long Day's Journey into Night*. She is said to haunt the cottage.

- **Lyman Allyn Art Museum** (625 Williams St.; 860-443-2545; lymanallyn.org) was established in 1926 at the bequest of Harriet Upson Allyn, the youngest of whaling captain Lyman Allyn's six children. The museum opened 6 years later with a small collection. Today the museum contains multiple galleries of more than 15,000 works, a research library, offices, and more. Also located on the museum grounds is the historic Deshon-Allyn House, a 19th-century mansion that was home to Lyman Allyn.

- The sea has always been at the heart of New London, so it's no surprise that it is home to the **US Coast Guard Academy** (31 Mohegan Ave.; 860-444-8400; uscga.edu). Visitors are welcomed year-round to tour the academy, but they need to make arrangements ahead of time through a link on the website. The public is also invited to attend public events but are subject to security measures (be sure to check the website so you'll have all the necessary paperwork). Also of note, any time you pass a marching formation on campus, they have the right of way. Do not pass them, just stop and stay out of their way.

- **Ledge Lighthouse** (ledgelighthouse.org) rises out of Long Island Sound at the beginning of the Thames River. Sometimes shrouded in early-morning fog, the lighthouse can have an eerie countenance, which fits right in with the rumor that the light is haunted by a ghost named Ernie. Some believe Ernie was a light keeper who, depressed by marital problems, cut his own throat and jumped off the structure. Some reports say the ghost is a tall, bearded man dressed in a slicker and rain hat. The ghost has been known to untie boats, hide coffee cups and radios, and slam doors. The lighthouse is atop a 65-foot, 3-story square building in the water at the meeting of the Thames River, Fisher's Island Sound, and Long Island Sound in New London Harbor. It was abandoned in 1987, and the structure took a beating from the elements. Once again, Nutmeggers jumped into action, and the New London Ledge Lighthouse Foundation was formed to save the iconic landmark. Today, fully renovated, the lighthouse once again stands in glory, complete with an interpretive museum and small theater. The foundation offers tours from July through Sept, details on their website. The New London Maritime Society and Cross Sound Ferry offer a variety of lighthouse tours that include Ledge Lighthouse. They can be pricey, but check them out.

Groton

The Thames River Heritage Park tour continues into neighboring Groton. There's so much history in this area, we think you'll need more than a 1-day pass to the taxi! Thank goodness, season passes are available.

Some of the Groton sites you can reach by water taxi include:

- **Fort Griswold Battlefield State Park** (Park Avenue; 860-449-6877) is the site of a 1781 massacre of American troops at the hands of a force of 800 British soldiers under the command of traitor Benedict Arnold. At that time, Yankee privateers based in New London were a thorn in the side of the British in New York, and Arnold came to burn the town, which he did, destroying 150 buildings. The part of his force that advanced up the east bank of the Thames suffered heavy casualties assaulting Fort Griswold, which was held by a force of 150 militia under the command of Colonel William Ledyard. When Ledyard finally surrendered, he was murdered with his own sword, and 80 of his men were slaughtered. Many of Fort Griswold's old emplacements remain, and there are some interesting historical displays. The 134-foot monument tower provides a nice view of the coast.

- **The Avery-Copp House Museum** (154 Thames St.; 860-445-1637; averycopphouse.org) is the little museum that started it all. They are the force behind the Thames River Heritage Park. The historic house in which they are located was built in the early 19th century by Rufus Avery. Remarkably, the house remained occupied by the Avery family for generations, with the last family member living there until his death in 1991 at the age of 101. Many of the original furnishings remain, providing a unique window into their lives.

- **Submarine Force Museum** (1 Crystal Lake Rd.; 800-343-0079; ussnautilus.org) houses the world's first atomic submarine, the **USS Nautilus**. The museum includes extensive exhibits tracing the history of America's submarine fleet and offers a pair of top-notch multimedia shows in two different theaters: one tracing the history of the submarine force from the days of David Bushnell's **Turtle** to the machines of today, and one dealing specifically with *Nautilus*.

If you're out with the kids (furred or otherwise) and don't have time for the water taxi tour but need to burn off some energy, Groton has some great state parks. **Haley Farm State Park** (Haley Farm Lane; 860-424-3200) is a great place to explore. It has 200 acres filled with trails near Palmer Cove. There is a bike trail (also wheelchair accessible) that winds its way along beautiful former farmland. The stone walls you see scattered across the property were a hobby of former owner Caleb Haley, who farmed the land in the late 19th century into the 20th.

From Halley Farm you can reach **Bluff Point State Park** (55 Depot Rd.; 860-424-3200) on a bridge over railroad tracks. Bluff Point is an 800-acre coastal reserve that offers a boat launch, shell (permit required) and saltwater fishing, and hiking. This place is also pet-friendly and a wonderful way to spend a day.

A strange place with a stranger name, **Gungywamp** in northern Groton is shrouded in mystery. Theories as to who created the strange rock formations on this land range from usual Yankee ingenuity to aliens. The fact that the land has not been readily accessible to the public added to the mystique. Archaeologists as well as ghost hunters have had their say. Strange phenomenon has been reported at the site, including sunlight strategically pouring through certain places of the stone chambers at certain times of the day, suggesting the chambers and stone rings were ceremonial. There's a large cliff called the **Cliff of Tears** that seems to elicit strong feelings of sadness or apprehension in some. Whatever the case, the stones have been dated and are considered to be centuries old; nearby pottery shards and arrow heads have been dated to the Paleo and Woodland time periods.

Since 2018, Gungywamp has been part of the Denison Pequotsepsos Nature Center (dpnc.org/gungywamp; 860-536-1216), which leads monthly hikes on the property. Private walks are available by appointment.

Mystic

Mystic Whaler Cruises (mysticwhalercruises.com) also conducts cruises out of New London from June through Oct. Choose from lobster dinner cruises, Sunday brunch cruises, sunset cruises, or even sailing vacations. Sail for a few hours or a few days.

The 45-acre **Coogan Farm** (162 Greenmanville Ave.) is the last parcel of undeveloped land in the village of **Mystic**. Obtained by **Denison Pequotsepos Nature Center** (109 Pequotsepos Rd.; 860-536-1216; dpnc.org), this land and its history are being preserved. The farm began with **Captain John Gallup** receiving 500 acres from John Winthrop Jr. for his work in the Pequot War. Parts and parcels of the land exchanged hands throughout the years, but today the farm can be enjoyed by everyone, with walking and biking trails throughout the property. The trails are free for the public to use year-round from dawn to dusk.

The nature center operates two nature stores, one at the DPNC headquarters on Pequotsepos Road and the other at Coogan Farm. All profits from the stores support their environmental education programs. You'll find a range of

mystictrivia

Mystic derives its name from the Pequot Native American word *mistuket*.

products, including bird feeders, nest boxes, books, items from local artisans, and more. The nature center is open year-round, Sun through Fri, 9 a.m. to 4 p.m.; Sat, 10 a.m. to 4 p.m. The store at the farm is open Sat and Sun, 10 a.m. to 4 p.m. Admission. Blue Star Museum.

If you are in Mystic in the autumn, no trip is complete without a stop at **B. F. Clyde's Cider Mill** (129 N. Stonington Rd.; 860-536-3354; clydescidermill.com). Built in 1881 and still family-owned and -operated, this is the oldest steam-powered cider mill in the United States. Come any day in season to try their hard or sweet ciders and apple wines, pies, jams, jellies, honey, maple syrup, fudge, pumpkin bread, gourds, pumpkins, candy apples, and kettle corn. The apple cider doughnuts here are seasonal classics. Open 7 days a week, Sept to late Dec, 9 a.m.–5 p.m. Demonstrations on Sat and Sun.

Mystic Drawbridge Ice Cream (2 Main St.; 860-572-7978; mysticdrawbridgeicecream.com) is a cute ice cream parlor that locals claim has the best ice cream around. The Mystic Mud, Mystic Turtle, and Seaport Sally Swirl are Drawbridge originals. Hours vary by season; check the website. By the way, that cute drawbridge is called a *bascule* (French for "seesaw"). You'll have plenty of time to contemplate its rare beauty because car traffic along Main Street goes into gridlock when it's raised to allow boats to pass.

One of the more unusual shops in Mystic is **Mystic Knotworks** (25 Cottrell St.; 800-889-3793; mysticknotwork.com), founded by Alton Beaudoin, who learned how to tie nautical knots as a bosun's mate during World War II. After the war he established himself as a nationwide expert on knotwork, so much so that the Smithsonian began collecting his work. Sailors came to his little shop for custom items, and the rope bracelets made here were copied around the world. Now the oldest knot shop in the United States, Mystic Knotworks operates out of an 1832 rigging and sail repair shop, and it supplies gift stores around the country. But why not get your crafted ropework here? Open Mon to Wed 10 a.m.–6 p.m., Thurs to Sat 10 a.m.–8 p.m., Sun noon–6 p.m.

The **Hoxie Scenic Overlook**, between exits 89 and 90 on the northbound side of I-95, offers a postcard view of Mystic Seaport. To the east you can see the seaport, home port to the *Charles W. Morgan* whaling ship, the *L. A. Dunton*, and the square-rigged *Joseph Conrad*, among others. The bluff on the right is where the Pequot Indian War was fought.

Stonington

Stonington is perched on a mile-long peninsula so narrow that you can stand on some cross streets and see the ocean on either side. Were it not for the town's protected harbor, it is unlikely that anyone would ever have chosen to build in such a confined space. That harbor, however, made Stonington a center of New England's whaling and sealing industries in the first half of the 19th century. It also helped make Stonington an important railroad terminus. In the early days of railroading, before rail bridges crossed the state's major rivers, Stonington was on the most direct route between Boston and New York, and 17 separate tracks once converged on the town. In those times, passengers arriving by rail from Boston had to board steamboats in Stonington Harbor for the trip to New York.

At the height of Stonington's fortunes, the town's two main streets were packed cheek by jowl with commercial buildings and the fancy homes of wealthy merchants. When whaling and sealing fell off, the railroad moved on, and Stonington, which lacked the real estate to expand into a bedroom community, was left frozen in the mid-19th century. Most of the beautiful Federal and Greek Revival homes are still there, only now they're B&Bs, restaurants, antiques stores, and crafts shops.

In 1820, Captain Nathaniel Palmer left from Stonington harbor and embarked on a sailing trip that resulted in the discovery of Antarctica. You can visit the 1853 **Captain Nathaniel B. Palmer House** (40 Palmer St.; 860-535-8445), which Captain Nat, as he was known, built with his brother, Alexander. Built in the late Federal style, the home has 14 rooms and a cupola that looks out over the shipyard and lighthouse. The worn floorboards of the lookout tower are a testament to how often worried family members paced the floors watching for sea captains to return. A restored outbuilding with an icehouse and workshop is located on the grounds, along with a genealogy library and a collection of oil portraits. This National Historic Landmark also has a permanent exhibit that traces the Palmer family's role in the state's maritime history. Changing exhibitions relate to Palmer, Stonington, and maritime history. The home is bordered by water on three sides, and the property has been naturalistically landscaped. Visitors are encouraged to stroll the grounds and bring a picnic lunch. The Palmer house is open May to Oct, Thurs through Mon 12 to 4 p.m. Admission.

Cannon Square, toward the south end of Market Street, marks the site where the Stonington militia successfully fought off the British in August 1814. Four British warships, the *Ramillies*, *Terror*, *Pactolus*, and *Dispatch*, along with the bombship *Terror*, sent cannonballs whizzing through the wooden walls of clapboard houses, bouncing along Water Street, and smashing through the meager defenses. For almost four days they kept up their attack, demanding surrender. But the only reply from the citizens of the town stated, "We shall defend the place to the last extremity; should it be destroyed, we shall perish in its ruins." From this small green near the south end of the peninsula, brave militia manned two 18-pound cannon, firing over the blue waters of the Sound at their adversaries. Ninety-four British died, while the American losses totaled somewhere between three and zero, depending on the count. American poet

ANNUAL EVENTS IN COAST & COUNTRY

FEBRUARY–MARCH

Eagle Watch Cruises
Essex
(860) 767-8269
ctriverquest.com/portfolio/wintereagle

JUNE

Antique & Classic Boat Rendezvous
Mystic Seaport Museum
75 Greemanville Ave., Mystic
(860) 572-0711
mysticseaport.org

Essex Shad Bake
Essex Island Marina
11 Ferry St., Essex
rotaryclubofessex.com

JULY

Guilford Art Center Craft Expo
411 Church St., Guilford
(203) 453-5947
guilfordartcenter.org/expo

North Stonington Agricultural Fair
21 Wyassup Rd., Stonington
northstoningtonfair.org
(860) 535-3956

AUGUST

Potato and Corn Festival
Augur Field
290 Forest Rd., North Branford
(203) 214-5566
nbpotatofest.com

Lebanon Country Fair
122 Mack Rd., Lebanon
lebanoncountryfair.org
(860) 642-6012

CT Renaissance Festival
Lebanon County Fairgrounds
122 Mack Rd., Lebanon
(860) 478 5954
ctfaire.com

Schemitzun
Mashantucket Reservation
(800) 396-2136
schemitzun.mptn-nsn.gov/gcphome.aspx

CT Maritime Heritage Festival
239 Bank St., New London
(860) 447-2519
ctmaritimefest.com

Hamburg Fair
Sterling City Road, Lyme
Hamburgfair.org

SEPTEMBER

Durham Fair
24 Town House Rd., Durham
(860) 349-9495
durhamfair.com

Guilford Fair
Guilford Fairgrounds
Stone House Lane and Lovers Lane
Guilford
(203) 453-3543
guilfordfair.org

Preston Scarecrow Festival
Preston City Congregational Church
321 Rte. 164
(860) 887-4647

Cruise, Blues, and Brews Festival
Chester Fairgrounds
11 Kirtland Terr., Chester
cruisebluesandbrews.com

Chester Fair
Chester Fairgrounds
11 Kirtland Terr., Chester
(860) 582-5947
chesterfair.org

Haddam Neck Fair
26 Quarry Hill Rd., Haddam Neck
(860) 267-5922
haddamneckfair.com

OCTOBER

Chowder Days
Mystic Seaport
75 Greemanville Ave., Mystic
(860) 572-0711
mysticseaport.org

Portland Fair
Exchange Club Fairgrounds
1348 Main St., Portland
(860) 342-4217
portlandfair.com

DECEMBER

Holiday Magic
Mystic Seaport
75 Greemanville Ave., Mystic
(860) 572-0711
mysticseaport.org

Philip Freneau wrote an amusing ode to the battle, saying of the British, "They kill'd a goose, they kill'd a hen/Three hogs they wounded in a pen/They dashed away and pray what then?/This was not taking Stonington."

Stroll up Main Street from the square (away from the point) and admire the architecture of the 1827 **Old Customs House** and the elegant 1780 **Captain Amos Palmer House**, both worth more than a passing glance, although privately owned. In fact, **James MacNeill Whistler**, who painted *Whistler's Mother,* spent part of his boyhood in this house.

Down at the end of Water Street is an especially popular local landmark, the **Old Lighthouse Museum** (7 Water St.; 860-535-1440; stoningtonhistory.org/visit/the-old-lighthouse-museum). It was constructed in 1823 but was moved to its present location in 1840 to protect it from erosion. It is now a museum housing six rooms of exhibits, whaling and nautical displays, a collection of pre-1835 pottery made locally, an ice-harvesting exhibit, and the popular lighthouse display, featuring a fourth-order Fresnel lens and photography of the lighthouses of Long Island Sound. If you care to climb the stone steps to the top of the lighthouse, you'll be rewarded with a stunning view of Long Island Sound, including Fisher's Island. If you're at the museum around day's end, linger awhile to see a spectacular sunset over Stonington Point. Open May to Oct, Thurs through Tues, 10 a.m. to 5 p.m. Admission includes a tour of the Captain Nathaniel B. Palmer House.

The **Mashantucket Pequot Museum and Research Center** (110 Pequot Trail; 860-396-6910; pequotmuseum.org) on the Mashantucket Pequot

Reservation in Mashantucket is without a doubt one of the most beautiful, stunning, and moving museums in all of Connecticut. The Mashantucket Pequots invested $135 million of the monies earned from the nearby Foxwoods Casino into building this state-of-the-art museum and research center. The museum brings to life the story and history of the Mashantucket Pequot people, a history spanning 20,000 years, from the last ice age to today, and that of other Native American tribal nations.

The life of woodland Native Americans is portrayed in stunning detail with dazzling multisensory dioramas and exhibits. Based on years of scholarly research and the works of Native American artisans, re-creations of life in a 16th-century Pequot village, a 17th-century Pequot fort, and an 18th-century farmstead were created. You can hunt caribou along simulated glacial crevasses—complete with howling winds and the sounds of creaking ice. When you visit the village, you'll hear the sounds of children playing and women working and smell the smoke of many campfires. The detail of each diorama is magnificent, especially the life-size, hand-painted Indian figures, cast from living Native Americans. In a specially designed theater, you can watch a 30-minute film called *The Witness*, which recounts the 1637 massacre of 600 Pequots at the Mystic fort.

Don't miss the 185-foot stone-and-glass observation tower, which gives you a sweeping view of the area. In fall, this is one of the best places in the state to take in the brilliant reds and golds of a New England autumn. It's best to visit the tower before going through the museum. Somehow seeing the sweep of the Pequot homeland makes the exhibits and dioramas all the more meaningful.

The museum is open Apr to Oct, Wed through Sat, 9 a.m. to 5 p.m. (last admission at 4 p.m.); Nov, Tues through Sat, 9 a.m. to 5 p.m. (last admission at 4 p.m.). Closed major holidays. Admission.

North Stonington

The microclimate in **North Stonington** is perfect for growing wine, and at least two stellar wineries have taken advantage of it. **Jonathan Edwards Winery** (74 Chester Maine Rd.; 860-535-0202; jedwardswinery.com) provides tasters with a unique opportunity—they have wines from California and from Connecticut to compare. Chardonnay, Pinot Gris, Gewürztraminer, and Cabernet Franc are all grown on-site. Their Napa Valley reds are big and bold, made with grapes like Petite Sirah that just aren't suited to Connecticut's growing season. But Cabernet Franc is a standout among the Connecticut reds, and the estate-bottled Chardonnay may just beat out the Napa version in your taste test. Open year-round, 7 days a week, 11 a.m.–5 p.m.

Nearby, **Stonington Vineyards** (523 Taugwonk Rd.; 860-535-1222; stoningtonvineyards.com) has been in operation since the mid-1980s and makes some of the best Chardonnay in New England. Try two versions, one fermented and barreled in oak, the other in steel, to experience why this grape is so versatile. The Sheer Chardonnay is comparable to the best versions of French Chablis, with mineral notes characteristic of the limestone terroir. The tasting room and facilities are a popular choice for weddings. Daily winery tours offer a glimpse of the state-of-the-art machinery and introduce visitors to the techniques behind their great wines. Open year-round, 7 days a week, 11 a.m.–4:30 p.m.

Griswold

What do you do with an acre of sunflowers? They're pretty, sure, but they don't have much use except for feeding the cows. The owners at **Buttonwood Farm** (473 Shetucket Tpke.; 860-376-4081; buttonwoodfarmicecream.com) had another idea. They started the Sunflowers for Wishes fundraiser to benefit the Connecticut chapter of the Make a Wish Foundation. The following year, they planted 10 acres that produced approximately 300,000 blooms. They sold those for $5 a bundle, and 100 percent of the $500,000 they raised went to the foundation. Now they are up to 14 acres. The event usually runs the third week of July, 10 a.m. to dusk. All bouquets are on a first-come, first-served basis. When they're gone, they're gone.

The farm also offers homemade ice cream and other products and sponsors events Mar through Oct. Summer hours: Mon–Fri 1 p.m.–8 p.m.; Sat–Sun noon–8 p.m. Hours vary depending on the time of year, so check their website before heading out. Be prepared to wait in line for the ice cream; it's often out to the parking lot. But the setting is so pleasant you really don't mind.

Places to Stay in Coast & Country

IVORYTON

Copper Beech Inn
46 Main St.
(860) 767-0330
Expensive
copperbeechinn.com
1890-vintage main building with 4 guest rooms with antique and country furnishings and a carriage house with 9 rooms with a mix of more modern amenities. Full American breakfast comes with all rooms.

MADISON

Madison Beach Hotel
94 W. Wharf Rd.
(203) 245-1404
curiocollection3.hilton.com
Expensive
Beautiful beach resort/hotel right on the water

MIDDLETOWN

Inn at Middletown
70 Main St.
(860) 854-6300
innatmiddletown.com
Expensive
Once a National Guard armory, this incredible building features 100 guest rooms and an on-site restaurant.

MYSTIC

Hilton Mystic
20 Coogan Blvd.
(860) 572-0731
www3.hilton.com
Moderate to expensive
Good bet for lodging with children; close to local attractions. Open year-round.

House of 1833 B&B
72 N. Stonington Rd.
(860) 536-6325
houseof1833.com
Moderate to expensive
An elegant and romantic Greek Revival mansion

Whaler's Inn
20 E. Main St.
(800) 243-2588
whalersinnmystic.com
Expensive
An old-style seaport inn in the heart of downtown Mystic by the drawbridge

OLD LYME

Old Lyme Inn
85 Lyme St.
(203) 434-2600
oldlymeinn.com
Expensive
Six rooms, all with private baths, with jazz club on premises

OLD SAYBROOK

James Pharmacy Bed & Breakfast
323 Main St.
(860) 395-1229
jamespharmacybnb.com
Expensive
1790 general store turned inn turned B&B, 3 guest rooms

PRESTON

Roseledge Country Inn and Farm Shop, LLC
418 Rte. 164
(860) 892-4739
roseledge.com
Moderate
Guests receive organic farm-to-table dining

WESTBROOK

Westbrook Inn
976 Boston Post Rd.
(800) 342-3162
westbrookinn.com
Expensive
An 1876 Victorian home built by a sea captain, now voted one of the most elegant inns in America

Places to Eat in Coast & Country

BRANFORD

Stony Creek Market
178 Thimble Island Rd.
(203) 488-0145
Inexpensive to moderate
This local hangout is a great place to have breakfast on the deck or pick up sandwiches and salads for an impromptu picnic.

CLINTON

Lobster Landing
152 Commerce St.
(860) 669-2005
lobsterlandingct.com
Inexpensive to moderate
Widely acknowledged as one of the best places to get a lobster roll in America, this seaside shack is open Apr through Dec.

EAST LYME

Flanders Fish Market and Restaurant
22 Chesterfield Rd.
(860) 739-8866
flandersfish.com
Moderate to expensive
Unpretentious place with good seafood, friendly service; other items on menu as well

GROTON

Paul's Pasta Shop
223 Thames St.
(860) 445-5276
paulspastashop.com
Inexpensive
You can take home prepared food or buy your own pasta and sauce.

MIDDLETOWN

It's Only Natural
606 Main St.
(860) 346-9210
Inexpensive
Award-winning natural food

Udupi Bhavan
749 Saybrook Rd.
(860) 346-3355
Inexpensive
Authentic Indian cuisine that is purely vegetarian

MYSTIC

Captain Daniel Packer Inne Restaurant & Pub
32 Water St.
(860) 536-3555
danielpacker.com
Moderate to expensive
Located in a 250-year-old inn; several menus to choose from; children's menu available

Oyster Club
13 Water St.
(860) 415-9266
Oysterclubct.com
Farm and sea to table with local specialties

NORWICH

Philly's Cheesesteaks
33 Sherman St.
(860) 886-9449
phillysct.com
Inexpensive to moderate
Best (and only?) place to get real Philadelphia cheesesteaks in Connecticut

OLD SAYBROOK

Al Forno
1654 Boston Post Rd.
(860) 399-4166
alforno.net
Moderate to expensive
Fine Italian cuisine and pizzas

Pizzaworks
455 Boston Post Rd.
(860) 388-2218
pizzaworksoldsaybrook.com
Moderate
Located in Old Saybrook Railroad Station, literally next to the train tracks so you can watch the trains come and go

WESTBROOK

Lenny and Joe's Fish Tale Restaurant
86 Boston Post Rd.
(860) 669-0767
ljfishtale.com
Moderate to expensive
Best fried clams around, huge servings

Haywire Burger Bar
730 Boston Post Rd.
(860) 391-8479
haywireburgerbar.com
Moderate
Family-owned and -operated restaurant, hand-formed 100 percent Black Angus beef burgers, meat ground in-house daily. Almost 30 local craft beers on a rotating basis to complement those burgers

The Quiet Corner

East of Hartford is an area the state's tourism promoters have nicknamed "the Quiet Corner." Bounded on the north by Massachusetts and on the east by Rhode Island, the Quiet Corner encompasses the lightly populated, slightly bucolic uplands of Tolland and Windham Counties. It is an area of peace and tranquility that has escaped both the bulldozers of the state's developers and the attention of the chic set. In truth, the Quiet Corner has such an air of serenity that in many places you can easily imagine that this is the way all of Connecticut looked 350 years ago. Fertile farmland abounds, and herb and flower gardens are among the region's most popular attractions. There are country inns that wouldn't be out of place in France. With some exceptions, the antiques here are neither quite as antique nor nearly as pricey as those sold in the trendier stores across the state in Litchfield County. And if other regions have more to offer the casual traveler, for the patient, the Quiet Corner has its own rewards.

THE QUIET CORNER

Nathan Hale Country

Marlborough

Seeing a small cluster of picturesque shops around a pond in **Marlborough** means you've reached the **Shops at Marlborough Barn** (45 N. Main St.; 860-295-1114; shopsatmarlboroughbarn.com). Actually, it's several barns and outbuildings that contain nearly 25 merchants. This is the place to shop for country furniture, crystal, antiques, knits, quilts, ironware, stoneware, collectibles, and more; many works are by local artisans. There's always something to pique your interest in the beautifully decorated room settings. Open Sun 10 a.m. to 4 p.m.; Tues through Fri 11 a.m. to 5 p.m., Sat 10 a.m. to 5 p.m.

Hebron

Hebron is a small town along Route 66 that is home to another example of Connecticut's roadside rock art, **Eagle Rock**, on the border with Marlborough. This rock had previous lives as a frog, a box turtle, and others, but it became an eagle in 1989 thanks to the talents of graduating RHAM High School student Jason Sawyer. Others now maintain the majestic bird, adding their initials and dates to its side.

Nearby on Route 85 is one of the most famous Connecticut ghost towns, Factory Hollow, nestled in **Gay City State Park** (Route 85; 860-295-9523; www.ct.gov/dep). Settled in 1796 by a religious sect named for the second leader, John Gay, the town once had 25 families, a sawmill, 2 gristmills, and a woolen mill. Along the Blackledge River straight up the main path from the parking lot you'll find the ruin of one of those mills, along with a cemetery filled with some of the abandoned village's residents. Wandering the trails here, you'll find many more stone foundations covered in grapevines and creepers.

Andover

Once in **Andover**, you will come across the **Hurst Farm** (746 East St.; 860-646-6536). If your kids have never seen livestock up close and personal, then we suggest a visit. The farm boasts gardens, hayrides, and a country store. You'll also find lots of standard farm critters, such as cows, goats, and lambs, as well as some of those exotic chickens with the punk-rocker hairdos. Adults will probably find more than enough to interest them at the food shop with James Hurst's own salsas, jams, and dried-herb blends, and lots of "only in Connecticut" food products. In fall, there are pick-your-own pumpkin and dig-your-own chrysanthemum patches. Open Tues to Fri 9 a.m.–5:30 p.m.; Sat 9 a.m.–4 p.m.; Closed Sun and Mon.

AUTHOR'S FAVORITES

Woodstock Fair, Woodstock

Willington Pizza House, Willington

UConn Dairy Bar, Storrs

Antiques Marketplace, Putnam

Diana's Pool, Chaplin

Coventry

Nathan Hale is Connecticut's official state hero, and there are Nutmeggers who feel about him kind of the way Tennesseans feel about Elvis. Hale (Yale class of 1773) was a fervent patriot who left his position as a local schoolmaster to join the rebellion against the British as soon as word arrived of the doings up at Lexington and Concord. He fought with the Continental army through most of 1776. In September of that year, he slipped into New York to gather information on British strength and deployments. After being caught (possibly as a result of being betrayed by a cousin), Hale was hanged by the British for spying. He was just 21. Our history books always reported his last words as "I only regret that I have but one life to lose for my country." However, the diaries of British captain Frederick MacKenzie, who witnessed Hale's execution, report young Nathan's final remarks as, "It is the duty of every good officer to obey any orders given him by his commander in chief."

The ***Nathan Hale Homestead*** (2299 South St.; 860-742-6917) was once Hale's home, which is sufficient to make it a landmark. Today, Hale might not recognize the house in which he grew up: It was rebuilt the year he died in the then-fashionable Georgian style. He'd probably recognize the surroundings, though. The house sits in the middle of the 1,219-acre ***Nathan Hale State Forest***, a wooded setting not too dissimilar from the surroundings of Hale's boyhood 300-acre farm. The farmhouse holds a collection of colonial antiques, including many of the personal possessions used by two generations of Hales. The homestead is the site of ***The Coventry Farmers' Market*** June through Oct on Sun 10 a.m. to 2 p.m. The homestead is open in May through Oct, Fri and Sat noon–4 p.m.; Sun 10 a.m.–2 p.m. Admission. Blue Star Museum.

While the nearby ***Nathan Hale Cemetery*** (Lake Street) in Coventry is a nice enough old graveyard—there's even an impressive marker for the man—Hale isn't buried there. After they hanged him, the British dumped his remains in an unmarked grave that now lies somewhere under 66th Street and 3rd Avenue in Manhattan.

Mansfield

Ballard Institute and Museum of Puppetry (1 Royce Circle, Ste 101B; 860-486-8580; bimp.uconn.edu), located on the University of Connecticut's Storrs campus, boasts a collection of more than 2,500 puppets and one of the country's largest collections of videotapes, films, and media about the art of puppetry. The institute is named for Frank W. Ballard who was hired as a set designer and technical director of the Jorgenson Theater when it was new in 1956. In 1962, Ballard added puppetry to the Drama, Art, and Music curriculum, which resulted in more than 400 student productions. He was responsible for the creation of the National Institute and Museum of Puppetry, which has morphed into the institute as it is today. More than half of the puppets in the institute's collection were created by Frank Ballard. Puppets and puppet lore dominate here. Some of the puppets are beautiful and charming; others are dark and disturbing; all are exquisite. Professor Ballard passed away in 2010, and the institute carries on in his memory. They offer workshops, tours, lectures, and performances year-round. Open Fri, Sun, and Wed 11 a.m.–5 p.m.; Sat 11 a.m.–7 p.m.; closed Mon and Tues. Admission by donation.

Groovy Like a Drive-in Movie

Like other states, Connecticut has a proud history as the one-time home of many drive-in movie theaters. There were at least 40 of them during the peak years of the 1950s. But, as has happened in the rest of the country, the drive-ins have gone dark town by town, leaving just two survivors. They're worth the trip.

Mansfield Drive-in (228 Stafford Rd.; 860-423-4441; mansfielddrivein.com) in Mansfield Center has been operating since 1954. It has three screens, all with double features. Open on weekends in April-May; in mid-June opens 7 days a week through Aug. It is recommended you arrive 30 minutes before show time. The theater also hosts an indoor/outdoor flea market end of Mar through mid-Nov every Sun from 8 a.m. to 2 p.m.

Southington Drive-in Theater (935 Meriden-Waterbury Tpke; 860-276-6219) opened in 1955. It has a single screen and operates June through mid-Sept. If their parking lot fills up, they welcome you to park your car in a recreation area down the road and bring chairs and/or blankets into their pavilion area to watch the movie. There's a per-person charge, with a family maximum equal to the price of a carload. It should also be noted that the Southington Drive-in as a business ceased to operate in 2002. Today the theater is owned by the town and is completely run by volunteers. All the profits go to various civic groups in the area. While they may not show current blockbuster movies, their line-up usually includes past favorites.

Regardless of which drive-in you choose, plan on arriving early; the parking lots can fill up fast.

With all the attention showered on UConn's famed basketball program, it's easy to forget that the school is also widely known for its excellent agriculture department. An offshoot of that department's activity is the ***UConn Dairy Bar*** (17 Manter Rd. #4263, Storrs; 860-486-1021; dining.uconn.edu), which has been around since the 1930s. Every day, about 25 flavors of frozen treats are on the menu, with old favorites such as chocolate, vanilla, strawberry, and coffee. Specialty flavors like Jonathan Supreme (named for the school's mascot) and peanut butter–swirled vanilla with chocolate-covered peanuts show up from time to time. According to more than one pistachio ice cream fanatic, the Dairy Bar is one of the few places in Connecticut that still churns up his favorite flavor with real pistachios, instead of green-dyed almonds. Servings are colossal. Open daily, 11 a.m.–7 p.m.

To work off some of that ice cream weight, try ***The Adventure Park at Storrs*** (2007 Storrs Rd.; 860-946-0606; myadventurepark.com/location/storrsct). This aerial forest includes zip-line, rope, tree-platform, and aerial bridge adventures with 9 different trails to try, all at different levels of difficulty, for a total of 60 different challenges throughout the park. Don't worry about falling; you will wear a harness and two clips that attach onto different ropes and cables. Open Apr to Nov, Fri 3 p.m.–8 p.m.; Sat 10 a.m.–10 p.m.; Sun 10 a.m.–6 p.m. It is also open during the week for groups.

Chaplin

A short distance from the busy UConn campus at Storrs, the Natchaug River rumbles through a shallow gorge and pours over a small waterfall into a clear pool at the center of a secluded, sun-dappled clearing. Winding over, under, and around the tumbled boulders on either shore are a handful of gentle walking trails. This is ***Diana's Pool***, and it is a secret picnic ground in ***Chaplin*** used mainly by local fisherfolk and UConn students.

Diana's Pool isn't easy to find, but it's worth the effort. Take US 6 and look for signs directing you to South Chaplin or Sherman Corners. Turn right onto Diana's Pool Road. This is a dead end, but about 100 feet up the road there's an unmarked parking area on the left (look for a No Swimming sign). From there walk about 100 feet down the trail; it branches a couple times, and if you're not sure which branch to follow, walk toward the sound of the water. At the end of the trail, you'll find yourself in a sylvan glade so perfect, you'll expect to see dryads and fauns frolicking. If you want to picnic, you'll have to do without picnic tables, but the sun-warmed rocks above the pool are a great place to spread a blanket and watch the play of sunlight and shadow on the water. Diana's Pool is relaxing at almost any time of the year. Cool autumn temperatures kill off the mosquito population and the fall foliage is in full color. Be sure to wear proper footwear for walking and rock climbing.

Tolland Area

Willington

Don't miss a meal at **Willington Pizza House** (25 River Rd.; 860-429-7433; willingtonpizza.com); it's a little slice of heaven with its small-town setting and decor running to carousel horses. Don't be fooled, though—the pizza selection is definitely big-city sophisticated. There's a broad selection of pies and toppings, including some low-fat pies for people watching their cholesterol. But the reason most people make the pilgrimage to **Willington** is the delicious Red Potato Pizza. This was the pie that gained nationwide attention. Although pizza pros in New Haven would disown it, the crunchy crust, garlicky roasted potatoes, and sour cream topping make for a rich and different pie that needs to be judged (repeatedly) on its own merits. You're always liable to come across picky pizza-pie mavens who claim that the only way to eat a Red Potato Pizza is with a side dish of iced caviar for topping each yummy slice. If nothing else, the folks at Willington Pizza give you choices. You'll find both the Heart Wise Pizza (tomatoes, onions, peppers, mushrooms, garlic, and broccoli on a red pizza; *no* cheese) and the Widowmaker Pizza (pepperoni, sausage, hamburger, bacon, Canadian bacon, cheddar and mozzarella cheese, all topped with Caribbean jerk spice). The choice is yours. Open Sun –Thurs 10:30 a.m.– 9 p.m.; Fri–Sat 10:30 a.m.–10 p.m.

There's now a second location, **Willington Pizza Too** (11 Phelps Way; 860-429-9030), because it's just that good.

Tolland

The lights are on, but nobody's home at Tolland's **Daniel Benton Homestead** (160 Metcalf Rd.; 860-872-8673; tollandhistorical.org/daniel-benton-homestead). A ghostly figure in a military uniform seems to appear at the front door. Footsteps echo through the east wing and then gradually trail off into silence. Occasionally the whole house shakes without making a sound.

A spokesman for the Tolland Historical Society, which acquired the Benton Homestead in the late 1960s, enigmatically notes that an old house plagued by a flying squirrel "can produce a lot of noise" but refrains from speculating on the subject of the supernatural. The society prefers to concentrate on the house's unusual architectural details, original paneling, and period furnishings, and the fact that it was the ancestral home of former US senator William Benton and used to house Hessian prisoners during the Revolution.

Area ghost watchers, on the other hand, have an abiding interest in the place and eagerly place the blame for certain strange goings-on at the homestead squarely on the shoulders of one Elisha Benton. In 1777, patriot Benton contracted smallpox while being held in a British prisoner-of-war camp. Sent home to Tolland to die, he was nursed by his 17-year-old sweetheart, Jemina Barrows. A little more than a month after Benton died in this house, Jemina succumbed to the same disease. Their graves lie 48 feet apart on the west lawn of the homestead.

During the years since this incident, the Benton Homestead is said to have played host to various ghostly activities. A member of the household staff claimed to have seen a weeping apparition in a white dress; a guest once reported hearing inconsolable sobbing at midnight; another common story has a uniformed figure wandering the house with arms outstretched as if pleading. The Benton Homestead opens in May and you should call to request a date and time for a tour. Donations appreciated.

Nearby, the 1856 **Old Tolland Jail Museum** (860-872-7718) on the green at the junction of Routes 74 and 195 housed prisoners until 1968. Today, the intimidating iron-and-stone structure houses the Tolland Historical Society's collection of antique manufactured goods, farm implements, furniture, and Native artifacts. The museum is open Memorial Day weekend through Sept, Sun 1 to 4 p.m., or by appointment. Admission. Blue Star Museum.

The **Tolland Military Museum** (749 Tolland Stage Rd.; 860-803-0034) opened in 2018 and includes the collection of Ashford resident Richard J. Provencher, including items relating to World War I, World War II, the Korean War, the Vietnam War, and Operation Desert Storm. Provencher is a retired Connecticut National Guard member. The museum is located in the building behind the Old Tolland County Jail and Museum and is open May through Sept, Sun noon to 3 p.m. Donations appreciated.

Vernon

As a rule, Nutmeggers understand delis as well as New Yorkers understand chowder. Which is to say that neither understands the other very much at all. A pleasant exception is **Rein's Deli-Restaurant** (435 Hartford Tpke.; 860-875-1344; reinsdeli.com) on Route 30 in **Vernon**. This is a large, noisy place, with brisk service and small tables that would be right at home in Gotham. The only reminders that you're still in Connecticut are the signs making witty references to New Yorkish things and places (with the restrooms naturally located in Flushing).

But never mind the decor. What counts is the authentic deli food you wouldn't be surprised to find at Manhattan's famed Carnegie. The half-sour pickles are crisp and briny. The firm, fat chips arrive smoking hot. The turkey, pastrami, and corned beef are eminently respectable and the Reubens rival the ones you get at the Manhattan deli from which that sandwich gets its name. If your taste doesn't run to deli meats and sandwiches, don't worry. The menu here is huge, and no matter when you stop by, you can get anything from blintzes to bagels, to lox and eggs, to a full dinner, to a diet plate. If you've ever wondered why New Yorkers rave about deli, here's your chance to find out without traveling to New York. Open daily, 8 a.m. to 8 p.m.

Union

North of Stafford, near the Massachusetts line, is Connecticut's smallest town, the diminutive settlement of **Union** (population 620). Most travelers pass by, but for bibliophiles, it's a standard stop en route to Massachusetts. For here resides one of the state's unique eateries, the **Traveler Restaurant** (1257 Buckley Hwy.; 860-684-4920). First and foremost a place for good, home-style cooking at decent prices, The Traveler has one special little twist. Not only can you order a decent meal here, but customers are invited to pick out three books from the shelves lining the walls, read while eating, and then take them home. That's right: Buy a meal, get a book. Children are well treated, and the supply of kids' books is great. The owners estimate they give away thousands of books a week. The Traveler serves breakfast, lunch, and dinner. Open Mon and Thurs 10 a.m.–8 p.m.; Fri 9 a.m.–8 p.m.; Sat and Sun 8 a.m.–8 p.m.; closed Tues and Wed.

Farther off the highway is **Bigelow Hollow State Park** (Route 171; 860-684-3430; ct.gov/dep), which hides a glacial valley that nestles Breakneck Pond. This is a haven for boaters and anglers—with some huge pike that roam the lakes—but also has 17 miles of blue-blazed trails. Listen for the sounds of beavers slapping their tails and pretend you are walking through the forests of post-glacial New England, thousands of years ago.

Eastford

Buell's Orchard (108 Crystal Pond Rd.; 860-974-1150; buellsorchard.com) in **Eastford** is a century-old farm stand par excellence. Starting in June with strawberries, the stand sells fresh produce throughout the growing season. August brings fresh peaches. Apples appear during the fall and can last well into the winter, depending on the size of the apple crop. The stand also sells cider, Vermont cheese, and pumpkins. The caramel apples are made with a special caramel sauce into which "firm late apples" are dipped. We guarantee that they are among the best you've ever tasted. The season for caramel apples

Gentlemen (and Women), Start Your Engines

You don't have to live in the Heartland or south of the Mason-Dixon Line to care a lot about NASCAR racing; it's a hugely popular spectator sport nationwide. Here in Connecticut, it also offers a welcome alternative to all the scenic vistas, quaint shops, historic homes, and nautical lore. In addition to Lime Rock, the racetrack that attracts the biggest names both on the track and in the stands, three other cozy, family-friendly NASCAR tracks in Connecticut offer weekly schedules of qualifying rounds, featured races, and special events:

Stafford Motor Speedway
55 West St.
Stafford Springs
(860) 684-2783
staffordmotorspeedway.com

Thompson International Speedway
205 E. Thompson Rd.
Thompson
(860) 923-2280
thompsonspeedway.com

New London–Waterford Speedbowl
1080 Hartford Tpke.
Waterford
(860) 574-9010
speedbowlct.com

starts about Labor Day and ends around Halloween. On Columbus Day weekend, the Buells celebrate the harvest with an open house that includes hayrides and free cider and doughnuts. Strawberry season begins in June: Mon–Sat 8 a.m.–noon, and Mon and Tues 6 p.m.–8 p.m. In mid-July, blueberry and peach season: Mon 8 a.m.–7 p.m.; Tues–Fri 8 a.m.–5 p.m.; Sat 8 a.m.–3 p.m. Apple and pumpkin season runs from Labor Day through Halloween: Mon–Sat 8 a.m.–5 p.m.; Sun 1–5 p.m. From Nov to Christmas Eve the farm is open Mon–Fri 9 a.m.–4 p.m.; Sat 9 a.m.–3 p.m. The farm is usually open after Christmas to January, Tues and Fri 9 a.m.–4 p.m.

Now that you've stocked up on yummy apples, cheese, and other goodies, you need a good place to have a picnic. Why not follow in the footsteps of tons of people and eat with the Frog. Yep, we're talking about another one of those great roadside pieces of rock art, only this one is probably the oldest in Connecticut and isn't exactly on the road anymore. The brainchild of ***Thomas Thurber***, a legislator in the 1880s who used to pass this rock every day, ***Frog***

Rock was on the side of the original Route 44. The story is that Thurber used to see it and envision a frog, so one day he stopped and painted it the way he saw it. It's been a frog ever since. Because it was along a heavily traveled road, it became a popular place for travelers to stop and picnic. When the new Route 44 was built, it no longer followed the same path, and Frog Rock faded into the background. In 1997, a group of Thurber's descendants gave Frog Rock a fresh coat of paint and included a memorial to their ancestor. Today, the Frog has company; in fact, he's pretty much presiding over a party these days.

The ***Frog Rock Summer Shack*** (212 Pomfret Rd. [Rte. 44]; 860-942-0131) now includes a children's playground with climbing equipment, a restaurant with standard roadside foods (burgers, fries, fried seafood, ice cream, etc.), and a gift shop with all the touristy items you'd expect. Sometimes there's even live music. The picnic tables are still there as well. While the Frog is always open, the rest stop is open Thurs through Sun, 11 a.m. to 8 p.m.

Old Woodstock

Pomfret

Christ Church (527 Pomfret St.; 860-315-7780; christchurchpomfret.org) on Route 169 in **Pomfret** is not the traditional white New England church with pointed steeple. Instead, this is a stone-and-brick building with a certain Byzantine influence. The interior, decorated in what one might call "High Victorian camp," makes an ideal backdrop for 6 extraordinary stained-glass windows, designed by famed Arts and Crafts designer ***Louis Comfort Tiffany*** early in his career and installed in the church in 1882.

Tiffany, a native of nearby Killingly, created the windows before moving to New York City, and all but one is an original Tiffany design. It is believed that Tiffany copied the Saint George window from an original Venetian design. Interestingly, the dedications and inscriptions in all six windows are rendered in lead, not in the more common paint, and the glass used is chunkier and more faceted than later Tiffany efforts. The themes here aren't typical to Tiffany, either. Instead of the common Tiffany floral and pastoral compositions, these items feature religious subjects like Saint George. There's also a window depicting the Parable of the Wise and Foolish Virgins and one depicting the Parable of the Talents, with the inscription, "Well done, my good and faithful servant." Finally, there is a rose window depicting Ezekiel and the wheel. Visit about an hour before sunset to get the full effect through the rose window. Call ahead or email the church office (christchurchpomfret@gmail.com) for a tour. Make sure you take a good look at the church's interior. It's a haven for gorgeous Arts and Crafts wood carving and tile work.

Route 169 weaves south from Woodstock through Pomfret, Brooklyn, and Canterbury and has been officially dubbed one of the 10 most outstanding *scenic byways* in the US. This section of the book wouldn't be complete without making adequate reference to Pomfret's favorite hangout, the **Vanilla Bean Cafe** (450 Deerfield Rd.; 860-928-1562; thevanillabeancafe.com). Housed in a renovated 19th-century barn, this is one irresistible place for lunch, dinner, or a midafternoon cup of cocoa. The soups here are fabulous—nothing fancy, just delicious, freshly prepared simple blends. The tomato Florentine paired with a salad is ideal for summertime weather. When winter comes, go for a warmer-upper, such as cheese-topped chili with beef or a vegetarian alternative. The black bean or herbed chevre burgers will fit the bill. The turkey sandwiches taste like the best of part of Thanksgiving dinner: day-after leftovers. They also offer a host of gluten-free options. The Vanilla Bean is run by the Jessurun family, and chances are you'll run into them when you visit. Unless you wind up being too full for dessert, the homemade ice cream really hits the spot after a chili lunch. In the evenings, patrons are often treated to entertaining poetry readings, folk concerts, and poetry slams. (The UConn campus at Storrs is close by, so creative talents abound.) Open Mon and Tues 8 a.m.–3 p.m.; Wed–Sun 8 a.m.–8 p.m.

Martha's Herbiary (589 Pomfret St.; 860-928-0009) on Route 169 at the junction of US 44 and Route 97 is a sweet-smelling treasure snuggled in the carriage house and servants' quarters of an 18th-century house. The gift shop is packed to the rafters with potpourri, soaps, essential oils, cooking herbs, and lotions. Cooking demonstrations and classes take place in the kitchen in the back. Outside, the gardens overflow with perennials, heirloom vegetables (vegetables grown from old strains of the plant, many dating back to colonial times), edible flowers, fish ponds, a sunken garden, and row upon row of herbs. Classes are offered throughout the year on a variety of topics, but reservations are required. The shop is open Tues through Sat 10 a.m. to 5 p.m.; Sun noon to 5 p.m.

The **Brayton Grist Mill & Marcy Blacksmith Shop Museum** (147 Wolf Den Dr.) off US 44, at the entrance to Mashamoquet Brook State Park, showcases two establishments that in 1857 made an agreement to jointly support a dam and flume on Mashamoquet Brook.

The 4-story Brayton Grist Mill is a reminder of long-ago days when every town on a river or creek had a water-powered mill to shell corn and grind grain. The gristmill on Mashamoquet Brook was operated by William Brayton from 1890 until his death in 1928. The equipment on display includes the turbine, the millstone, and a corn sheller patented in 1888.

woodstock & pomfret trivia

During the mid- to late 19th century, Woodstock and Pomfret were dubbed "inland Newports" due to their popularity with the rich and ostentatious, who trained up from New York or down from Boston to build lavish summer "cottages" in the Quiet Corner.

The Marcy Blacksmiths also plied their trade in a shop along Mashamoquet Brook; in fact, the area became known as Marcy Hollow. In 1830, Orin Marcy of Pomfret opened the shop, which used a water-powered bellows and trip-hammer. The next two generations of Marcys prospered, perfecting their craft. Darius, Orin's son, won first prize for his horseshoes at the Chicago World's Fair in 1893. A number of antique tools are displayed at the blacksmith shop; some are farrier's tools, and others are wheelwright's tools. Several tools are specially made and stamped "O. Marcy." The museum doesn't have a telephone, but it is open May through Sept, weekends 2 to 5 p.m. Admission is free.

Finish the day at **Sharpe Hill Vineyard** (108 Wade Road; 860-974-3549; sharpehill.com), which produces the best-selling wine in New England, Ballet of Angels, a semisweet summer pleaser, cool and refreshing. But don't neglect their other wines, such as the crisp Chardonnay or the St. Croix, which tastes like spiced roses. Walk up the hill behind the winery through the rows of grapevines and enjoy a view of Windham County and beyond into Massachusetts and Rhode Island. Open for tastings and sales, Fri through Sun 11 a.m.–1:30 p.m.

Ashford

Continuing west along US 44, you'll wind up in the quaint community of ***Ashford***, home to a wonderfully thrifty, only-in-New England version of recycling: a library in the old town dump! It's a metaphor for the regional motto, "Use it up. Wear it out. Make it do or do without." Which makes this "library" at the **Ashford Transfer Station** such a practical idea. It happened this way: A few years back, folks began remarking that a lot of perfectly good books were being sent to the dump, so the people down at the town's **Babcock Public Library** put their heads together to come up with a way to get some more mileage from these castoffs. What they came up with was an "annex" of the library at a central location—the, er, dump—where people could drop off or pick up used books free of charge.

So the Ashford Transfer Station, where residents take their recyclables and trash, gained a plywood shed with simple plank shelving. Now, when residents drop off their recyclables, more often than not they stop by the "annex" to browse the shelves and pick up a couple novels. The arrangements are simple. Books are divided into broad categories such as "mysteries," "westerns," or "romance," with titles running the gamut from those of Stephen King and Tom Clancy to books of philosophy and children's books; drop off what you've read and take as many other books as you want. People from outside of Ashford—such as you—are welcome to use the library, but trash services are for Ashford residents only. The transfer station "library" (232 Upton Rd.; 860-429-3409) is open Wed 2 to 8 p.m.; Sat 8 a.m. to 4 p.m.; Sun 10 a.m. to 4 p.m.

Woodstock

Merchant and publisher **Henry Chandler Bowen** had two great obsessions: roses and the Fourth of July. He indulged both at his summer residence in the center of **Woodstock**, in the northeastern corner of Connecticut. There, in 1846, he built himself a board-and-batten-sided, gingerbread-encrusted Gothic Revival palace. Outside he planted a rose garden, and inside he upholstered much of the furniture in pink. The house itself he painted a fashionably subdued light lavender, but it was later repainted pink with green shutters and dark green and red trim, reminiscent of the flowers that Bowen loved. He named this classic Victorian "painted lady" **Roseland Cottage** (556 Rte. 169; 860-928-4074; historicnewengland.org/property/roseland-cottage), but today, most folks in Woodstock just call it "the pink house."

During the latter half of the 19th century, Roseland hosted the most extravagant series of Fourth of July celebrations that America had ever seen. On the day before each celebration, prominent guests from all over the country would arrive by train in neighboring Putnam, whence they would be transported by carriage to Woodstock for an evening reception that featured (what else?) pink lemonade. The next day, a huge American flag would be displayed on one side of the house. The guests would then parade down Route 169 to Roseland Park, where they would amuse the public and each other with exchanges of high-flying rhetoric until it was time to return to Roseland for further diversions of a nonalcoholic nature. (Bowen was a temperance man.) What makes all of this so remarkable is that no fewer than four US presidents—Benjamin Harrison, Ulysses S. Grant, Rutherford B. Hayes, and William McKinley—participated in these shenanigans; two of them—Harrison and Grant—while in office, the others while they were congressmen.

gloriousfalldrive

In the Quiet Corner, there's no prettier fall drive than Route 169. Start at the intersection of Rocky Holly Road in Lisbon and head off to Woodstock and points north.

> ### No Clothes, No Kidding
>
> *Solair Recreation League* (65 Ide Perrin Rd., Woodstock; 860-928-9174; solairrl.com) is what our mothers in their most shocked voices used to call a "nudist camp." It's been around since the 1930s and offers 360 acres of wooded solitude. Amenities include a lake, rental cabins, pool, tennis and volleyball courts, and a social hall. Visitors are welcome provided you make reservations in advance. The office welcomes visitors daily but suggests you come in on a weekend between 10 a.m. and 2 p.m. to meet with a staff member who can show you around.
>
> You'll find the Solair Recreation League off English Neighborhood Road in Woodstock. Before dropping in, call for directions, hours, more information, and reservations. Open June to Labor Day, Sun–Wed 9 a.m.–4 p.m.; Thurs and Sat 9 a.m.–6 p.m.; Fri 9 a.m.–8 p.m.

Today, Roseland Cottage and its grounds and outbuildings are maintained by Historic New England and open to the public. The rose garden is still there, along with an 1850s maze of boxwood hedges, and so is most of the original Gothic Revival furniture. The famous flag is displayed in its traditional location each Fourth of July. Even the bowling alley out in the barn, thought to be the oldest such facility in a private residence in America, is still as it was. One can almost imagine Ulysses Grant—who seems to have coped well at Roseland even though he was most definitely not a temperance man—bowling his famous strike there during his July 4 visit. Open June through Oct, Thurs through Sun, 11 a.m. to 4 p.m. (last tour at 3 p.m.). Admission.

The Christmas Barn (835 Rte. 169; 860-928-7652) is more than just a red barn full of Christmas paraphernalia. The year-round display of Christmas decorations upstairs is balanced by displays of country furniture, crafts, lace curtains, curios, collectibles, quilts, craft supplies, and Victoriana suitable for all seasons. Besides, owners Joe and Kris Reynolds are that rare breed of people who seem able to keep the Christmas spirit alive all year. Open Aug through Dec, Thurs, Fri, and Sat, 10 a.m. to 5 p.m.

Putnam

Woodbury may boast Connecticut's "Antique Avenue," but in **Putnam** you've got a whole Windham County town full of antiques shops. Okay, some carry merchandise that's somewhere just above "tag-sale stuff" on the antiques food chain, but most are chockablock with high-quality, well-maintained furnishings, collectibles, and jewelry.

When its main industries quite literally went south, the community and its citizens could have held a pity party and thrown in the towel. Instead, they transformed Putnam into one of the hottest antiques shopping districts in New England. Now more than 400 dealers do business here; most are scattered throughout the Main Street area in a former mill, the old courthouse, and an 1880s Victorian department store.

The anchor attraction is the 4-story **Antiques Marketplace** (109 Main St.; 860-928-0442; antiquesmarketplace.tumblr.com) in what used to be the C. D. Bugbee Department Store. Jerry Cohen, a transplanted Californian, accomplished the changeover. There are 350 dealer spaces in the 22,000-square-foot building, and the vendors are as varied as the goods they carry. Their profiles are on the marketplace's website and, if you read them, you'll see the wealth of knowledge and passion they bring to the items they collect. A trip here is as much about learning as it is about shopping. The entire antiques district is open Wed through Mon from 10 a.m. to 5 p.m.

Arts and Framing (136 Main St.; 860-963-0105) is the place to visit for antique mirrors and frames, custom hand-gilding, and glass as well as some antique furniture and accessories. Open Thurs through Sun, 11 a.m. to 5 p.m.

Jeremiah's (26 Front St.; 860-928-0666) is a large, multi-dealer shop, with an ever-changing display of estate jewelry, china, and glass, in addition to Victorian and country-primitive furniture. Open Wed through Mon, 10 a.m. to 5 p.m.

If you are celebrating (or regretting) some of your purchases, take a walk along the **River Mills Heritage Trail** (Kennedy Drive; 860-963-6811), which winds along the Quinebaug River. Park near the corner of Kennedy Drive and Pomfret Street and you will see the 1868 Monohansett Mill, where 2.75 million yards of cotton sheetings and shirtings were produced every year. Crossing the bridge on Pomfret Street, you will get great views of Cargill Falls. On Church Street, you will pass the 1868 Morse Mansion, a brick Victorian Italianate villa, and the 1874 Old Putnam High School, now the town hall. The path turns right

Stone Walls

When you venture off the beaten path in Connecticut, one of the first things you'll notice is the labyrinth of stone walls that snake across the landscape. Glaciers that inched their way across the region close to 20,000 years ago scraped the earth as they went, carrying tons of rocks and boulders with them. Farmers had to remove this debris so they could till the soil and plant their crops. The mortarless stone walls you see throughout the area were originally built to make use of the rocks that had been liberally deposited everywhere and to mark field boundaries. Today they serve as elegant property accents, adorning many of the state's most opulent homesteads. These days, craftsmen who have mastered the ancient art of stonewall construction are well compensated.

off of Church Street into a riverside park, where you'll find the 1861 Morse Mill, another textile manufacturing plant. Turn right onto Providence Street and cross the river again near the upper falls. The Belding and Powhatan Mill is on this side of the street, incidentally where the office of the Last Green Valley National Heritage Corridor is located today. After observing two more mills, the 1842 Rhodes and 1861 Nightingale, you can continue back along the river to your car.

If all that walking has left you a tad peckish, central Putnam offers a modest selection of handy eateries for lunch and light noshing. A recommendable luncheon choice, with homemade soups and a selection of artful sandwiches, is the **Courthouse Bar & Grille** (121 Main St.; 860-963-0074; courthouse barandgrille.com). Open Sun–Thurs 11:30 a.m.–10 p.m.; Fri and Sat 11:30 a.m–midnight.

Windham Area

Killingly

You know you've found **Zip's Dining Car** (725 Hartford Turnpike; 860-774-6335; zipsdinerct.hibuwebsites.com) when you see the neon sign that towers over the building advertising with commendable brevity: eat. Located at the junction of Routes 101 and 12 (exit 93 off I-395) in the Dayville section of **Killingly**, Zip's is an original O'Mahoney diner, built in 1954.

The diner is actually a New England invention. Its progenitor, the lunch wagon, was invented by Walter Scott in 1872 in Providence, Rhode Island. More improvements followed, and in 1906 the Worcester Lunch Car Company was born. It soon was the primary popularizer of the Art Deco, neon-crowned, nickel-alloy (later stainless-steel) structure that we now associate with the American diner.

Zip's is one of the last of the original stainless-steel diners still in operation and is especially notable for its pristine condition. The quilted and beveled stainless steel and the blue-accented chrome just gleam. This is a family-run restaurant that has been in the same family for three generations.

Zip's menu is classic diner fare, featuring freshly prepared food, most of it made from scratch. The roast turkey with all the trimmings and the Yankee pot roast are both big dinner favorites. For lunch hoist a huge Zip's Burger (an especially good cheeseburger on a bulky roll) or a turkey club (made with freshly roasted turkey); these examples of the sandwich-making art are as well executed as you will find anywhere. Open Mon to Thurs 6 a.m.–2 p.m.; Fri–Sun 6 a.m.–4 p.m.

Head south from Zip's on Route 12 and you'll hit **Logee's Greenhouse** (141 North St.; 860-774-8038; logees.com), which has been a family operation since 1893, so when it comes to plants, they speak gospel truth. The six greenhouses feature a range of plants, including herbs, house plants, passion flowers, bonsais, and more. Logee's publishes a mail-order catalog that's available at a small charge. Logee's is open Wed–Sun 9 a.m.–5 p.m.

Plainfield

If you're into fishing, consider putting **Plainfield** on your itinerary. The modern **Quinebaug Valley State Trout Hatchery** (141 Trout Hatchery Rd.; 860-564-7542) in the township's Central Village is one of the largest hatcheries in the East. The operation is open to the public year-round, Mon to Fri 8 a.m. to 3 p.m., and visitors can view the hatchery through a big glass wall. The state allows restricted fishing in the nearby waters weekends from Mar through Memorial Day. And there's a fishing pond at the hatchery that is often stocked.

Keep driving west from the Plainfield area on Route 14A until you're almost in Rhode Island. There, in the hamlet of **Oneco** (where Route 14A is known as Pond Road), you'll find something called **River Bend Campground** (41 Pond St.; 860-564-3440; riverbendcamp.com), which offers the Lucky Strike Mine and Gemstone Panning Sluice. While you won't exactly find the treasure of the Sierra Madres here, children can don miners' hats and delve into an aboveground man-made mine in search of gemstones, fossils, or shells, or try their luck panning the sluice. Open Mon to Thurs 9 a.m.–8 p.m.; Fri and Sat 9 a.m.–9 p.m.; Sun 9 a.m.–6 p.m. from mid-Apr to mid-Oct. Admission.

Moosup (pronounced MOOSE-up) may be Connecticut's most patriotic village. On the Sunday closest to August 14 (V-J Day, the day Japan surrendered), the entire town turns out for its ***"Victory over Japan" Parade.*** Sadly, this is the last of its kind in the country. You'll see flags, brightly costumed marching bands, and baton twirlers, but the day really is for the vets. Marchers parade from N. Main Street to Prospect Street, starting at 1:01 p.m. (the time Japan surrendered) and lasting until around 3:30 p.m. The parade is free; come early and bring your own lawn chairs. Call (860) 564-8005 for more information.

Canterbury

In 1832, at the request of the **Canterbury** community, **Prudence Crandall** opened an academy on the Canterbury Green to educate the daughters of local wealthy families. The school flourished until the following fall, when Crandall admitted Sarah Harris, a 20-year-old African American woman. Outraged parents withdrew their daughters, forcing the school to close. But Crandall reopened it as a school for the education of "young ladies and little misses of color." The state responded by passing the "Black Law," which made it illegal for Crandall to run her school. Crandall was arrested and spent one night in jail. She was taken to court, but the case was dismissed for lack of evidence. Despite her legal victory, she ultimately closed the school after it was attacked by a mob. Although Crandall's school was open for less than two years, it stands as a powerful symbol in the fight for racial equality and civil justice.

The 1805 building in Canterbury where Miss Crandall's academy was housed is preserved as the **Prudence Crandall House Museum** (1 S. Canterbury Rd.; 860-546-7800), a site for both permanent and changing exhibits on the history of Black Americans in pre–Civil War Connecticut. There are also exhibits dealing with the life of Prudence Crandall and the development of Canterbury. The museum has a gift shop and a research library. Open May through Oct, Wed through Sun, 10 a.m. to 4 p.m.; open for 2 tours on Sundays from mid-Nov to the end of Apr. Admission. Blue Star Museum.

ANNUAL EVENTS IN THE QUIET CORNER

FEBRUARY
Essex Ed Groundhog Day Parade
Main Street, Essex
essexct.com

MARCH
Hebron Maple Festival
22 Main St., Hebron
(860) 228-5971
hebronct.com

JULY
Willimantic Boombox Parade
Main Street, Willimantic
wili.com

AUGUST
Brooklyn Fair
15 Fairgrounds Rd., Brooklyn
(860) 779-0012
brooklynfair.org
Founded in 1809, the oldest continuously operating fair in the United States

SEPTEMBER
Hebron Harvest Fair
Hebron Lion's Fairgrounds
347 Gilead St. (Route 85)
(860) 228-0542
hebronharvestfair.org

Woodstock Fair
Routes 169 and 171
(860) 928-3246
woodstockfair.com

Four Town Fair
56 Egypt Rd., Somers
(860) 749-6527
4townfair.com

NOVEMBER
Northeast Connecticut Region Ember Art Festival
nectrct.org

Brooklyn

Creamery Brook Road in bucolic **Brooklyn** is bordered by the usual Quiet Corner collection of quaint stone walls and verdant pastures. That's as expected. What's completely unexpected is the herd of shaggy bison. After all, Connecticut isn't exactly known for being where the buffalo roam—except that they do now. Austin and Deborah Tanner started out buying one bison for their dairy farm and ended up with a small, shaggy herd of American bison on their **Creamery Brook Bison Farm** (19 Purvis Rd.; 860-779-0837; creamerybrookbison.net).

The Tanners offer prearranged tours of their working farm; you just need to call and schedule. They also sell healthful, lean, red bison meat, and you can purchase various cuts of bison meat at the farm or you can order online and have it shipped. The Tanners suggest bison burgers are a good way to start. Fresh eggs and souvenirs are also sold at the farm store. The Tanners participate in local fairs and hold events throughout the year. A complete calendar can be found on their website.

The **Brooklyn Town Hall** (4 Wolf Den Rd.; 860-779-3411) was built in 1820 as the Windham County Courthouse. It was here in 1833 that Prudence Crandall was tried for violating the "Black Law" by running a school for African American students in nearby Canterbury. Taking a stand against discrimination, Crandall pleaded not guilty and refused to post bail. She defiantly spent a night in a cell in the basement of the courthouse, but she wasn't alone. Mary Benson, daughter of prominent abolitionist George Benson, volunteered to stay with her. The next day, George Benson and Rev. Samuel May paid the bond for her release. May also spoke for her at a Canterbury town meeting since at that time it was not considered appropriate for women to do so, while Benson allowed her to remain at his house during her two-day trial.

You can still see the **Benson family home** (60 Pomfret Rd.), where Reverend May officiated the 1834 wedding between George Benson's daughter Helen and William Lloyd Garrison, the publisher of *The Liberator* of Boston. You can also see the **Unitarian Meeting House** (7 Hartford Rd.), the first church of its denomination in the state, where May served as the first pastor starting in 1822. All these places are on the Freedom Trail. While you can visit the town hall and meetinghouse, please respect the privacy of the owners of the Pomfret Road homes, which are not open to the public.

Scotland

On the north side of Route 14, just west of **Scotland**'s town green, is the **Huntington House Museum** (36 Huntington Rd.; 860-423-1547; huntingtonhomestead

.org). This is the birthplace of Samuel Huntington, an important but too often forgotten Founding Father of the nation. Born in 1731, he grew up here before apprenticing as a cooper and studying law part-time. Elected to the Connecticut General Assembly in 1764, Huntington was appointed to Governor Trumbull's Council of Safety and then the Continental Congress, where he was named president in 1779. While in this position, Huntington and the rest of Congress ratified the Articles of Confederation, making him technically the first president of the States. Later, he became governor of Connecticut, adopted the Constitution, and served in the office until his death. Open May through Oct on the first Sat of each month, 11 a.m. to 3 p.m.

Windham & Willimantic

Willimantic ("Willi" to locals), a village in Windham, is home to the largest thread mill in America and is sometimes called the "Thread City." So where else would you locate a museum dedicated to the history of the textile industry? The **Windham Textile and History Museum** (411 Main St.; 860-456-2178; millmuseum.org) occupies two 1877 buildings inside the mill complex of the old Willimantic Linen Company on Main Street. Dugan Mill is a 2-story brick building housing a factory setting re-creating conditions of a century ago. There's a fully equipped shop floor with a spinning frame, carding machine, loom, and 1880s cast-iron proof printer. Overlooking the shop is an 1890-vintage overseer's office.

The museum's 3-story main building houses a re-creation of the company store that once occupied the site; it's now set up as a gift shop. The museum also offers re-creations of a 19th-century mill owner's mansion and a mill worker's home. The Dunham Hall Library, on the third floor, contains a one-of-a-kind collection of books, photographs, and manuscripts, including a collection of old textile industry pattern books. Open Sat and Sun, 10 a.m. to 4 p.m. Guided tours offered the second Sun of the month at 2 p.m.; self-guided at other times. Admission. The museum sponsors special events throughout the year.

The sleepy village of **Windham** isn't well known these days. Two centuries back, however, the **Windham Frog Pond** was famous throughout England and her colonies. During the long hot summer of 1754, war and drought endangered Windham. As that summer drew to a close, ponds and streams across Connecticut were almost dry, a catastrophe for an agricultural community. That year, though, Windhamites had other worries. With the French and Indian War in full swing, they could expect especially ferocious Indian raids at the end of summer. One hot night, worried residents heard an uproar coming from a marshy pond outside the village. It sounded, they thought, like the chanting of hundreds of Indians working themselves up to an attack. Some even thought they heard someone utter the words "Colonel Dyer and Elderkin, too." Dyer and Elderkin were the community's leaders.

All night long the sound continued as the town marshaled its defenses. In the last hour before dawn, the noise rose to a crescendo before dying out at first light. Their nerves drawn taut as bowstrings, the desperate colonists prepared to fend off the expected attack. But it never came. After a while, a scouting party crept through a swamp to the pond from whence the startling noises had come. There, they found not the expected French and Indians, but thousands of dying bullfrogs choking in the shallow waters of the pond. No one could explain what had happened, but it was a wonder and no mistake.

The Frog War story eventually became well known in Europe, so much so that it was made into a popular operetta that brought notoriety, if not fame, to the small town of Windham. In honor of the frogs, the town renamed the site Frog Pond. Windham Frog Pond can be seen today about a mile east of Windham Center on the Scotland Road (Route 14); the pond is on your left as you cross Indian Hollow Brook.

A few years ago, Windham announced that it was adopting a new town seal. The winning entry featured—you guessed it—a frog.

To that end, the town has another frog attraction: **Frog Bridge** just outside of downtown Willimantic. Completed in 2000, this bridge cost the city $13 million. On this bridge are four 11-foot frogs atop spools of thread. The bridge crosses the Willimantic River and connects Routes 66 and 32.

Places to Stay in the Quiet Corner

ASHFORD

Henrietta House Bed and Breakfast
125 Ashford Center Rd.
(860) 207-4001
historichenriettahousebnbct.com
Moderate
1700s house with 5 working fireplaces, hand-sawn paneling, and beehive oven

COVENTRY

Daniel Rust House B&B
2011 Main St.
(860) 742-0032
thedanielrusthouse.com
Moderate to expensive
Located in a lovingly restored pre-Revolutionary homestead on 2 acres

WOODSTOCK

Inn at Woodstock Hill
94 Plaine Hill Rd.
(860) 928-0528
woodstockhill.com
Moderate to expensive
Twenty-one guest rooms, 8 with working gas fireplaces

Mansion at Bald Hill
29 Plaine Hill Rd.
(860) 974-3456
mansionatbaldhill.com
Wedding venue with bed-and-breakfast guest rooms and a stellar restaurant

Woodstock Sustainable Farms and The Manton-Green Bed and Breakfast
211 Pulpit Rock Rd.
(888) 788-8726
wssfarms.com
Expensive
B&B on a 200-acre "farm for the future" with pasture-raised animals and heirloom vegetables

Places to Eat in the Quiet Corner

COVENTRY

Bidwell Tavern
1260 Main St.
(860) 742-6978
Thebidwelltavern.com
Moderate
Long-standing 1822 tavern serving some of the best chicken wings in the state

PUTNAM

85 Main
85 Main St.
(860) 928-1660
85main.com
Moderate to expensive
New American fusion cuisine, including a full sushi menu

The Stomping Ground
132 Main St.
(860) 928-7900
the-stomping-ground.com
Moderate
Pub grub and live music; craft beer

MANSFIELD

Fenton River Grille
135A Storrs Rd.
(860) 786-7870
Fentonrivergrill.com
Moderate to expensive
Twenty draft lines plus local craft brews, flatbreads, salads, seafood, burgers

WILLIMANTIC

Willimantic Brew Pub
967 Main St.
(860) 423-6777
willimanticbrewingcompany.com
Moderate
Located in a former 1909 post office, seven-barrel brewery

Index

1760 Sheldon Tavern, 86

A

Aaron Burr, 87
Abbey of Regina Laudis, 93
Abigail's Grille & Wine Bar, 45
Abijah Rowe House, 39
Academy Hall, 26
Adventure Park at Storrs, The, 199
African-American Memorial, 15
Airline State Park Trail, 165
Alanson Freeman, 73
Albany Turnpike, 68
Aldrich Contemporary Art Museum, 129
Alexander Calder, 95
Allegra Farm, 169
Allis-Bushnell House, 151
Alpheus Quicy, 30
American Clock & Watch Museum, 63
American Mural Project, 71
American Steamed Cheeseburgers, 125
Amistad, 118
Amistad Center for Arts & Culture, The, 13
Amistad Memorial, 119
Ancient Burying Ground, 15
Andover, 196
Anne Conover Nature Education Trail, 149
Antique and Artisan Center, 104
Antique Avenue, 94
Antiques Marketplace, 209
Antiques on the Farmington, 47
Arnold Family Homestead, 177
Arrigoni Winery, 166
Arts and Framing, 209
Ashford, 206
Ashford Transfer Station, 206
Austin House, The, 14
Avery-Copp House, 181
Avery-Copp House Museum, 184
Avery's Beverages, 60
Avon, 48
Avon Old Farms School, 48

B

Babcock Public Library, 206
Bafflin Sanctuary, 165
Bakehouse of Litchfield, The, 85
Ballard Institute and Museum of Puppetry, 198
Bantam Bread Company, 91
Bantam Cinema and Arts Center, 90
Barker Character, Comic, and Cartoon Museum, 122
Barkhamsted, 69
Barnum Museum, 109
Bart's Drive-In, 33
Battell Memorial Chapel, 73
Battle of Ridgefield, 129
Bear Mountain, 75
Beatrix Farrand, 55
Beaumont home, 176
Beinecke Rare Book and Manuscript Library, 115
Bellamy-Ferriday House and Garden, 93
Benedict Arnold, 176
Benedict Arnold Walking Trail of Colonial Norwichtown, 177
Benjamin Tallmadge, 85
Benson family home, 213
Bethany, 122
Bethel, 132
Bethlehem, 92
Bethlehem Christmas Town Festival, 93
B. F. Clyde's Cider Mill, 186
Bigelow Hollow State Park, 202
Big Red Gift Barn, 41
Bishop's Orchards Farm Market & Winery, 151
Bishop's Orchards Winery, 151
Bittner Park, 147
Black Pond State Park, 125
Blue Slope Country Museum, 176

Bluff Head Trails, 147
Bluff Point State Park, 185
Board & Brush, 61
Bolton, 31
Book Barn, 173
Book Barn Downtown, 173
Books on the Common, 130
Boothe Memorial Park and Gardens, 113
Bradley Mountain Farm, 61
Braemore Preserve, 147
Branford, 141
Branford's Stony Creek, 141
Branford Trail, The, 143
Brayton Grist Mill & Marcy Blacksmith Shop Museum, 205
Breakwater Books, 148
Bridgeport, 109
Brignole Vineyards, 39
Brookfield, 134
Brookfield Craft Center, 134
Brooklyn, 213
Brooklyn Town Hall, 213
Brownstone Exploration & Discovery Park, 165
Bruce Museum, 102
Buell's Orchard, 202
Bull's Bridge, 82
buried treasure, 114
Burlington, 51
Burlington Fish Hatchery, 51
Burlington Land Trust, 52
Burr Pond State Park, 84
Bushnell Carousel, 16
Bushnell Park, 15
Bushnell Park Foundation, 17
Buttonwood Farm, 191
Byrd's Books, 132

C

Caboose Ice Cream Stand, 162
Cambridge House Brew Pub, 41
Camille's Way, 161
Campbell Falls State Park, 73
Canaan, 73
Canfield Corner Pharmacy, 94
Cannon Square, 187
Canterbury, 211

Canton, 47
Canton Historical Museum, 47
Captain Amos Palmer House, 189
Captain John Gallup, 185
Captain Nathaniel B. Palmer House, 187
Captain Richard Pitkin, 28
Captain William Kidd, 141
Cass Gilbert, 124
Cato Corner Farm, 174
Center Church on the Green, 116
Central Connecticut State University, 59
Chamard Vineyards, 154
Chaplin, 199
Chapter Three, 173
Charles Henry Boebe, 180
Charles Island, 114
Chatfield Hollow State Park, 158
Cheshire, 121
Chick Austin, 95
Chief Waramaug, 96
Childe Hassam, 102, 129
Children's Museum of Southeastern Connecticut, 173
Children's Museum, The, 22
Christ Church, 204
Christmas Barn, The, 208
Christmas Shop, The, 41
Cindy's Unique Shop, 126
City Fish Market, 24
Clarke Outdoors, 77
Cliff of Tears, 185
Clinton, 153
Coffee An', 107
Colchester, 174
Collins Company, 47
Collins Creamery, The, 37
Collinsville, 47
Collinsville Antiques Co. of New Hartford, 68
Collinsville Canoe and Kayak, 48
Colten-Hayes Barn, 40
Commerford Zoo, 83
Comstock Bridge, 174
Connecticut Antique Fire Apparatus Association, 33
Connecticut Antique Machinery Association, 81

Connecticut Audubon Birdcraft Museum, 108
Connecticut Audubon Society, 108
Connecticut Department of Energy and Environmental Protection Marine Fisheries Headquarters and Boating Division, 172
Connecticut Electric Railway Association, 32
Connecticut Firemen's Historical Society, 30
Connecticut Fire Museum, 32
Connecticut Forest and Park Association, 161
Connecticut Freedom Trail, 70, 103, 116
Connecticut Freedom Trail Quilt Project., 10
Connecticut Motor Coach Museum, 32
Connecticut Museum of History and Culture, 19
Connecticut River Foundation's Connecticut River Museum, 155
Connecticut's Beardsley Zoo, 110
Connecticut's Old State House, 11
Connecticut's State Capitol, 10
Connecticut Trolley Museum, 32
Connecticut Veteran's Memorial, 21
Coogan Farm, 185
Cook-Fowler House, 160
Cooley School House, 39
Copernican Observatory and Planetarium, 59
Corning Fountain, 17
Cornwall, 76
Cornwall Bridge Pottery Store, 78
Cornwall Farm Market, 78
Country Quilt Llama Farm, 79
Courthouse Bar & Grille, 210
Coventry, 197
Coventry Farmers' Market, The, 197
Creamery Brook Bison Farm, 213
Crying Child Rock, 74
Crystal Ridge Winery, 27
Custom House Maritime Museum, 180

D
Danbury, 133
Danbury Museum and Historical Society, 133
Danbury Railway Museum, 134
Daniel Benton Homestead, 200
Daniel Lathrop School House, 177
David K. Leff "Hidden in Plain Sight Trail", 71
Deacon John Grave House, 152
Deep River, 157
Deep River Ancient Muster, 157
Deerfield Farm, 161
Denison Pequotsepos Nature Center, 185
Derby, 112
Devil's Hopyard, 170
Dewey-Granby Oak, 40
Diana's Pool, 199
Dinosaur Place at Nature's Art Village, The, 179
Dinosaur State Park, 25
Discovering Amistad, 119
Discovery Museum and Planetarium, 109
Dr. Anselm Franz, 113
Dr. Dolittle, 158
Dr. Hezekiah Chaffee House, 33
Dr. Jonathan Rothberg, 154
Dr. Reuben Smith's 1781 Apothecary Shop, 85
Dr. Reuben Smith's house, 86
Dr. William Beaumont, 176
Dudley Farm Museum, 146
Dudley Farm,, The, 146
Dudley Foundation, 146
Dudleytown, 79
Durham, 159
Durham Market, 159
Dwight Hall, 114

E
Eagle Rock, 196
Earthplace, 107
Eastern National Ski Jumping Championships, 76

Eastford, 202
East Granby, 37
East Granby Farms Recreation Area, 38
East Haddam, 166
East Hartford, 28
East Haven, 119
East Windsor, 32
Edith Morton Chase, 89
Elephant's Trunk Flea Market, 82
Elias Austin House, 160
Eli Whitney Museum, 119
Elizabeth Park, 18
Elizabeth Park Conservancy, 18
Empower Leadership Sports & Adventure Center, 164
Enders Falls, 43
Enders State Forest, 43
Enfield, 36
Eric Sloane, 81, 137
Eric Sloane Museum & Kent Iron Furnace, 81
Essex, 155
Essex Steam Train and Riverboat, 156
Ethan Allen Way, 79
Eugene O'Neill, 182
Eunice Mauwee, 82
Evergreen Cemetery, 158

F

Fairfield, 108
Fairfield Museum and History Center, 108
Fairfield Town Green, 108
Fair Weather Acres, 27
Fair Weather Café, 161
fall foliage, 69, 137, 155
Falls Village, 73
Famous 50's Diner, 110
Farmington, 53
Farmington Canal Greenway, 121
Farmington Historical Society, 56
Farmington Memorial Town Forest, 54
Farmington River Tubing, 68
Farmington Valley Arts Center, 49
Farmington Valley Railroad Society, 47
Faulkner's Island Lighthouse, 150
Faulkner's Light Brigade, 150

Ferris Acres Creamery, 135
Firehouse 12, 118
Fire Museum, 30
First Baptist Church (Greenwich), 102
First Baptist Church (Milford), 114
First Church of Christ, 167
First Company of the Governor's Horse Guards, 49
First National Bank of Litchfield, 85
Fisher Gallery and Shop, 49
Fisher Meadows, 48
Five-Mile Point Light, 118
Flamig Farm, 46
Florence Griswold Museum, 171
Flutterby, 148
Fort Griswold Battlefield State Park, 184
Fort Trumbull, 182
Founders Bridge Promenade, 28
Frances Osborne Kellogg, 112
Franklin, 176
Frank Pepe Pizzeria Napoletana, 117
Freedom Forest, 179
Fresh Salt, 155
Frog Bridge, 215
Frog Rock, 204
Frog Rock Summer Shack, 204

G

Gardner State Park, 174
Gay City State Park, 196
Gelston House, 167
General David Humphreys House, 112
geocaching, 43
George Dunkelberger, 103
Giles Kilborn, 86
Gillette Castle, 168
Glastonbury, 27
Glebe House Museum and Gertrude Jekyll Garden, 94
Goatboy Soaps, 91
Gold's Pines, 78
Goodman Green, 21
Goodspeed Opera House, 166
Goodspeed's Station Country Store, 158
Gordon Van Tine mail-order house, 39
Goshen, 82
Gouveia Vineyards, 128

Granby, 39
Granby Artists Association, 40
Grand-Am Championship Weekend, 75
Granny's Pie Factory, 28
Grassroots Ice Cream, 40
Great Mountain Forest, 74
Great River Park, 28
Greenwich, 102
Greenwood Glass, 70
Griswold, 191
Griswold Inn, 156
Guilford, 146
Guilford Green, 147
Guilford Harbor, 148
Guilford Land Conservation Trust, 150
Guilford Salt Meadows Sanctuary, 149
Gungywamp, 185
Gunntown Cemetery, 122
Gutenberg Bible, 115

H

Haddam's Whole Harmony 4 U, 159
Haley Farm State Park, 184
Hamden, 119
Hammonasset Beach State Park, 152
hand-carved oak pews, 18
Hartford, 10
Hartford Stage, 17
Hartman Park, 171
Hart Porter House and Its
    Outbuilding, 31
Harvest Kitchen, The, 111
Headless Horseman of Canton, 47
Hearthstone Castle, 134
Hebron, 196
Heirloom Market at Comstock Ferre, 25
Helga J. Ingraham Memorial Library, 86
Hendrick Cottage, 45
Henry B. duPont III Planetarium, 110
Henry Chandler Bowen, 207
Henry Whitfield State Museum, 148
Heublein Tower, 46
Hickory Stick Bookshop, 97
Hillside Historic District, 123
Hill-Stead Museum, 55
Historic Waterfront District, 180
Hockanum River Linear Park Trail, 28

Holcombe Farm, 43
Holmberg Orchards, 180
Hopkins Inn, The, 98
Hopkins Vineyard, 98
Hop River State Park Trail, 31
Horace Wells, 17
Hotchkiss-Fyler House, 84
Housatonic State Forest, 78
House of Books, 80
House of Hayes, 42
Hoxie Scenic Overlook, 186
Hubbard Park, 125
Hugh Lofting, 158
Huntington House Museum, 213
Hurst Farm, 196
Huxley's Bookmark Café, 125
Hyland House Museum, 148

I

Igor Sikorsky, 113
Indian Burial Grounds, 178
Indian Hill Cemetery, 162
Indian Springs Golf Course, 161
Institute for American Indian Studies, 97
Israel Putnam, 17
Ivoryton, 156
Ivoryton Playhouse, 157
Iwo Jima Survivors' Memorial Park and
    Monument, 60

J

Jackie Robinson Park, 104
Jacob Weidenmann, 15
J. Alden Weir, 128
James Blackstone Memorial Library, 145
James Fenimore Cooper, 178
James MacNeill Whistler, 189
James Mars, 73
Jeremiah's, 209
Jessie Gerard Trail, 70
J. Gregory Wiggins, 18
John Brown, 84
John C. Calhoun, 87
Johnny Ad's, 154
John Tantaquidgeon, 178
Jonathan Dickerman House, 120
Jonathan Edwards Winery, 190

Jonathan Trumbull, 175
Jonathan Trumbull House, 175
Jonathan Trumbull Jr. House, 175
Jones Family Farms, 111
Jones Winery, 111
Joseph Battell Fountain, 73
Joseph Preli Farm & Vineyard, 27
Joshua Hempsted House, 182
J. Seitz & Co, 96
J. Timothy's Taverne, 62

K
Karabin Farms, 60
Kasulaitis Farm and Sugarhouse, 69
Keeler Tavern, 129
Keeler Tavern Museum, 129
Keeney Memorial Cultural Center, 24
Kelley Preserve, 143
Kellogg Environmental Center, 112
Kent, 79
Kent Falls State Park, 80
Kidcity, 164
Killingly, 210
Killingworth, 158
King House Museum, 36
K LaMay's, 124

L
Lake Compounce, 62
Lake Waramaug State Park, 96
LaMothe's Sugar House, 53
Lamson Corner Cemetery, 53
Laurel Ridge, 90
Laurel Ridge Foundation, 90
Laurel Ridge Grass Fed Beef, 90
Lebanon, 175
Lebanon Historical Society, 176
Ledge Lighthouse, 183
Ledyard, 180
Ledyard Up-Down Sawmill, 180
Legacy Theater, The, 144
Lemuel Camp Tavern, 160
Les's Dairy Bar, 124
Library Wine Bar and Bistro, The, 127
Lighthouse Archaeological Site, 70
Lighthouse Point Park, 118

Lime Rock Park, 75
Litchfield, 85
Litchfield County, 66
Litchfield County Choral Union, 72
Litchfield County Jail, 85
Litchfield Distillery, 87
Litchfield Green, 85
Litchfield Hills, 66
Litchfield History Museum, 86
Little Bethel A.M.E. Church, 102
Lobster Landing, 153
lobster roll, 154
Lock 12 Historical Park, 121
Logee's Greenhouse, 211
Loomis-Chaffee School, 34
Loomis Institute, 34
Lost Acres Orchards, 42
Lost Acres Vineyard, 42
Louis Comfort Tiffany, 204
Lourdes in Litchfield Shrine, 88
Love Heart's Bakery and Cafe, 91
Lucius Pond Ordway/Devil's Den Preserve, 128
Lutz Children's Museum, 31
Luxor, The, 56
Lyman Allyn Art Museum, 183
Lyman Trumbull, 174
Lyme, 170
Lyme Art Association, 171

M
Mabel Osgood Wright, 108
Madison, 151
Madison Historical Society, 151
Madison Mile of Outdoor Art, 152
Main Street Market, 164
Manchester, 28
Manchester Historical Society, 29
Mansfield, 198
Maritime Aquarium at Norwalk, 106
Marketplace at Guilford Food Center, 147
Mark Twain, 19
Mark Twain House and Museum, 19
Marlborough, 196
Martha A. Parsons House Museum, 37

Martha's Herbiary, 205
Mashantucket Pequot Museum and Research Center, 189
Masonic Hall, 124
Mattatuck Museum, 124
McLean Game Refuge, 43
Medad Stone Tavern Museum, 150
Meigs Point Nature Center, 153
memorial to US Army pilot 2nd Lt. Vincent H. Core, 54
Meriden, 124
Merritt Parkway, 103
Middlefield, 161
Middlesex County Chamber of Commerce, 163
Middlesex County Historical Society, 162
Middletown, 162
Middletown Heritage Trail, 162
Middletown Police Station, 163
Milford, 113
Miller Farms, 50
Mill House Antiques & Gardens, 94
Mill Pond Falls, 23
Mine Hill Distillery, 95
Minnie Island State Park, 174
Miss Porter's School, 55
Mohawk Mountain, 79
Mohawk Mountain Ski Area, 79
Mohegan Congregational Church, 178
Mohegans, 178
Mohegan Sun Casino, 179
Monroe, 136
Monster Rock, 77
Monte Cristo Cottage, 182
Montville, 178
Moosup, 211
Mount Riga, 74
Munson's Chocolates, 32
Museum of Connecticut History, 10
Museum of Contemporary Art Connecticut, 107
Museum of Curiosities, 11
Museum of Fife & Drum, 157
Museum of Fire History, 64
Music Mountain Chamber Music Festival, 73
Music Shed, 72

Mystic, 185
Mystic Drawbridge Ice Cream, 186
Mystic Knotworks, 186
Mystic Whaler Cruises, 185

N

Narragansetts, 178
Nassahegon State Forest, 51
Nathan Hale, 197
Nathan Hale Cemetery, 197
Nathan Hale Homestead, 197
Nathan Hale Schoolhouse, 167, 182
Nathan Hale State Forest, 197
National Helicopter Museum, 112
National Railroad Historical Society, 106
National Register of Historic Places, 103, 105
Naugatuck, 122
New Britain, 57
New Britain Bees, 60
New Britain Industrial Museum, 59
New Britain Museum of American Art, 57
New Canaan, 103
New Canaan Farmers Market, 104
New England Air Museum, 35
New England Brewing Company, 144
New England Carousel Museum, 16, 63
New Guida's Restaurant, 161
New Hartford, 68
New Haven, 114
New Haven Harbor, 119
Newington, 22
New London, 180
New London Historical Society, 182
New Milford, 82
New Park Brewing, 22
New Preston, 96
Newtown, 135
Niantic, 173
No. 109 Cheese & Wine, 130
Nodine's Smokehouse, 83
Norfolk, 72
Norfolk Center Cemetery, 73
Norfolk Chamber Music Festival, 72
Norfolk Library, 72
Norfolk Town Hall, 73

North Branford, 145
Northford Congregational Church, 145
North Stonington, 190
Norwalk, 105
Norwalk Transit District, 105
Norwich, 176
Norwich Heritage and Regional Visitors Center, 176
Norwich Heritage Groups, 176
Norwich Historical Society, 176

O

Old Avon Village, 49
Old Campus, 114
Old Customs House, 189
Old Horse Guard Barn, 50
Old Lighthouse Museum, 189
Old Lyme, 171
Old Mill Pond Village, 41
Old New-Gate Prison & Copper Mine, 38
Old Norwichtown Burial Ground, 177
Old Saybrook, 154
old stone jailhouse, 51
Old Tolland Jail Museum, 201
Old Town Hall Museum, 37
Old Wethersfield Country Store, 24
Oliver Ellsworth House, 34
Oneco, 211
Operation Desert Storm, 179
Orford Soap Company, 29
O'Rourke's Diner, 6
Orsamus Roman Fyler, 84
Osbornedale State Park, 112
Osborne Homestead Museum, 112

P

Painting Sites Trail, 129
Paul Mellon, 115
People's State Forest, 69, 70
Perk on Main, 163
Perrotti's Country Barn, 162
Pettibone's Tavern, 44
Phelps Barn, 45
Phelps Gate, 114
Phelps Tavern, 45
Philip Johnson's Glass House, 103
Phillip James Jones, 111
Phineas Taylor (P. T.) Barnum, 109
Phoenix Mutual Life Insurance Building, 12
Pickin' Patch, 48
Pinchot Sycamore, 46
Pitkin Glass Works, 28
Pitkin Tavern, 29
Plainfield, 211
Plainville, 62
Pocketful of Posies, 164
Podlasie, 57
Pomfret, 204
Portland, 165
President Andrew Jackson, 178
Privet House, 97
Prudence Crandall, 211
Prudence Crandall House Museum, 212
P. T. Barnum, 83
Putnam, 208
Putnam Memorial State Park, 132

Q

Quinebaug Valley State Trout Hatchery, 211

R

Redding, 130
Redscroll Records, 127
Rein's Deli-Restaurant, 201
Reverend Dr. Samuel Seabury, 94
Reverend Elizur Goodrich House, 160
Rev. Horace Bushnell, 15
Revolutionary War Office, 176
Richard Dana, 89
Richard N. Mather, 29
Rich Farm Ice Cream Shop, 137
Ridgefield, 129
Ridgefield Playhouse, 130
River Bend Campground, 211
Riverdale Farms Shopping, 51
River Mills Heritage Trail, 209
Riverton, 70
Riverton General Store, 70
Riverwalk, 12
R. J. Julia Bookseller, 152
Roaring Brook Falls, 121

Roaring Brook Nature Center, 47
Rocky Hill, 25
Rocky Hill–Glastonbury Ferry, 26
Rocky Hill Historical Society, 26
Rocky Neck State Park, 173
Roger Tory Peterson Estuary Center, 172
Roger Wilcox, 105
Roseland Cottage, 207
Rowanwood Farms, 135
Roxbury, 95
Roxbury Land Trust Trails, 95
Russell Library, 163

S
Salem, 174
Salem Valley Farms, 174
Salisbury, 74
Salisbury Outing Club, 75
Salisbury Winter Sports Association, 75
Sally's, 117
Salmon Brook Historical Society, 39
Salmon Brook Shops, 41
Sandra Boynton, 77
Sankow's Beaver Brook Farm, 170
Satan's Kingdom State Recreation Area, 68
Saville Dam, 69
Saybrook Point, 154
Saybrook Point Inn, Marina, & Spa, 155
scenic byways, 205
Schaghticoke Indian Reservation, 82
Scotland, 213
Seaside Park, 111
Second Company of the Governor's Horse Guards, 135
Selectman's Stones, 143
Seventh Day Baptist Cemetery, 52
Shade Swamp Sanctuary, 53
Shanks Waterfront Dining, 153
Shantok, Village of Uncas, 179
Sharpe Hill Vineyard, 206
Shaw Mansion, 182
Sheffield Island Lighthouse, 106
Shelton, 111
Shelton Lakes Recreation Path, 112
Shepaug Dam Bald Eagle Observation Area, 136

Shops at Marlborough Barn, 196
Shore Line Trolley Museum, 119
Silk City Model Railroad Club, 30
Silver Sands Beach, 114
Silver Sands State Park, 114
Simsbury, 44
Simsbury Historical Society, 45
Skull and Bones, 115
Slater Memorial Museum and Converse Art Gallery, 177
Sleeping Giant State Park, 120
Small Boat Shop, 105
Soldiers Monument, 114
Soldiers & Sailors Memorial Arch, 17
SoNo, 105
SoNo Switch Tower Museum, 106
Southbury, 136
Southford Falls, 136
South Norwalk, 105
Spanish American War Memorial, 17
Sperry Farm, 122
Spice & Tea Exchange, The, 147
Spirit of Victory, 17
Stamford, 104
Stamford Cone, 104
Stamford Museum and Nature Center, 104
Stanford White, 55
Stanley-Whitman House, 56
Steep Rock Reservation, 97
Stegosaurus, 13
Stepney Cemetery, 136
Stewart B. McKinney National Wildlife Refuge, 154
Stewart McKinney National Wildlife Refuge, 150
Still Hill Brewery and Tap Room, 26
Stone Field, 14
Stone House, 158
Stonington, 168, 187
Stonington Vineyards, 191
Stony Creek Museum, 144
Stony Creek Quarry, 142
Stony Creek Quarry Preserve, 143
Stowe Center, 20
Stratford, 112
Stratford Antique Center, 113

Strong-Howard House, The, 34
Submarine Force Museum, 184
Suffield, 35, 36
Sunset Meadow Vineyards, 83
Sweet Pea Cheese, 42
swinging bridge, 166
Sycamore, 132

T
Taine Mountain Preserve, 52
Talcott Mountain, 45
Talcott Mountain State Park, 46
tallest tree in the state, 78
Tantaquidgeon Museum, 178
Tapping Reeve House & Litchfield Law School, 86
Tapping Reeve Meadow, 87
Tarrywile Mansion, 133
Tarrywile Park, 133
Ted's Restaurant, 124
Thames River Heritage Park, 181
Theodore S. Gold, 78
Thimble Islands, 141
Thomas Thurber, 203
Thorncrest Farm and Milk House Chocolates, 83
Time Machine Hobby, 30
Tolland, 200
Tolland Military Museum, 201
Tomb, The, 115
Topsmead, 89
Topsmead State Forest, 89
Torrington, 83
Torrington Historical Society, 84
Totoket Historical Society, 145
Trail Wood Sanctuary, 165
Traveler Restaurant, 202
Trinity College, 18
Trinity College Chapel, 18
Trust for Public Land, 52
Tulmeadow Farm Store and Ice Cream, 46
Tunxis Trail, 51
Turtle, 184
Two Roads Brewing, 113
Two Wrasslin' Cats Coffee House, 167

U
UConn Dairy Bar, 199
Uncas, 178
Uncle Aaron's Tackle Shack, 70
Union, 202
Union Cemetery, 136
Union Park, 163
Unionville, 56
Unionville Museum, 56
Unitarian Meeting House, 213
US Coast Guard Academy, 183
USS Nautilus, 184

V
Vanilla Bean Cafe, 205
Van Wie Preserve, 143
Van Wilgen's Garden Center, 145
Vernon, 201
"Victory over Japan" Parade, 211
Viets' Tavern, 38
Village Chocolatier, The, 147
Village Creek Historic District, 105

W
Wadsworth Atheneum, 12
Wadsworth Mansion, 164
Wadsworth Stable, 175
Wallingford, 125
Walnut Beach, 114
Walter Bunce House, 30
Warren, 98
Washington, 96
Waterbury, 123
Webb, Deane, and Stevens Museum, 24
Weed-Enders House, 39
Weir Farm, 128
Weld Thayer Chase, 103
Wentworth Homemade Ice Cream Company, 120
West Avon Congregational Church, 49
Westbrook, 154
West Cornwall Covered Bridge, 76
West Hartford, 21
Westmoor Park, 21, 22
Weston, 128
Westport, 107

Westport Country Playhouse, 107
WestWoods Trail System, 149
Wethersfield, 23
Wethersfield Heritage Walk, 23
Wethersfield Historical Society, 23
Whale Oil Row, 180
White Flower Farm, 88
White Lady, 136
White Memorial Foundation, 87
White Memorial Foundation and Conservation Center, 87
Whiting Mills, 72
Whitlock's Book Barn, 122
Wickham Park, 31
Willimantic, 214
Willington, 200
Willington Pizza House, 200
Willington Pizza Too, 200
Willoughby Adelbert Wallace, 143
Willoughby Wallace Memorial Library, 143
Wilton, 128
Windham, 214
Windham Frog Pond, 214
Windham Textile and History Museum, 214
Winding Drive Jellies and Jams, 91
Windsor, 33
Windsor Historical Society, 33
Windsor Locks, 35
Windsor Locks Canal, 35
Winsted, 71
Wisdom House Retreat & Conference Center, 89
Wish House, The, 78
Witch's Dungeon Classic Movie Museum, 64
Woodbury, 94
Woodbury Pewter Factory Store, 94
Woodstock, 207
Works Progress Administration, 105

Y

Yale Center for British Art, 115
Yale Peabody Museum of Natural History, 116
Yale University, 114
Yale University Art Gallery, 116
Yale Visitor Center, 115
Yantic Falls, 178

Z

Zip's Dining Car, 210

About the Author

Cindi D. Pietrzyk is a freelance writer and editor based in Connecticut, where she has lived since she was four years old. She is the author of several books, including Globe Pequot's *Short Nature Walks in Connecticut* and *Boston's Freedom Trail*. She and her family enjoy exploring history on back roads and in small towns as well as in cities with all the culture they offer. Follow her on Facebook and be sure to let her know about your adventures in our state.

Eric D. Lehman is the award-winning author and editor of 23 books of travel, fiction, and memoir, including *New England at 400*, *New England Nature*, *Connecticut Town Greens*, and *Connecticut Farms and Farmers Markets*.

www.ingramcontent.com/pod-product-compliance
Ingram Content Group UK Ltd.
Pitfield, Milton Keynes, MK11 3LW, UK
UKHW021849210426
5322IPUK00022B/569